Business Process Management:
Profiting from Process

Roger T. Burlton

800 East 96th St., Indianapolis, Indiana, 46240 USA

ASSOCIATE PUBLISHER
Linda Engelman

ACQUISITIONS EDITOR
Loretta Yates

DEVELOPMENT EDITOR
Susan Shaw Dunn

MANAGING EDITOR
Charlotte Clapp

PROJECT EDITOR
Carol Bowers

COPY EDITOR
Mary Ellen Stephenson

INDEXER
Sandy Henselmeier

PROOFREADER
Candice Hightower

TECHNICAL EDITOR
Ankur Laroia

TEAM COORDINATOR
Pamalee Nelson

MEDIA DEVELOPER
Dan Scherf

INTERIOR DESIGNER
Anne Jones

COVER DESIGNER
Aren Howell

PAGE LAYOUT
Gloria Schurick

Overview

Contents

About the Author

Roger T. Burlton is the founder of the Process Renewal Group and President of the Process Renewal Consulting Group, Inc., which he formed in 1993. He is a respected thought–leader and an accomplished strategic consultant when it comes to managing business change. He has extensive strategic and tactical experience in a broad spectrum of industries, and his successes span business strategy and architecture, process renewal, knowledge management, and a number of enhanced systems development methods.

He is considered a global industry leader in the introduction of innovative methods for change and is recognized internationally for his pioneering contributions in Relationship Management (1997), Knowledge Management (1996), Business Process Management (1991), Strategic Alignment (1993), Prototyping and Rapid Systems Development (1984), and people-based Project Management Methodologies (1980).

Roger has conceived and chaired several high-profile conferences on advanced business and information management globally, including Knowledge and Process Management Europé 98 and 99, and the Knowledge Management 99 conference series in the United States. He was the chair of the National BPR Conference in the United States and Software World Canada, which was Canada's largest IT management conference for five years running.

Roger also presents these concepts to managers and professionals in public and private seminars through prestigious seminar houses, such as DCI and IRM UK. To date, he has conducted more than 500 sessions and has presented to more than 15,000 professionals around the world. His sessions have been translated for French, Spanish, Portuguese, Italian, and Japanese audiences and are offered by partners in some non-English speaking countries.

Roger has been a frequent contributor to Ed Yourdon's *American Programmer* periodical, published by Cutter. He has also published articles *in Knowledge Management* magazine and the *Data-to Knowledge Newsletter*.

Roger graduated with a B.A. Sc. in Industrial Engineering at the University of Toronto in 1971. He is a certified Professional Engineer in the province of Ontario (1973). He functioned as an Industrial Engineer and Systems Analyst in manufacturing and government organizations before joining the consulting ranks in 1980. In 1986, he founded SRI Strategic Resources, Inc., which was acquired by BC Telephone (a subsidiary of GTE) in 1988. He served as Director of Productivity R & D, Branch Manager, and Director of Advanced Technologies until his departure to set up Process Renewal Group in 1993.

Currently, Roger is developing a new offering that will deal with the convergence of relationship management and knowledge management. In addition, in collaboration with Ptech Inc., he has completed the automation of the process management methods that are be featured in this book. The software product is available now.

Dedication

To my wife, Angie, who has always been supportive of my choices. This book would not have happened without your understanding. Also, to my children, Lindsay and Stephanie, who make what I do worthwhile.

Acknowledgments

I want to thank many people for their contribution to this book. First and foremost, a long-time associate in Process Renewal Group, Mary Lowe, was invaluable in reading my often-cryptic drafts and asking tough questions to make sure that it made sense. As an experienced practitioner with the framework described in the book, she also organized a lot of my materials in Part II and put it into a great structure. Without Mary, this book would never have been written.

I also want to thank two other Process Renewal Group associates, whose insight over the years has kept me from taking my work too seriously. Kathy Long's unrivaled world-class knowledge and experience in the analysis and design of business processes has kept me practically focused. Sandy Foster's constant search for the repeatable science in the methods has ensured that what I write and advocate can be done again by others.

I also want to thank Doug Kirkpatrick from the Morningstar Packing Company, who enlightened me on what a truly empowered organization can do.

I want to thank all the staff at Ptech, Inc., especially Jeff Goins and Hossam Elgabri, for their support in providing models, illustrations, and examples developed in Ptech's FrameWork™ technology. I believe this technology to be the most complete and progressive of all process management technologies today. I also want to thank them for developing and making available to everyone a more complete HTML example of the case study in the book. This can be found on the Web at www.samspublishing.com. (Type this book's ISBN in the Search field.)

I would also like to thank Jim Montoya, who was the Dean of Admissions and Financial Aid at Stanford when Mary Lowe and I worked on the financial aid project referred to in this book. He is currently the Vice Provost for Student Affairs at Stanford. Jim's vision and leadership have made and continues to make a real difference for the students at Stanford. Working with him was an inspiration to both of us.

Tell Us What You Think!

As the reader of this book, *you* are our most important critic and commentator. We value your opinion and want to know what we're doing right, what we could do better, what areas you'd like to see us publish in, and any other words of wisdom you're willing to pass our way.

As an Associate Publisher for Sams, I welcome your comments. You can e-mail or write me directly to let me know what you did or didn't like about this book—as well as what we can do to make our books stronger.

Please note that I cannot help you with problems related to the topic of this book, and that due to the high volume of mail I receive, I might not be able to reply to every message.

When you write, please be sure to include this book's title and author as well as your name and phone or fax number. I will carefully review your comments and share them with the author and editors who worked on the book.

E-mail: `feedback@samspublishing.com`

Mail: Mike Stephens
Associate Publisher
Sams Publishing
800 East 96th Street
Indianapolis, IN 46240 USA

Introduction

Process Management Comes of Age

The time for process management is unquestionably upon us. It might not be discussed with fad-like hysterics as it was in the early 1990s when Michael Hammer and James Champy wrote the book about business process re-engineering that got a lot of people's attention.[1] However, many organizations are finally starting to understand its value.

My seminars in practical Business Process Management (BPM) started in 1990—a couple of years before Hammer and Champy published their book. These seminars have been well attended ever since. There have been peaks and valleys in attendance as the subject has matured. From 1990 to 1994, everyone was curious and just wanted to educate himself on what the terms meant. From 1994 to 1997, attendees came looking to try it out for themselves. Many of them still struggled since they were really searching for a silver-bullet solution to all the problems that they had, which weren't solved by their previous attempts at silver-bullet solutions. For some of them, the hard work part of the process management message didn't sink in. They also didn't want hear that it would be complex and involve significant human change. The published materials at the time didn't tell them that. For this reason, around the mid-'90s, survey after survey reported that two-thirds of the re-engineering attempts failed to deliver anticipated or promised results. The word on the street was that process re-engineering was dead. This was reflected in a dip in seminar attendance below earlier numbers. It seemed the fad would pass.

From 1997 to 1999, in many organizations, attention was drawn away from enterprise processes by the very expensive and resource-hungry year 2000 software crisis. Many enterprises did little in the way of process renewal during this time because they couldn't afford to. The fad seekers, moreover, had moved on to something else. For some, it was Internet technology, enterprise resource planning (ERP), sales force automation, supply-chain management, data warehousing with business intelligence, or knowledge management. But, by the late '90s, organizations had also discovered, as they did with prior fads, that these also weren't simple solutions and certainly not just about technology.

I found myself preaching to organizations that issues such as knowledge management aren't centered on information technology (IT). I also reminded them that their focus must be on their business processes and the changes required of people such as changes in beliefs, behavior, incentives, roles, jobs, culture, and structure. From 1997 onward, new or emergent ideas

---

[1]*Reengineering the Corporation: A Manifesto for Business Revolution, Michael Hammer & James Champy, HarperCollins, 1993*

such as ERP, customer relationship management (CRM), business-to-consumer (B2C) e-business, and business-to-business (B2B) e-business all demanded complete end-to-end process design and management to be effective.

By the time the year 2000 crisis came and went, it was clear that the focus had returned to business process, but in a less flamboyant way. In 1993, Hammer and Champy missed the mark with their fiery message of radical redesign at all costs. However, what they got right was the enduring message of the importance of processes. Today, I can safely say that Business Process Management isn't a fad—it is here to stay. It's a new fundamental management requirement through which enterprises can run their organizations to survive and thrive.

The challenge today is to use business processes as reusable enterprise assets that align the complex set of other enterprise assets. People, technologies, facilities, information, and knowledge must be synchronized and work in harmony through processes to support the enterprise outcomes that deliver value to the organization's stakeholders. Managing the performance of the processes and the ever-changing alignment among other enterprise assets is now the *challenge du jour*. Organizations are figuring out the importance of business process management (BPM), as witnessed by the growth in conferences dealing with enterprise architecture and Process Renewal Group's Business Process Management seminars. Attendance at these events, I am happy to say, is the highest it has ever been, even outperforming the heydays of business process re-engineering (BPR). Business Process Management is here to stay.

It's my mission to help organizations truly understand how to succeed with BPM. I hope this book will help you strive toward your mission. For many of you, it will guide your actions well. Unfortunately, for others, managing business processes and enterprise change will be seen as too hard to do and too much work. It has been my experience that companies which are serious about solving problems and providing great results for external stakeholders find the methods very valuable and worth the effort. For those looking for a quick fix, those that are internally focused or looking for a simple way to implement technology without commitment to business issues first, this book will either change your mind or disappoint you. I hope it is the former.

Who Should Read This Book

This book is for executives, strategists, managers, project leaders, and business analysts involved in process-based organizational change. It's also suitable for educational institutions that want a complete coverage of process management theories and practices.

How This Book Is Organized

The book is divided into two major sections:

- Part I, "A Management Guide," consists of the first nine chapters and is aimed at anyone planning to conduct process projects and everyone involved in delivering services to customers as part of day-to-day process management. It's a good introduction to the major issues and approaches of process renewal and ongoing process management. I recommend that all managers and all practitioners read this section.

- Part II, "A Practitioner's Guide," is organized according to the major phases of process management. It's intended to be used as a phase-by-phase reference for those planning and conducting the work of the particular phase. All project staff should be intimately familiar with its contents.

A Management Guide

PART

I

IN THIS PART

Drivers of Business Change

IN THIS CHAPTER

During the time that I was writing this book, I was involved with a company that was very successful in its consumer products marketplace—number one in North American market share. During the year, however, it changed its prime consumer focus to an e-commerce approach, changed its sales incentive scheme to a new network marketing model, and dropped the prices on its products by an average of 40% in anticipation of competitor response. It also opened up or consolidated operations in five new countries, each with different regulatory mandates. The company then was acquired by a large global competitor that didn't have an e-commerce solution or a network channel. Together, they became the dominant player in their industry in the world. This firm then acquired another network marketing company in the same industry with some complementary products to secure its position and merged with it. The company did all this and managed to maintain a growth trajectory that continues today.

This company isn't all that unusual. The things it did, and continues to do, are typical of the type of changes happening in the world today in many organizations. The firm is very unusual in that it managed to pull these changes off without major damage to its stakeholder relationships. Like many enterprises today, this company faces incredible pressures.

This chapter examines some of the most pressing of these business drivers. In doing so, I will start to show that managing your processes constantly is a key factor in navigating the difficult transitions that arise. Your enterprise's specific responses to these drivers will vary depending on its mission, value proposition, and its current situation in the marketplace. However, these pressures for change can't be ignored. Change isn't an option—you will change whether you like it or not.

When enterprises make investments in change, they expect to receive a fair return on their investments. These investments should pay off in terms of the business performance results that they are chartered to deliver. Figure 1.1 depicts the challenge for managers everywhere.

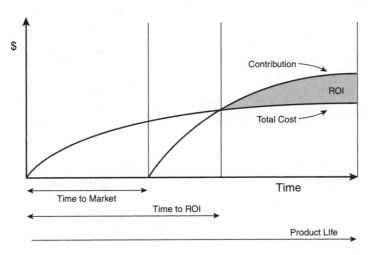

FIGURE 1.1

Return on Investment (ROI).

As changes are made, new organizational capability is put in place. This can be in the form of new products and services that allow the organization to meet its mandate better. After spending an amount of time and money and utilizing other resources, the capability is ready for use. This time is referred to as *time to market*. The organization then realizes the benefits of its investments and at some point reaches the break-even point, when the accumulated investments and operating costs are exceeded by the contribution made through the availability of the product, service, or capability. I will refer to this point as the *time to ROI (Return on Investment)*. The enterprise then continues to reap rewards until the product reaches the end of its useful life and is retired or renewed. Positive return is achieved unless the contribution never catches up to the investment and cost line when products miss the mark or projects fail. This can happen as shown in Figure 1.2. Variations on this model will be used elsewhere in this chapter to illustrate the pressures on organizations today.

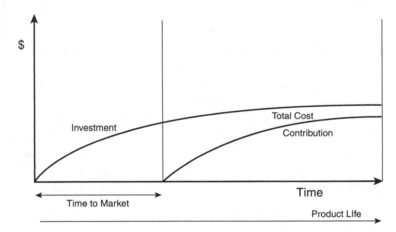

FIGURE 1.2
Return on Investment never reached.

It's becoming harder and harder to achieve the ROI expected for several reasons. The prime business challenge faced by enterprises around the world is to manage complexity and to deliver capability—both the ability to perform and the capacity to scale. This task isn't trivial as the business environment becomes even more complex. A traditional response by organizations has been to conduct some form of strategic planning by doing SWOT (strengths, weaknesses, opportunities, and threats) analysis. With this approach, organizations would proceed directly from a weakness and start up a project to strengthen it or from an opportunity and build the capability to exploit it. These types of approaches, of which SWOT is just one, are devoid of real strategy formulation from an enterprise perspective. It's how many organizations ended up with 25 databases with the same data in them but with no integrity, and how enterprises produced many Web sites with conflicting or confusing messages. Today, these approaches clearly lag because they miss the concept of organizational asset alignment.

In the past, corporations have paid for this lack of integrity in the time and cost to make further changes. Today, many are still paying because they can't deliver capability to the front lines fast enough. Many organizations have responded by introducing information architecture and systems planning approaches. From the business strategy, they build architectures of the total information technology (IT) environment: data, applications, and infrastructure. From this they establish an IT transformation plan and establish budgets to implement the program. This has been a step in the right direction, but more often than not it's still not linked to any process view that connects their stakeholders to the business.

Business architectures that identify stakeholders, processes, and organizations, and link them to the products and services of the organization are now very much the focus. Many organizations are aligning all elements with one another. What's proving to be more challenging is the allocation of resources across functions such as IT and human resources (HR) as well as business units. Defining a program of change for all components is what some of the more insightful companies and government agencies are trying to address.

The most courageous enterprises are stepping up to the problem that faces many of them today: Even those who design their strategies well and produce aligned architectures for all their organizational assets often don't deliver what they said they would. The resources required don't actually get allocated to the required work. A major cause is that an organization doesn't have in place a vetting process to take rogue initiatives and assess them against the approved plans. Likewise, the required resources simply aren't available because they are doing other things. Also typically missing is a cross-functional process that reviews and approves resource allocation based on the current program of approved projects and their requirements. This process assesses the appropriateness of implementation proposals other than those already approved.

Nirvana for organizations is to close the loop through a learning cycle that feeds back to strategic planning and architecture. Monitoring progress against the planned program initiatives and also measuring ongoing business performance will allow priorities to evolve and be reset realistically.

Figure 1.3 depicts the full process of delivering enterprise asset capability. It answers the who, what, when, where, why, and how regarding the enterprise being managed. And, it does so in a logical order. It starts with why and then progresses to what, where, when, who, and how. Lastly, it re-addresses why again in a never-ending cycle.

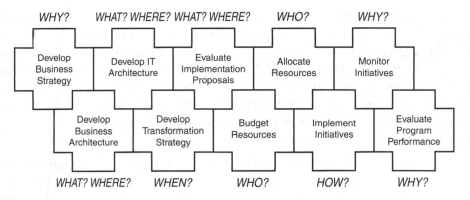

FIGURE 1.3
The process to deliver enterprise asset capability.

Critical decisions are made during the process of managing these assets. They vary from organization to organization, depending on the drivers that each organization faces. The following sections address some of the more common drivers found today in many organizations' business landscape. I haven't tried to be exhaustive in this list, nor will I attempt to drill into significant detail on each. You all recognize the issues. Instead, I've focused on defining the major factors from business and technological viewpoints so that you can evaluate which are particularly relevant to you. Any of these could represent an opportunity, or potentially a risk, for the organization. Your choices of response are covered in Chapter 2. How you respond will be the key factor in your success.

New-Age Business Drivers

As the economy changes, the context for all private and public sector businesses changes with it. I feel that four major forces are causing upheaval for many enterprises:

- Hyper-competition
- Growing organizational complexity and reach
- Rising external stakeholder power
- E-business technology

Hyper-competition

The term *hyper-competition* simply implies that competition is happening more quickly and more aggressively than ever before. The tearing down of barriers is allowing new entrants into traditional markets and playing havoc with the old rules. Competitors are also playing harder than ever before. Many new players are entering the economy and taking over a larger and larger share of markets. Many are driving out unresponsive incumbents. However, other incumbents will do anything to keep what they have and squeeze out new threats.

The airline industry's experience is a case in point. As existing large carriers merge, creating a few major players, competition often disappears on certain routes, most notably to small communities. In many cases, the newly merged carrier reduces the number of flights and increases average fares for travelers, who have little choice. Often, new competitors then enter the marketplace with lower cost structures and rates. It doesn't take long for the major carrier to respond with special low fares to keep their control over the routes. It does this at a loss and has the staying power to squeeze out its new competition in a war of attrition. When that occurs, the major carrier often then raises the prices again and recovers its position.

Air Canada was accused of this behavior before it acquired its weakened main competition, Canadian Airlines. In the United States, most major carriers have been accused of the same tactics. The behavior of Northwest, United, and American airlines will be interesting to watch as other carriers, such as TWA and USAir, are taken over. However, this arrogant behavior has also backfired at times, allowing new entrants to be successful as long as they are well funded and remain profitable through incredible efficiency. Southwest Airlines, Alaska Air, and others have been very successful in developing alternatives to the major carriers by offering lower fares and great service. They also are growing their business profitably. Competitors with high overhead structures often abandon the routes to the upstarts.

Opportunities and threats exist in all industries. Initial responses to some minor player challenges occurred in the early 1990s with massive cost-cutting exercises by the big players. Figure 1.4 shows the planned impact on competitiveness through cost reductions from business process re-engineering (BPR) programs. This was a good short-term fix, but, in many cases, it was done by reducing—not enhancing—capability, which was treated as a non value-added cost, not an investment. This capability proved to be a key factor when the business world became more competitive after 2000.

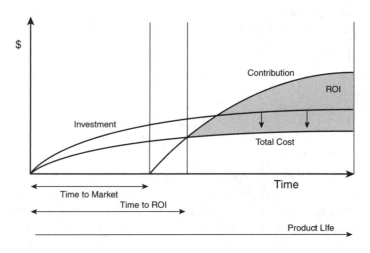

FIGURE 1.4

Improved ROI through cost-based business process re-engineering.

Some of the main reasons for an increasingly competitive world are

- Shrinking business cycles
- The commoditization of products and services
- The provision of knowledge as a product or service

I will deal with each of these.

Shrinking Business Cycles

It has become clear that products and services don't remain constant for very long any more. From the 1950s through the mid-1980s, it wasn't unusual to expect a new product or service to remain fairly consistent for a number of years. Since the mid-1980s, however, the in-market time, or product life, has continued to shrink. Figures 1.1 and 1.2 depicts the dilemma that executives face in trying to maximize return on their investments. These curves were manageable when there was sufficient time to earn the ROI—that is, when the product lifeline was sufficiently far to the right.

But, today, the in-market opportunity is rapidly vanishing because of two main factors. First, products and services now last for months, not for years, before they have to be dropped or renewed. This can be equated to the product lifeline racing dramatically to the left in Figures 1.1 and 1.2. When this occurs, it means that there's less opportunity to recover investment costs unless the second factor is dealt with: The time to market point must also be moved to the left to maintain a fair ROI. Figure 1.5 shows the challenge. This means that you can no longer take years to deliver a new capability that the marketplace would have loved a year ago. In one year, the market's desire has doubtlessly moved on to something else.

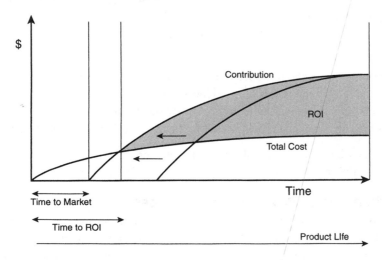

FIGURE 1.5
Improved ROI through faster time to market.

Product development cycles must shrink, and we must think about delivering changeable capability. (This will be dealt with in more detail in Chapter 2, "Organizational Responses to Business Drivers.") The pressure to do this requires us to be more adaptable in our ways of working. The old Industrial Revolution model of invest, invent, and mass produce is no longer valid because it assumes that what we deliver is stable, as is the way that we deliver it. Instead, today's challenge is to be flexible enough in generating our products and services to allow significant delivery variations. At the extreme, it means that every instance of a service or product configuration can be unique. Customers receive customized, individualized treatment. Strangely enough, in looking at this extreme, the need arises for some sort of stability because it's clear that we can't reconfigure our work methods every time a customer places an order. The trick is to design, develop, and implement capabilities that are innately adaptable and scalable. Facilities, technologies, and people must be able to deliver results, each of which might be different.

This has a strong impact on how we set up our organizations. Some of the requirements are

- To adopt a customer and process focus, not a product focus, because the product will vary
- To design products as basic, customizable modules that can evolve and change
- To use adaptable technologies whose rules and workflows can be changed declaritively without programmers getting involved
- To focus on the continuous enhancement of the knowledge of workers
- To build flexible, responsive processes

A good example of these organizational characteristics can be found at Dell Computers, where new designs of computers reach the market very quickly. All Dell customers can configure their own machines on the Internet or by talking to a knowledgeable agent, and corporate customers can work through their own personalized Web pages. Dell's advantage lies more in its capability to change quickly than in great designs for its machines.

Another good example is Levi Strauss & Company's custom jeans service. Under this program, for a few dollars more than the full price of a pair of Levi jeans, you can be measured for fit in a store and have the factory thousands of miles away cut a single thickness of fabric by computer-controlled lasers. From this, a pair of jeans is expertly sewed and shipped to you in a few days. And they fit. Levi's makes much more per unit profit from these than standard jeans.

In both cases, the design was for an infinitely adaptable product using a standard process and technology that didn't require downtime to get to market after a change or a customization.

Commoditization of Products and Services

Unlike products of just a few years ago, many of today's products and services look much alike. It's hard for individuals and organizations to pick and choose among them because their features are similar. Most organizations have learned from one another and have incorporated the best of the breed into their own offerings. To add to this, many products work well, and added features seem to be marginal in their value to customers. Businesses no longer add significantly new concepts or capabilities as they once did. Many of these products are becoming mature. An example is the last few releases of Microsoft Office. Most people were already only using a small percentage of the capabilities of the product suite when new releases were introduced and, if it weren't for the requirement to be able to read new incompatible file formats, many people may not have purchased the new versions. A few more advanced users might have welcomed some of the features, but a larger and larger proportion of users didn't find much functional advantage in new versions relative to the price charged. This scenario is repeated with other maturing products and services. When products are all hard to differentiate in functionality and performance, some other factor will determine what will be bought.

The next factor in attracting customers will usually be the quality and reliability of the product or service. The confidence that you can place in the successful operation of the offering becomes key. In the 1970s and '80s, quality differentiated products from each other in the marketplace. Products with similar functionality were assessed by their quality. Conformance to customer needs was paramount. This was apparent in the automobile industry. Japanese quality allowed companies such as Honda, Toyota, and Nissan to capture significant market share over GM, Ford, and Chrysler because of the perceived unreliability of North American automobiles. During this period, Total Quality Management was king, and quality commanded and received higher prices and profits. Today, I have confidence that Microsoft's operating systems have sufficient functionality, but I am not so confident that I can trust Windows $9x$ to work when I want it to. The advent of the competing Linux operating system was somewhat fueled by this lack of trust.

Reliability is no longer an option for companies. It's becoming a price of entry into the global marketplace. In many economic sectors, customers won't accept poor quality. Their expectations for performance are higher, and their tolerance of poor execution is lower. Companies with quality problems simply don't last any more. Historical customer loyalty won't overcome a lack of trust in reliability. Competitors with superior quality will eventually win out.

If products' functionality and quality are comparable, customers will look to convenience and customization next. The ability to meet specific and unique requirements is of value to many organizations and individuals. As mentioned earlier, the ability to customize still provides competitive advantage and price protection.

Given parity of all the previous factors and an equivalent level of trust, price will rule. If prices are more or less the same, the level of recognition and trust of the company providing the product or service will prevail.

Figure 1.6 shows what many organizations are now doing. They are trying to hang on to their existing customers and increase their loyalty through the relationships the organizations are building with the customers. Terms such as *share of wallet* and *share of book* (meaning how much of the customers' total spending your company earns) are replacing *share of market*. This is the aim of branding programs in many organizations and the reason that many upstart companies in the e-business world have struggled or failed. There are just so many places to buy, all with the same prices and terms. It's easier to buy from a name you know when everything else seems the same. It's also the aim of customer relationship management (CRM) programs aimed at increasing loyalty.

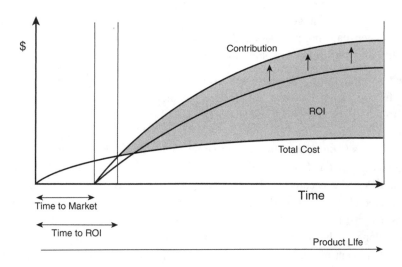

FIGURE 1.6

Improved ROI through greater share.

In summary, customer relationship criteria will move .

> From product functionality/performance
>
> To quality and reliability
>
> To convenience and customization
>
> To price
>
> To trust, treatment, and branding

The rapid commoditization of products and (to some degree) services has become clear in a number of industries such as telecommunications service, technology supply, banking, retail, automobiles, and even financial services such as insurance and mutual funds. What differentiates one product from another is now becoming relationship-based: the confidence that customers have with the supplier, the ease of doing business, and the level of trust in the relationship.

You must ask yourself what business you really are in. If it isn't possible to quickly move up the value chain, it might be better to purchase commodities from an organization that provides high quality yet low cost and work in partnership with that organization while focusing on your distinct capabilities. No one is making a success of being mediocre any more.

Products or Services Differentiated by Knowledge

Consistent with what we have found in the last section, loyalty is tied to relationships and trust. Organizations are now realizing that doing a good job or providing a great product is required but by itself is no longer sufficient. A major component of service is knowledge. The knowledge provided to customers can be in the form of accessible, knowledgeable staff or in the form of great reference materials in a multitude of media and formats.

Many organizations also are in the business of providing knowledge as a product. Training organizations, consulting firms, encyclopedia and reference materials publishers, and others sell knowledge. For them, the currency and availability of relevant and accurate knowledge are their distinguishing characteristics. Trust in the source is critical.

The Brazilian weekly newsmagazine *Veja*, published by Abril, has by far the largest market share in its segment because it has established a reputation of providing trustworthy news perspectives. *Veja* isn't afraid to take on controversial issues and stand strong against the government. If this publication didn't show up on time on people's doorsteps early Saturday morning, there would be a national uproar. Reading it has become a Brazilian habit.

For other organizations, knowledge is associated with the prime products and services of the business and is used to differentiate the business from competitors. This ancillary knowledge is a key requirement of customer awareness and satisfaction.

Businesses that offer commodities must provide relevant knowledge about their products and services to make it easy for customers to buy and use them with confidence. This is a major area of competitive attention for many companies. If you want to make chocolate chip cookies, perhaps you will buy M&M's instead of standard chocolate chips. To do so, you might need to find a Web site or an 800 number that will give you a great recipe as well as all the nutritional information needed to evaluate how many cookies you can eat as part of a healthy diet. At the same time, you might want to confirm that you can serve them safely to family members who might have specific allergies.

This scenario plays out in many ways. One notable example is Progressive Insurance, an automobile insurer, documented in Michael Hammer and James Champy's first book[1] because of its breakthrough model of service to policyholders. Since the early 1990s, Progressive's insurance adjusters have been on the road in technology-equipped vehicles so that they can go to

---

[1]Reengineering the Corporation: A Manifesto for Business Revolution, *Michael Hammer and James Champy, HarperCollins 1993*

the accident scene, survey damage, arrange for personal transportation and towing, and give a check to close the claim at the scene. Progressive, as its name suggests, is now going even further with another previously unheard of idea. By going to its Web site (www.progressive.com) or by calling its 800 number, you can get a quote for its insurance coverage. Progressive will also give you up to three other rates from its competitors for similar coverage. This attracts a lot more potential customers and establishes a high degree of trust. Progressive couldn't do it without a significant program of constant knowledge gathering in the background. Its service isn't a commodity; it provides extra value for its customers.

The drive to incorporate knowledge also applies to new marketing and sales models that don't try to sell too much too soon. Permission marketing advocate Seth Godin points out that you usually don't ask an acquaintance to get married when you first meet.[2] A number of steps happen in between, each of which requires permission to go to the next step. The approaches to accomplish this attempt to build confidence and trust, and then move up through levels of permission to finalize a sale. Many e-business companies have adopted this evolutionary model, offering regular e-mail broadcasts of new knowledge to customers. It's an attempt to build familiarity. It doesn't advertise products and services explicitly too soon. Similarly, many organizations are offering *webinars* —that is, online seminars on a topic of interest that gets customers closer to the organization. Web sites offer lots of guidance, hints, and sources of related information, all to build trust so that buyers will buy, and organizations can build wallet share. Competing has become more sophisticated than ever, but it requires the infusion of knowledge into business processes.

Growing Organizational Complexity and Reach

Outside pressures are pushing organizations to get bigger and enter unknown markets. Consequently, enterprises are also struggling with incredible changes in their own structure and how to go to market. These changes are becoming harder to manage, especially with hyper-competition and shrinking business cycles. Added organizational complexity makes it harder for businesses to anticipate and respond to competition. I will discuss four factors that contribute to organizational complexity:

- E-business
- Corporate globalization
- Corporate consolidation
- Partnerships, virtual organizations, and extended value chains

---

[2]Permission Marketing: Turning Strangers into Friends and Friends into Customers, *Seth Godin, Simon & Schuster, 1999*

The E-Business Factor

E-business, or business conducted over electronic networks, is having an enormous effect on all organizations today. It allows service to be provided and business to be transacted anywhere at anytime. In many ways, organizations are expected to be everywhere all the time. As a marketplace supplier, you can be in a business-to-consumer e-business relationship or a business-to-business one; e-business is opening up a wider and more extensive range of opportunities and expectations. The same is true on the supply end coming into your business. Much is now being done electronically. Cisco now sells more than 80% of its products over the Internet. Other businesses are rapidly trying to emulate its success. E-business is faster and cheaper than traditional "bricks and mortar" transactions, and customers like it better because it's more convenient. It allows them to reach globally without having to be there all the time. Growth happens faster. Scarce resources have greater leverage. E-business can be scaled upward to accommodate growth.

The implications of e-business for organizations are significant. Due to the heightened expectations of speed that come with it, supporting business processes must be cross-functional and work incredibly well. Traditionally, an order placed by mail might take weeks to deliver. This allows time for internal hand-offs across organizational boundaries to get things done and for mistakes to be worked out without impacting the customers' results and perceptions. Now, when a customer clicks a commercial Web site's "Place Order Now" button, she expects to receive the goods in hours or, at most, a few days. Disconnected processes will be apparent right away in terms of failed performance and loss of customer loyalty. Seamless value chains are mandatory regardless of the organizational structure if e-business is to be successfully supported. This factor alone is sufficient to convince an enterprise to organize and manage around processes.

Corporate Globalization

In a seminar I gave a few years ago in Europe, I was discussing some best practices in business and business process benchmarks from a global viewpoint. I used a number of examples of American, Canadian, and Asian companies as well as European ones. During the discussion, some audience members maintained that many of these ideas weren't relevant because they weren't planning to operate a global company. In response, I asked them to look at the delegates in the meeting in the next hotel conference room. That meeting was being held by a Japanese multinational. My question to my group was simply, "Do you think that the group next door is here to visit the cathedral?" The local country workshop then turned the discussion to how to become as good as the global competitors in terms of their local markets.

Many management gurus have claimed that companies have a choice of becoming truly global or a just being a smaller focused niche player. They claim that there will be little in between.

As more organizations try to manage globally, they are requiring their suppliers to do the same. One of my clients is a significant supplier to Wal-Mart. In the past, the supplier's operations in different countries each had responsibility for its own national sales. However, Wal-Mart Germany discovered that it could buy more cheaply from another European country operation and demanded the same pricing and terms from its supplier in Germany. This quickly escalated into having to treat Wal-Mart as one organization with a set of global terms. It also meant that the supplier organization's processes for sales and service had to change significantly from country-based to global customer-based. The supplier soon realized that, although it already was an international company with sales, manufacturing, and distribution all over the world, that didn't qualify it as a global entity. Working globally was quite different. The transition to truly behaving globally was even more difficult as constraining and misaligned incentives and cultures had to be overcome.

Likewise, a large bank with operations in more than 70 countries discovered that its clients wanted to be treated as one entity globally. Although every one of their country operations was governed by different central bank regulations, customers wanted one deal globally. That also meant that, rather than sell to the local country customer, a relationship had to be formed under the direction of a global relationship manager. This led to the philosophy of one global balance, one global credit limit, and one set of terms operating globally in near real-time for real-time decision making. The impact on processes was and still is widespread. The changes in locations of processing from country centers to global centers is having a large impact on staff and each local country's operations. The technological upheaval is significant. Despite the cultural implications, it must be done if the bank wants to gain competitively against the other handful of banks that could possibly succeed in treating global customers with a truly global service.

Globalization is both a threat and an opportunity. The biggest danger is to ignore the trend. The biggest risk, after you have recognized it, is to not go far enough in reconfiguring your internal capabilities because of compromises and internal power struggles.

Corporate Consolidation

Tied in with the other aforementioned trends is the seemingly unstoppable tidal wave of consolidations, mergers, and acquisitions.

The organization mentioned in the last section that's now dealing with Wal-Mart globally also had to consolidate its sales, support, and operations across internal divisions. Previously, each division dealt with Wal-Mart and other large retailers independently because their products were different. Now it has become one relationship and one process regardless of product. This model is now being rolled out to other large multinational and national customers.

Time Warner and AOL, Exxon and Mobil, US West and GTE, Pfizer and Warner Lambert—these are just a few of the massive recent mergers or acquisitions prevalent on the financial news pages. Add to this the steady stream of deals that Intel, Cisco, and thousands of others participate in as part of a steady appetite for growth. Organizations that do this well have significant advantage in the market. However, not all are so good at the game. A recent study by Hedgerow Mergers and Acquisitions concluded that

- Sixty-six percent to seventy-five percent of all mergers and acquisitions (M&As) actually destroyed market value.
- Thirty percent substantially eroded shareholder returns.
- Twenty-three percent failed to recover the costs of the deal.
- Fifty percent resulted in lowered productivity, profits, or both.
- Thirty-three percent to fifty percent of acquisitions were divested within five years.

Hedgerow's conclusion was that only one in five mergers is considered financially successful. This is frightening in light of the number of mergers taking place currently. Clearly the risks are great, but the feeling is that these organizations must take the gamble.

Some companies have gained incredible advantages by being turnaround artists. For them, M&A is actually a core process. Bombardier has become the third largest aircraft manufacturer in the world by taking over others that were all but abandoned by their shareholders as a lost cause. They have done the same in other forms of transportation. Celestica has outperformed the high-tech market significantly by taking over manufacturing from the likes of Toshiba, Motorola, and others that decided to pull back and focus their efforts elsewhere. This implies that doing M&A right is key. It's possible to win in acquisitions, but there must be a focus on integration of processes and culture more than anything else. The successful organizations avoid the common pitfalls that lead to disaster. Again, the results from Hedgerow Mergers and Acquisitions have shown that the causes for failure are

- Confusion, debate, and positioning around roles and responsibilities
- Confusion and debates around positioning for resources
- Sluggish execution/disagreement on priorities
- Exodus of key talent (not just the dead wood)
- An inward focus (away from markets and customers)

All these issues of process, project, risk, and change management are covered in this book.

Partnerships, Virtual Organizations, and Extended Value Chains

Closely related to the restructuring associated with mergers and acquisitions and to the wave of e-business formation is the significant number of new partnerships that are being established. Partly because of timing and quality of service drivers, organizations have found that they can't meet higher customer expectations if they do everything on their own. Many couldn't get off the ground with new services fast enough without help. Others have concluded that they couldn't scale to higher levels of business volume if there was too much to do without enough human resources. For many, it's simply a matter of avoiding the risk of staffing to high levels while the economy is good. Suppose it doesn't stay that way?

In any case, each and every organization must anticipate or respond to business events affecting customers and meet their expectations when they do. There's no mystery in figuring this out. The mystery is often in designing and developing the set of workflows and enablers required to meet those expectations. From the triggering event through to the closing outcome, collaboration across internal and external corporate boundaries is required. Processes must work on behalf of the process customer regardless of internal structure but also regardless of external partners. Dell, Toshiba, and others don't make all their own computers; they have contract manufacturers such as Celestica build the computers for them. Rexall.com doesn't ship its own health supplements; it uses UPS. DCI doesn't develop and teach its own seminars; it uses experts on topics currently in demand and changes them continuously as new technology and information management approaches reach the marketplace. Many mutual-fund and insurance companies don't sell directly; they equip and train independent financial advisors and agents. Cisco's success with this model is spurring others to mimic what's seen by many as the current best practice in strategic organizational design.

To do this effectively, organizations have to ask themselves what business they are really in. What is their value proposition to their customers and to their customers' customers? What can they be good at, and what should they have others do on their behalf?

> **NOTE**
>
> Value propositions will be covered in more detail in Chapter 2.

Some people might wonder what the difference is between real partnerships and traditional outsourcing. I believe that many well-conceived and executed outsourcing arrangements have all the hallmarks of true partnerships. The main one is that of trust among the partners. In a partnership arrangement, all parties involved must have a shared interest and incentive in the outcome of value to the ultimate customer. The business processes to make this happen are shared as one.

External Stakeholder Power

There is no doubt that organizations today, whether private or public sector, closely or widely held, are feeling a lot more external pressure from outside stakeholders. These interested parties are having a strong say in what happens. Customers, consumers, and service users can't be ignored without risking the existence of the organization. Suppliers are so intertwined with your value chain that their failure or lack of cooperation will stop you cold. Owners and share-holders are the vehicle for financing your future. Their lack of confidence can compromise your plans. Skilled staff members are hard to attract and retain. They are your means. How you are seen by other influential outsiders is becoming more and more significant. One word from them could see the organization scrambling to recover.

Customers/Consumers

Customers are getting smarter more quickly. This means that it isn't possible to fool them any-more. They have to be kept informed of products and the status of services. They know more about how your products can be used and the nature of your business than ever before. They learn more quickly, so you must do the same to stay ahead. If you miss a market trend that they see and demand that you do business that way or provide new products that you don't have yet, you will lose them. Your difficulty in staying with your customers' growing aware-ness is exacerbated by the shortening of business cycles that make it hard to exploit a body of knowledge.

Along with greater customer awareness has come greater customer demand for responsiveness and higher intolerance of lack of performance. Most customers want more choice and flexibil-ity. Each customer wants to be served when he wants and in his own way, which might change from time to time. Many of these changes will require the supplier to take on responsibilities that they would not have done before. Inventory management, direct shipment, and customer support are examples of these responsibilities. Mass customization or individualization pro-grams are expected. Many customers feel that they don't need an intermediary to initiate or provide service; they would prefer to help themselves directly.

Often, it's a matter of customers becoming caught in the time crunch where faster service is mandatory for their own customers and hence for them. Twenty-four-hours-a-day self-service is required because business never stops globally. Both physical and virtual sites must be convenient.

Automating as much of the process as possible provides timesavings to the participants in the business process and allows fewer people to do the existing work or the same people to do more work. For example, Rexall.com allows online automatic ordering of health supplements on an "easy ship" order that sends the same order each month. This saves time for both customer and supplier.

For the reasons mentioned here, segmentation of customers and consumers is critical so that you can understand each one better, serve them well, and assign staff with the right set of matched skills. It will save them and you time. Time is their scarcest resource and one that they can never get back. It's also yours, so be prepared to consider getting rid of those cus-tomers that don't warrant your effort.

I had a client in Europe that manufactured drinks and drink machines. After careful segmentation, this company concluded that the top tiers of customers were those who bought the most repeatedly. They chose to continue to provide personal service to that top tier. The bottom tier, however, was comprised of many small customers, such as hairdressing salons or small businesses, that bought very little and required a lot of support to manage orders and deliver small volumes of supplies. It was decided that the cost of supporting these customers was prohibitive relative to their business contribution. They were a losing proposition financially and from a management attention perspective. It was recommended, instead, that this segment be served by individually licensed franchisees, who would manage a defined local territory. The company would serve the franchisees with volumes consistent with those of their top segment customers.

Some customers demand that the organization take ownership of their entire set of needs all at once and consolidate all actions to deliver a consolidated result. Again, this will save time and worry. Travel services and Web sites that allow travelers to book all aspects of a trip are more valuable than those that handle only car or limousine rental, hotel, or air travel. This total response is in the best interest of many customers, who don't want to deal with many people or technologies. One-stop shopping is in demand.

It's clear that customers' and consumers' needs are becoming more complex. These stakeholders are also less loyal when their needs aren't met. Clearly, they are more demanding that their suppliers meet these commitments, and less tolerant if the supplier doesn't.

Supplier Focus

Although there is more pressure on suppliers to anticipate needs, respond to them, and perform better than in the past, there also are pressures on customers to treat their suppliers consistently well.

The best suppliers are those that meet their customers requirements well. They are also key partners in cross-company value chains. In this role, they are also the best at meeting their customers' requirements by working as part of a larger process. In many cases, the partners in the value chain might have a different value proposition from one another. They might be very focused on being an operationally excellent manufacturer of components for their customer, who, in turn, is focused on truly new and innovative products for the marketplace. They both bring their relative strengths to the partnership in such a way that neither could accomplish the same high level of customer results on their own.

The best suppliers aren't idle—they are in demand. They won't do a poor job. They solicit their customers carefully to ensure that they can do the best and work together most effectively. Top-notch suppliers might not offer the lowest price, but their customers often end up paying the least total cost when errors, defects, or mistakes are taken into account. The best suppliers are almost always the most reliable in terms of products and services. They can be trusted to deliver what is expected. They reject requests for corner cutting and instant fixes when they feel that such measures will cause bigger problems in the long run.

The bad news for some companies trying to acquire the services of the best suppliers is that they won't accept customers who aren't as committed to success as they are. They don't have to. There are plenty of other customers that value commitment to quality and service.

The Investment Market Speaks

Investors traditionally have looked at a company in light of its longer-term potential. There have always been speculative investments with high risks, but the tendency to jump in and out of stock ownership has never previously applied to the larger firms as much as it does today. Clearly, this lack of patience by investors is having a large impact on organizations of all types. For government organizations, the same is true and it manifests itself in political interference and allocated budgets. These can change dramatically depending on the day's political regime.

Investment money walks away easily, and, when it does, it has a dramatic effect on organizations that require new funds to grow and change. The pressure on the CEO and board of directors is almost unbearable. A drop of 35% in share prices means that it's hard to raise new capital. An organization seen as having upside potential and as having a strong management team can raise the money needed to capture new markets and develop new products. But one small slip can drop it to the bottom of the pile.

On the day I wrote this section of this chapter, Nortel Networks dropped one third of its market capitalization, wiping out more than $30 billion of valuation for individual investors and mutual funds. This happened not because Nortel is weak, but because its growth rate projection was scaled back for 2001. The rate of growth, however, wasn't the real issue. The investment market reacted more to the loss of faith in Nortel's management team's ability to see the future and on a perception that the news was known earlier but kept from analysts, fund managers, and investors. This is obviously a serious breach of trust in investors' and analysts' minds.

Many people look toward profits and return on equity as ways of evaluating a company's worth. A major contributing measure to this is Return-on-Assets (ROA). In traditional organizations, this was a valid metric measuring the contribution made as a proportion of balance sheet assets. However, in information or knowledge-based companies, knowing the ROA isn't sufficient to help the investor understand the true value of the knowledge created. Another perspective, fortunately, is gaining attention. Typically named *Return-on-Management*®[3] (ROM), it measures the payback of a company's scarcest resource: management time and attention.[4] *Management*, in this sense, is anything not directly involved with core production. It includes functions such as research and development, marketing, sales, information technology, and human resources management, among others. The investment marketplace knows that ROM is important and seems to correlate valuations reasonably well to this factor, even if it does so

---

[3]*Return-on-Management*® *is a registered trademark of Strassmann, Inc.*
[4]*How* High is Your Return on Management?, *Robert Simons and Antonio Davila,* Harvard Business Review, *January–February 1998*

qualitatively. Noted author and industry observer Paul Strassmann claims that ROM and Knowledge Capital®[5] can be calculated[6] more precisely to aid investors to produce valuations. New economy enterprises must manage Return-on-Management to the satisfaction of investors.

Scarce Human Resources

In our knowledge-oriented economy, human issues are gaining attention again. Strassmann's ROM arguments and financial evidence strongly support the observation that humans are assets.

However, letting go of an employee with years of experience has no immediately evident negative effect on the balance sheet, even though her company has invested hundreds of thousands of dollars in her education to get her to the productive level that she is at the time of her layoff. There is no write-off of an asset as there would have been if 100 two-year-old computers were retired. As far as the official books are concerned, furniture has a value; staff doesn't.

Fortunately, many organizations learned from early misguided, cost-focused re-engineering efforts achieved primarily through staff reductions that were good only for a year or two. They learned that no one could build market share or sustain innovation by cutting smart people.

This type of careless staff reduction has translated to a genuine skills crunch, wherein the scarcest of all resources is knowledgeable and capable humans with the appropriate attitudes. They are hard to find and harder to keep. The loyalty of skilled humans with lots of career choices, who feel that they are treated poorly, is fleeting. Without a strong program of compensation, rewards, and recognition of personal preferences, hiring and retention will be a constant headache that robs the organization of its productivity and adaptability. Those companies that handle their associates well, such as SAS Institute, the software and services solution provider, also perform well in the market. SAS's remarkable performance of less than 5% annual turnover in staff is a direct reflection of sensitive human resource policies and practices that focus strongly on the customer yet recognize the importance of a balanced lifestyle and family values as well as a strong work ethic.

Because there is an obvious skills shortage in most knowledge-intensive industries, paying attention to employees as stakeholders is a critical factor for success.

Ethical Agenda

Other indirect stakeholders might influence the organization's success very dramatically. The image and perception of a company in the eyes of outside groups can make a difference, either good or bad. The public, regulatory agencies, special interest groups, funding groups, professional associations, lobbyists, and other community stakeholders can be key players. These

---

[5] *Knowledge Capital® is a registered trademark of Strassmann Inc.*
[6] *"Measuring and Managing Knowledge Capital," Knowledge Executive Report, June 1999, Paul Strassmann*

stakeholders are becoming more powerful and sometimes militant. The company's actions in response to—or in anticipation of—outsiders' pressures can make a big difference.

In British Columbia, where I live, there is no better example of this than the forestry industry. This industry is the prime employer in the province, and in many towns and communities is the only real opportunity for work. Meeting the community expectations of job continuity is a key factor for this organization (as it is for many businesses). Also, the forestry employers face tremendous confrontational actions by environmental lobbyists. Traditionally, these groups have blocked roads, spiked old growth trees to prevent cutting, and conducted other visible radical activities to publicize their beliefs. These protests worked well to raise awareness for a while but also served to alienate the workers in the communities affected and some other members of the public. Logging firms rarely responded positively to the demands of the groups, and their cause moved forward more slowly than the environmentalists had hoped.

More recently, however, tactics have changed. Many of the environmentalists moved their focus from the logging companies to forest product customers. For example, a major market for BC forest products can be found in Europe. Lobby groups spent a lot of time with European forest products buyers to convince them that the forestry companies' practices—such as clear cutting and old-growth extraction in the last temperate rain forest in the world—are environmentally dangerous and not sustainable. The consequences have been the cancellation of many contracts and much publicity associated with these cancellations. The forest product companies clearly took note and were forced to answer to their owners on these issues. As a result, some of the more advanced and more process-mature companies now are certifying finished wood products by tracing specific trees throughout the process, starting with logging through to the finished product delivery. This practice, which is well defined and governed by an international standards and certification agency, has led to surprise advantages of higher-than-average prices and a high demand for products from those companies that can comply. The environmental stakeholders clearly are wielding their powers and can't be ignored.

There are numerous other examples such as the pressures and lawsuits on tobacco companies from state governments and class-action litigants, public reactions to companies that have experienced oil tanker spills, and public expectations of integrity and honesty in utilities or charities, to name just a few.

There are even Web sites in existence where individuals can check an organization's ethical behavior and performance against its social responsibilities. Users of these sites can also update the sites with their perceptions and experiences.

Clearly, what counts is not just the increasing pressures that come from the members of the business' community that affect an organization's performance, but also the organization's understanding and readiness to deal with all community stakeholders. These groups won't go away by ignoring them.

E-Business Technology Drivers

As business product cycles change more and more rapidly and each organization is required to form an individual and unique relationship with each of its customers and other stakeholders, only flexible processes and maneuverable technologies can enable knowledgeable staff to make the commitments required to continuously adapt. Technology can also provide a great opportunity for business change, perhaps one of the most important opportunities, as long as we don't deal with technology in isolation of the other factors of process, knowledge, and stakeholder relationships. Figure 1.7 shows how these are related. Note that all arrows are bi-directional, requiring a two-way examination of opportunities and impacts.

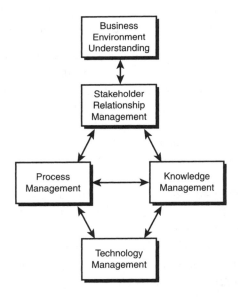

FIGURE 1.7
Interplay among critical competencies for performance improvement.

Without quality and productivity improvements made possible by strategic technologies, enterprises can fall behind competitively. Production technology improvements can take the form of new production capabilities, such as manufacturing process improvements and better production management solutions that allow ongoing feedback through real-time programmable logic controllers (PLCs) (These controllers link equipment into control rooms or virtual control rooms to monitor and automate production processes.)

In general, organizations are becoming more mature in their information technology applications and are building on their legacy. Some advanced organizations are approaching a new maturity level in the realm of Process Management ("What do I have to do?") and Data

Management ("What do I have to know to do it?"). As these organizations mature, they get closer to the business and data; process perspectives converge to the point that stakeholder relationships, business process, and knowledge are dealt with concurrently. Figure 1.8 shows how this approach to IT is converging around business issues.

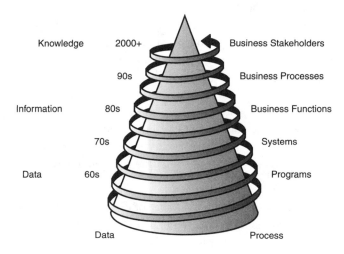

FIGURE 1.8

The Burlton Data/Process Management Maturity Model.

An analysis of Figures 1.7 and 1.8 led me to look at what technology can do to serve business process stakeholders better. I will look at technology potential from these points of view:

- How technology can provide access to information that has more integrity, whenever and wherever it's needed
- How technology can initiate, track, and automate process execution
- How technology can help create and distribute the latest knowledge

The following sections look at the effects that these technologies can have on business—not in excruciating detail, but as examples of the types of enablers to search out.

Information Accessibility and Integrity

The availability of information that can be trusted, where and when it is required, means that new business approaches and processes can be imagined and designed without technological constraints. It's always a good starting point to gain agreement that accessibility constraints won't be factored into our thinking too soon. Let's imagine that all information will be trustworthy and available. Technologically, there's no reason not to.

The pressures of globalization and rising customer expectations means that information must be accessible by anyone, located anywhere, whenever that person chooses. This requires exploiting today's scalable information management technologies to store data, new information appliances to present it, and reliable network infrastructures to transport it.

Because information sharing is the key issue for many external stakeholders and internal staff, building a foundation of robust database management systems (DBMS) is a fundamental. Scalable relational DBMS for the transactional part of the business and object-oriented DBMS for the more complex types of data such as voice, graphics, maps, and video are now available to all organizations. These technologies are the storage mechanisms for information assets. Choose a system that can be a central coordination site across a number of applications, connecting many of their users. Other storage mechanisms are data warehouses and data marts that extract and consolidate data from a number of non-integrated data sources from inside and outside the enterprise. These mechanisms make data accessible to be manipulated and presented as if from one consistent source. The complexity of the provisioning process and infrastructure must be hidden from those gaining access.

This information can be presented through a number of different front-end technologies and user interfaces. Classical multimedia desktop computers for office workers provide a high-resolution, multiple-window environment for graphical and textual information and other rich data types such as spatial, sound, and video. Sophisticated analysis tools can also be accessed from there, to provide an online information management service. When assembled intelligently, a number of functions can be provided through one-stop shopping portals, making it easy for users to find all they need to know.

These integrated access sites are enabled by internetworked technologies for outsiders (Internet), trusted customers and suppliers (extranet), and internal staff (intranet). Delivering these technologies isn't difficult as compared to organizing the information that they must make available.

Providing information to anyone who needs it requires abundant communications bandwidth for anyone and from our sources anywhere. High bandwidth local area networks hooked to wide-area networks hooked to global networks must all be built or rented. Also, *anyone* and *anywhere* imply that the air and space become places for electronic information messages to traverse. Wireless networks using emerging standards such as digital cellular, wireless application protocol (WAP), infrared, radio, and satellites all support the use of mobile devices. These include Palm Pilots and digital telephones in our pockets, displays in our cars, and anything else that moves and can be located with digital cellular networks and global positioning devices. We can already push a lot of information through high-speed wireless networks. These will soon be faster and cheaper than they are today. They should be planned for now.

It's one thing to have enterprise information available whenever you want it. It's something else for that information to have integrity. *Integrity* for data management purposes means that, if information is redundant, it must be consistent. That means that it can be trusted. The simplest form of data integrity is to be able to update a single data field in a single record in a single file. By definition, there will never be any redundancy issues if this is the case. Integrity in the information that is accessible to anyone you choose, regardless of location, is key if you want to avoid different people making decisions based on information that varies but that should be the same. Integrity of information means that relationships will be managed consistently, and that the costs of wrong decisions and corrective actions will be significantly reduced.

One major trend supporting the concept of key enterprise information integrity is enterprise resource planning (ERP), as enabled by technologies such as SAP, Baan, Oracle, and PeopleSoft. This approach strives to provide a single place to store and manage information about enterprise assets. Components that handle information about financial, human resource, and fixed assets are common. This integration of asset information has significant process implications. The difficulty of making ERP work lies more in the process and business changes required than in the concept of shared data with integrity. One shortfall of most ERP implementations is the difficulty of getting the information out in meaningful ways after it's captured. Data warehouses are often used to solve this problem.

Likewise, another significant trend deals with relationship management. Integrity of customer relationship information has also been a concern for a long time. Now there are significant software offerings from vendors such as Seibold, Vantive, and I2 that provide the mechanisms for customer relationship management (CRM) solutions. Pivitol has taken it one step further by broadening its offerings to cover a range of stakeholders, not just customers. I believe that others will do the same by extending their CRM and supply-chain management software to manage the integrity of all stakeholders' information in a more balanced way.

Business Process Automation

If business must be supported from anywhere 24 hours a day, 7 days a week, processes must also be accessible and executable in the same timeframe. Technologies that help navigate entire processes are now available to support this. Embedding the business's rules and its human knowledge into the organization's executable processing software can change your way of working. Figure 1.9 shows the requirements for complete business process automation—from initial business event through final business outcome.

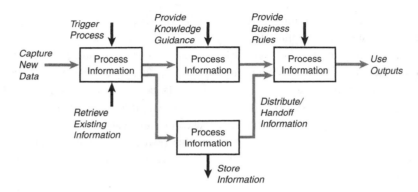

FIGURE 1.9

A business process view of information management.

To initiate the automated process flow, triggering events must be sensed or recognized. Some technologies that recognize triggers have been around for a while, whereas others are relatively new. Office workers have long been able to launch a workflow through their desktop computers' Enter keys or mouse clicks. The order process agent might take in a lot of information, but until the agent confirms the order, the bulk of the order process isn't initiated. Today, humans can use a handheld event recognition device to trigger process flows as part of a wireless network to do essentially the same thing.

Most of us are very used to swiping a credit or membership card in a reader to initiate self-service processes. Many airlines provide kiosks that take your frequent flyer cards and securely allow you to initiate the issuing of your seat assignment and boarding cards as well as luggage tags. Smart cards can go one step further by carrying information that might be relevant upon the triggering event.

Other devices, such as bar code scanners, also trigger automated action. When you scan your library card and the library book that you want to take out, the technology recognizes an event involving the codes, invokes the rules for that type of book and you, and tells you when the book is due back. Later, on return of the book, your record of liability is cleared, and the process instance is closed. If you don't return the book on time, other parts of the process are invoked to send you reminders and calculate penalties for lateness.

The capability of bar codes to initiate action should be examined for productivity and reliability. However, the process that follows it must be thought through to its conclusions.

The principles behind the bar-code style of triggering processes apply beyond the technology itself, whereby the reading device doesn't have to find the bar code to read it. Self-identifying tags can allow stationary sensors to identify the presence of a triggering event. These tags are essentially tiny computer chips that emit their own unique electronic message from the chip.

When the chip is in range of an energizing source, it sends out its fingerprint to initiate action. These devices have been used on personal ID tags so that, no matter where you go in the work site, you can be located. Farmers routinely use them to identify their animals at automated feeders and prevent them from overeating by dispatching just the right amount of food and water. All railcars have them to allow tracking and expediting of movement across the country. The uses are limited only by your imagination.

After it's initiated through these triggers, the complete business process flow can be automated through to process termination. This would include the movement and management of the multimedia information required to achieve a satisfactory outcome of value to the initiating stakeholder. Overall workflow technologies play a management role. These technologies pass inputs and control to specific applications that perform specific functions and then return outputs and control back to the transaction manager function of the workflow engine. Work is prioritized and delivered to users' in baskets for execution, or is sent to standalone applications for processing. The work products can be text, numbers, forms to be circulated and filled out, or even electronic approvals. The workflow environment is a flexible multimedia push technology requiring standards and openness across platforms and locations. It's based on a set of predefined business rules; the steps of the navigation can vary from instance to instance. The workflow engine determines the needed sequence. It also tracks and traces and reports back status.

Traditionally, workflow capabilities were found in imaging and forms management software; today, it's the opposite. Imaging and forms are just two types of data that can navigate a networked environment with the control of a workflow engine. When well designed, this engine assembles and controls reusable software components and invokes them using navigation rules documented separately from computer logic. Business people, not technicians, do the management and modification of the navigation rules. They define them in business language, not technology constructs. Adaptability is the consequence.

Knowledge Creation and Distribution

As business cycles shrink and time-in-market opportunities diminish, those organizations that can create and exploit knowledge faster and better will succeed. Making knowledge accessible to business processes as guidance is a make-or-break process in its own right. Technology can play a key role in delivering the latest knowledge to the people doing the work or can deliver encoded knowledge that software can automatically execute.

In customer interactions, as well as internal interactions, learning never stops, and the business environment never rests. For these reasons, finding ways to improve the support of human knowledge is starting to get a lot of attention.

The concept of just-in-time (JIT) training isn't new. It recognizes that the best application of training occurs when it's provided just before it's applied. Consider what it would take to keep training courses and reference guides up-to-date using traditional media development methods. Also think about how you would deliver the new messages quickly. It would almost be impossible. By utilizing technology available to all organizations today, this problem can be solved. Through intranets, you can widely, quickly, and inexpensively distribute the latest guidance to front-line staff members who are part of a workflow. Likewise, new knowledge can be delivered to customers. These environments are multimedia in nature and can update documents, graphics, voice messages, and video to show what business changes are occurring and how to deal better with current scenarios. This replaces training courses and procedural guides, which become the same thing in this multimedia delivery environment. In structured or transaction-oriented situations, the training can be linked to specific aspects of the workflow and available through a function key or drop-down list. Notification of new knowledge can also be prominently displayed the first time someone enters into an application after the knowledge has been posted.

For less structured work, providing access to knowledge portals can be valuable. In this situation, knowledge is structured according to some form of knowledge "yellow pages" that segments the knowledge in indexes understood by the knowledge seekers. Hierarchical and hypertext relationships of knowledge concepts are shown in the structure, as is a map of all known human sources and knowledge stewards. The map can also depict the cognitive authority (trustworthiness) of the source. These portals would include access to relevant documents and search engines to find other internal or external sources. They also contain mechanism for knowledge feedback and the use of lessons learned.

Another way to use technology to support the leverage of knowledge is to embed it in the software that runs the business applications.

As we saw with workflow software navigation, business rules can capture a subset of knowledge. Business rules–based application development engines are available in the marketplace from a number of proven vendors. These technologies separate business rules from data definitions and workflow. This ideally allows ease of updating rules, based on lessons learned and marketplace changes, because no software coding is required. Rules and business event triggers are stored in a layer between normalized databases and the workflows or applications that use them. Ideally, the rules and the knowledge that they depend on reside in a shared rule repository and are executed from a rules server.

Expert systems have been with us for some time. They are gaining attention again in domain-specific situations in which expert knowledge is required but not available in all staff members. Call centers and help desks provide typical opportunities to exploit these technologies, especially those that use case-based reasoning approaches. In these, knowledge and best practices are generalized and transformed into useful rules. The difference is that case-based approaches aren't just strict rules—they reflect and recognize patterns and then guide the service provider through a most likely path of action or questioning. New patterns arise and are inferred from new situations.

Knowledge, like all organizational assets, must be created or discovered and then acquired before it can be distributed and used. Some technologies can support the creation of new knowledge in collaborative communities, as well as its distribution to those in day-to-day work processes. Although collaborative creative work is primarily a human endeavor, communications technologies can be very helpful when it comes to iterating ideas across a wider community, either inside or outside the enterprise.

Technologies that support person-to-person, team-to-team collaboration include

- E-mail and messaging
- Group calendars and scheduling
- Electronic meeting systems
- Desktop video and real-time data conferencing
- Group document handling
- Groupware services to support collaboration

Groupware solutions identify and connect knowledgeable people through the mechanism of living discussion documents or reference databases. This form of technology is particularly useful when it's built on a replication mechanism, so that globally all interested members of a work group or a virtual community of practice can contribute concurrently. These varied technologies—such as Lotus Notes, Microsoft NetMeeting, and other collaborative, Internet-based applications and products—are best used when complex, fast-changing knowledge must be shared in an iterative knowledge creation cycle. For sharing lessons learned and knowledge feedback, these technologies maximize human interaction while minimizing technological interference.

Summary

This chapter described some of the major pressures facing enterprises today. It looked at hyper-competition, growing organization complexity and reach, rising external stakeholder power, and e-business technology. Each of these is changing the face of how business is transacted globally. No organization is immune from the changes that these driving forces are bringing. Business in all industry segments must respond now to head off the risk of falling behind forever.

Chapter 2 will cover a range of possible responses to these challenges. It will ask a number of questions to help you determine what choices you have and to pick from among them.

Organizational Responses to Business Drivers

IN THIS CHAPTER

Given the myriad pressures facing organizations today, many organizations are either changing their reason for being or renewing their commitment to their current approach. For all, the question of purpose and strategy must be revisited. A number of questions must be asked:

- Is our mission and value proposition still suitable?
- How much of a time horizon is appropriate for our planning process?
- Will we be followers or leaders?
- Will everything have to change all the time, or can we isolate some stable aspects?
- Can we control everything, or do we have to relinquish control and trust others more?

This chapter will delve into some of the choices that might be considered.

Questioning the Mission and the Value Proposition

The prime question that must be dealt with is, "What are we really in business to do?" All other choices will emanate from this answer. It's the root of the traceability tree.

The mission of the organization succinctly describes what the organization is striving to do. For example, at the Process Renewal Group, our mission statement reads

> *The Process Renewal Group* is a consulting organization committed to helping its clients successfully manage business change. Our mission is to help dramatically improve our clients' performance through the renewal of business strategies and business processes as well as the innovative application of information technologies.

Mission statements must get the point across and guide all strategies and actions. It's incumbent on all organizations that they revisit their mission periodically to ensure that it's still suitable for the foreseeable future.

A deceptively simple aspect, closely related to questioning the mission, is determining the organization's *value proposition*. This describes the set of products and service characteristics, relationship styles, and branding perceptions that the organization is striving to create. It's the basis for its differentiation in the marketplace, for what gets done and how. Value proposition has a strong affiliation with the company culture, and the degree of fit with each other will help determine success.

Michael Treacy and Fred Wiersema's work has proposed that businesses choose one of three major types of value proposition for organizations:[1]

---

[1] The Discipline of Market Leaders: Choose Your Customers, Narrow Your Focus, Dominate Your Market, *Michael Treacy and Fred Wiersema, Addison-Wesley, 1995*

- Operational excellence
- Product leadership
- Customer intimacy

It's generally accepted that an organization today must select a primary focus and might also pick a secondary one. Trying to be all things to all people doesn't allow rational strategies to be developed and executed and provides no focus or leadership.

Not surprisingly, the best manufacturers are focused on operational excellence, the best pharmaceutical providers, on product leadership (product-to-market), and the best high-end retailers, on customer intimacy. The choice has a big impact on the customers served as well as on the nature of the relationships with all other stakeholders. The chosen proposition drives the processes that internally deliver the desired result. It doesn't mean that the other propositions are ignored, but one will dominate a business's thinking, decision making, and behavior.

Switching value propositions might be called for in the market in which a company finds itself. For example, because of the inability to find sufficient appropriate resources, telecommunications technology providers such as Cisco and Nortel have had to choose to grow in all aspects of customer relationship management, manufacturing growth, and innovation. Management attention and funding can't cover all fields. Being good at all of them isn't sufficient when others are great at one.

Cisco Systems has never manufactured its own equipment. It has reached a globally envied position because of its ability to get leading internetworking products to market fast. Nortel, once a manufacturing powerhouse, has decided it needs to out-Cisco Cisco if it wants to reach its market share goals, so it outsourced much of its production. Its value proposition is changing. Celestica, one of the world's top high-tech outsourcing manufacturers, does little product R&D compared to the days when it was part of IBM, but it does manufacture for many high-tech innovators. For Celestica to keep its business and to grow, it must remain the best and most reliable supplier in its field. Celestica must also maintain a low-cost structure as its prime differentiation in the marketplace, even as it acquires the manufacturing capabilities of its new partners/customers.

Regardless of the specific choice of a primary and perhaps a secondary focus, a choice is required because to be anything but the best today means losing your position and perhaps your business itself.

A challenge is and will continue to be that, because of their own responsibilities and background, different executives and staff in the company often have different views of what the value proposition is or should be. They might also be out of step with each other because of differences in understanding between historical drivers and today's business drivers. This gap typically translates into an internal inability to focus corporately and to allocate resources to the most important requirements. The unyielding communication of the value proposition and the mission is critical when things change or when internal confusion and lack of consensus is apparent. Eliminating this chasm in cultural focus will become a critical factor for success in transitioning to a new proposition—if it's not already critical.

Questioning the Time Horizon

The question here is, "Are we in it for the long haul or out to exploit a short-term opportunity?" The answer will drive completely different behaviors.

Business professors James Collins and Jerry Porras published a seminal work in 1994[2] that dealt with the sustainability of organizations while everything around them was in flux. They crystallized a few key factors that allow organizations to become sustainable over the long term. The term they coined was "built to last." It looked like a winning philosophy, but was it?

Recent history of new-economy organizations has challenged some of the premises behind this thinking. Lately, Collins has been forced to question his strategy of building great companies to last, and he has started to ask whether sustainability is for everyone.[3] The choices that organizations must make regarding the planned life are influenced by the ownership strategy of the company and the nature of the rate of consolidation of the organization's industry.

The technology-driven stock market has witnessed many new entrants that weren't "built to work" and, consequently, have failed. Many of these new organizations today don't intend to last forever. They were "built to flip"—to be acquired by a new entrant or competitor or to float a public offering for great initial gains. The planning choices made by the corporate entity in question must identify which approach is appropriate because the value proposition, strategies, and stakeholder relationships will vary for each. Let's look at the attributes of the choices: "built to last," "built to work," and "built to flip."

"Built to Work" Versus "Built to Last"

The criteria for "built-to-work" organizations center around excellence in whatever the business is about. "Built-to-work" organizations might be intended to become great, long-term companies in their own right (that is, "built to last"), or they might fully anticipate that they will be gobbled up by a major player in the marketplace. Regardless, all work is done according to the highest possible standards, and value added is clearly demonstrated. These organizations make a distinct contribution to their markets, investors, and customers. They provide meaning to staff and associates through the intrinsic value of the work itself.

---

[2]*Built to Last: Successful Habits of Visionary Companies*, James C. Collins and Jerry I. Porras, Harper Collins, 1994

[3]*"Built to Flip,"* James C. Collins, Fast Company, *March 2000, Issue 32, page 131*

"Built-to-work" and "built-to-last" organizations are unconditionally committed to their principles and values. They are passionate about their relationships and the trust that makes them work. They develop strong brands and teach the market their beliefs. They develop their organizations through leadership and teach their staff their beliefs. They invent products and services that make a difference and build a sustainable business engine around them. They nurture their culture at an evolutionary pace but never stop doing so. This requires time, constancy, and consistency, but process efficiency and speed are always being sought.

This might sound like a romantic view of an old-economy business, but the essence of this view is just as important today. In a new-age "built-to-last" organization, partnerships become paramount because of the need to focus on a core competency associated with a value proposition. But, the organization must still be part of a world-class value chain. The difference between the old and new "built-to-last" models is simply that, today, the set of partners must have complementary value propositions and a commitment "to last" together.

For "built-to-work" organizations, global consolidation, mergers, and acquisition frenzies can't be ignored. Established, "built-to-last" organizations often will have a strategy of acquiring solid new ventures with new ideas while they are small, and the culture isn't yet rigid. This can be an efficient source of R&D for more established firms. The new-venture, "built-to-last" organization must choose whether it wants to be acquired or to take on the attributes of a long-time, successful entity. For some, there's little interest in building a great, long-lived company but more interest in quickly creating something of value while it's still valuable. The strategies, relationships, and processes will vary greatly.

This view is completely consistent with the thinking of Clayton Christensen, who describes what happens to markets when a disruptive technology or way of working arrives on the scene.[4] According to Christensen, the marketplace incumbent can choose to resist and watch the competitor take market share, or it can acquire the upstart competitor, as Microsoft and other market leaders have done so well in the recent past. The new kid on the block can choose to sell or to fight, but ultimately not every one will last. There will be a shakeout. A good example of this is the handful of automotive companies we see today, compared to more than 450 in the early 1900s.

For some companies, life is the extent of the product development cycle, and, once that is done, the company ceases to exist. It's all about products, and the company is simply a means to bring an innovation to market to be exploited by others. Japanese electronics R&D consortia fall into this category, whereby the commercialization of the product is performed by organizations other than those who developed the concept. The idea generators make their income from royalties and rights, not by selling products. This practice is commonplace in medical devices

---

[4]The Innovator's Dilemma: When New Technologies Cause Great Firms to Fail, *Clayton M. Christensen, Harvard Business School Press, 1997*

and biotechnology as well as in university-based research firms. Many large firms looking for innovation can purchase this form of R&D without significant risk. In this scenario, companies are often acquired by some entity with sales and marketing capability that has the economic structure and wherewithal to allocate strategic resources to exploit the opportunity. The acquiring entity will be able to leverage faster, better, and cheaper than the developer. This is a different value proposition. This model is hard to beat for companies trying to do it all. Managers have too many variables to focus on, and too many things can go wrong. Trying to be best at everything means that they are trying to be better than a partnership of companies, each of which is doing everything to be the best at only one aspect. It's an argument as old as business itself: How can I best allocate my scarce resources? Today, the resources in question are the time and effort of our skilled, experienced human managers and professionals.

"Built to Flip"

For "built-to-flip" organizations, the company's life is merely the idea life. What's for sale is the potential of the idea—the business plan, not the business itself.

"Built-to-flip" organizations depend on their ability to attract the right skills with the appropriate incentive plans. It was easy when every dot-com company could launch an IPO, creating instant millionaires within the newly traded company. However, after the rush, these companies are having a harder time attracting those who don't want to accept what's now seen as a higher risk. This short-lived phenomenon clearly wasn't a sustainable model. I believe that, although there's significant opportunity in the new economy, it will be for those who are developing "built-to-work" organizations, and the "built-to-flip" propositions will be more transparent than they were previously. Workers will look for meaningful work as an intrinsic measure, not just for financial gain.

Establishing a Time Horizon

Regardless of the life span anticipated for the organization, the approach will remain the same:

- Know the mission and value proposition
- Know your principles
- Understand your stakeholders
- Weight your stakeholders' emphasis
- Develop your criteria
- Evaluate your priorities
- Pick your processes
- Make them work

The emphasis on a number of key factors will vary depending on the organization's choice of approach. Table 2.1 points out the likely emphasis for each type of business, although it won't be universally true for all businesses.

TABLE 2.1 Organizational Choices in Strategy and Performance Management

Built To...	Likely Value Proposition	Key Stakeholders	Measures
Last	Customer intimacy or operational excellence	Customers and consumers, suppliers, staff and owners	Customer loyalty, return on equity, staff retention
Work	Product leadership	Partners, staff	Rate of innovation, time to market, staff acquisition
Flip	Product leadership	Venture capitalists, founders and staff	Staff acquisition, time to takeover or IPO, return to founders and shareholders

Another critical factor in determining the planning horizon is the incentive plan for the organization's senior management. Robert Kaplan and David Norton's balanced scorecard[5] defines four major types of measures that can be used as incentives:

- Financial
- Customer
- Process
- Innovation

If the executive-reward horizon encourages a short-term return, we can expect to see decisions and behavior that focus on the short-term financial and process efficiency aspects at a possible cost to customers and innovation in the long run. The financial and process measures will focus on productivity and optimization of existing assets, not on revenue and market share growth. Cost reduction and lean operations will prevail even if it's at the expense of staff loyalty and retention of organizational learning. The opposite could also be true if the leadership has an incentive for pursuing market growth and longer-term sustainability. Knowing the personal drivers of those at the top will be a leading indicator of behaviors and measurement results to come.

---

[5] "Having Trouble with Your Strategy? Then Map It," Robert S. Kaplan and David P. Norton, Harvard Business Review, September/October 2000, pages 167–176

Questioning the Leadership Style

A key question for many organizations very much related to that of their value proposition is whether they will lead change or follow change. Each approach has had its share of significant debate on its relative merits and risks. Especially in the new economy, Wall Street has changed its mind more than once. As the promise of new ventures with new ideas fails to live up to the IPO hype, value-based companies have come into favor again. Earlier dot-com companies with little in the way of profit—or hope of achieving it—soared to incredible valuation heights, only to crash back to earth after the reality that they might never make a profit sunk in. Some seemed to have made the grade, but many haven't. Many traditional, established companies that took a go-slow approach and are now adopting newer tactics seemed to do better, but not all. So what's the right strategy? Is there even a right or wrong way, or is it more about execution than strategy? These are all good questions that each organization has to ask itself.

A good question is whether there really is anything new about this in the new economy. E-business is just business but at a faster pace with new channels. Organizations, especially successful ones, have always had to deal with the question of *when* to change, not whether to change. Should they risk their current market leadership with something new? Historically, their branding might have provided something that delivers superior margins. Should they compete with themselves with a lower-cost product or service? Where is the business case and what's the risk?

There might not be a right or wrong way, but you have to pick a way. McDonald's carefully researches new sites, and then Burger King locates a new restaurant nearby. Both ways seem to work. Pfizer will pour billions into drug R&D. In time, when the patents expire or licensing agreements are reached, the generic manufacturers will make cheaper alternatives to Pfizer's best sellers. Neither is wrong. It's just a choice of strategy, but you have to have one.

There is a risk, however, in becoming too complacent when it might be time to try something new. Legendary companies such as Nordstrom and Federal Express are hard to match because they are moving targets, always learning from their loyal customers. At the right times, this is a good strategy. But what do Apple, IBM, DEC, Compaq, and Barnes and Noble have in common? They all missed huge marketplace opportunities. They listened to their customers at a time when their customers were unaware of a fundamental shift occurring in products or services and, as a result, didn't ask for the new product or service.

This thinking, brought to the surface by Clayton Christensen,[6] has shown us the "dilemma" that comes with success and the importance of not blindly clinging to one strategy at all times. In the case of Apple, IBM, and the four other previously mentioned companies, some new

---

[6]*See note 4 earlier in chapter.*

product, service strategy, or channel appeared in the marketplace. The firms considered the new offering novel but not a threat because it wasn't "relevant" to their most profitable customers. The initial market was relatively small with unattractive margins and typically comprised different customers with different needs. It also involved a product or approach that existing high-end customers and owners would deem inferior by all existing measures of value. The emerging market was easy to dismiss, hard to support from a cost benefit and risk perspective, and consequently ignored until it matured elsewhere and threatened the status quo.

Apple Computers is a fascinating study in the ups and downs of new versus existing strategies. The Apple II appealed to a market segment ready for a small, inexpensive personal machine to support educational objectives. This was an unrecognized market, and the Apple II didn't threaten existing computer companies, which didn't want such a poor performer by existing standards compared to their mainframe business. In the first two years, Apple sold 43,000 units—a huge success for a startup then but a revenue-rounding error to the more established computer manufacturers. Likewise, the Macintosh was introduced based on technology developed but not commercialized by Xerox, whose existing customers didn't see the value. Xerox couldn't make a compelling business case for a personal computer with a user-friendly graphic interface. Again, Apple scooped a large win with a disruptive technology that its competitors were slow to value in a marketplace they saw as being too limited. The strategy to do this didn't come from existing customers but from an internal vision and an open mind.

The success that Apple had with the Mac moved it to more upscale markets with competitive products for customers of the traditional firms. The upwardly mobile Apple became a threat and, in the process of growing larger, started to assume many of same decision-making criteria that paralyzed its competitors early on. The idea for a new pocket-computing product took form with the Newton, but, unlike in its prior initiatives, Apple adopted a different set of criteria for judging the Newton's success. Despite sales of 140,000 in its first two years, the Newton was considered a failure and abandoned because it contributed only a miniscule percentage of revenue, as compared to existing customer income. This decision left 3Com with a huge opportunity for the Palm Pilot.

Paradoxically, Apple's later crisis of survival—along with its vision, which was reignited with the return of Steve Jobs—opened the door for the iMac, G3 Power Mac, and G4. This return to a value proposition of leadership and innovation was appropriate for Apple. The iMac exhibited what can go right by not asking existing sophisticated product or service users what to do. By introducing a product with less functionality than existing ones and targeting a different market, a new leadership business model was created. In the process, a new market emerged.

Similar examples abound in almost every industry, proving that there isn't necessarily a right choice but sometimes it's a matter of the appropriate strategy for the right time. Just ask the competitors of Southwest Airlines, Amazon.com, Autobuytel.com, Progressive Insurance, Dell

Computers, and the like. None of them saw a serious threat coming, and, when they did, they still didn't act in time. They were too busy looking backward at existing competitors and today's customers when it was time to transition.

Consider what others have done. General Motors couldn't have made the Saturn line work inside GM proper, so it set up shop in Spring Hill, Tennessee, and moved its best assembly line employees there. Hewlett-Packard chose to compete with its own LaserJets by also marketing ink-jet printers. 3M gives researchers untethered R&D time and money for anything they want to work on. But also consider what Microsoft has done by being second in learning from the pioneers and building evolving solutions in word processing, graphics, browsers, and operating systems or, if that fails, buying out the competition.

Questioning Stability

A key question regarding a fast-changing business world is how we can rapidly respond to the need to change when everything is connected, and end-to-end integration is mandatory for processes to deliver value to customers. Many organizations have proven that process-based solutions that must work across the organization, people, technologies, and sites can't be changed quickly unless the infrastructure itself is architected for change. They must know what aspects of their capability can provide stability and what must be designed for adaptability. They must also know how to make sure that stable and adaptable aspects don't become inter-woven in a convoluted mess in which a change to anything automatically means a change to everything.

Clearly, most products and services have a very short life now when compared to the past. They must change quickly and easily. Also, our customer/consumer and other stakeholder expectations will be much shorter lived than previously. Products and services must be under-stood and updated frequently because the bar is constantly being raised by the competition and technology continues to advance. Keeping things the same through inactivity will result in an ever-decreasing level of fit with stakeholder expectations.

Because so much of what we do is now supported by software, it's impossible to effect changed processes and deliver new products if the software change constrains time to market. My experience in telecommunications was often frustrating because there was never any short-age of good ideas for rate plans to support new customer expectations. These new telecom "products" were easily conceptualized by marketing and customer segmentation strategists. They weren't easily implemented, however, because it was nearly impossible to update the billing systems with the new algorithms, rules, and formats in a short time frame. Instead, mas-sive, risky system development efforts had to be launched, which included significant analysis just to find the code to change. Alternatively, a new, redundant billing system would be built from scratch. When these systems were initially designed, no one thought beyond the stated needs of the functional users. They just deeply embedded all the day's logic, not anticipating that it would change. Software designers focused on getting an accepted specification and didn't look beyond expressed needs to distinguish the stable from the changeable. Neither did they attempt to separate the two and cross-reference them.

As we now have with Data Independence, Normalization, and Separation, I expect that within a few years we will see the total adoption of Rule Independence, Normalization, and Separation from the software. Processes will invoke the rules, and businesses will act on the derived results. Technologies now exist to allow rules to be declared outside of computer programs, and rules to be generated into referenceable software. Rules will become another corporate intellectual asset to be managed like data and business processes. We can't adapt otherwise.

Some organizations maintain that everything is in flux all the time, and that nothing can be planned. Experience has shown, however, that some things shouldn't be changing all the time, that there must be some unchanging base to start from. If businesses can isolate these stable aspects, they can avoid chaos and thrashing. They can concentrate on handling the other more changeable aspects with less complexity. What remains to be dealt with is simpler because the number of variables is reduced, and the number of interfaces is significantly fewer.

I believe that an organization's principles and values, fundamental trust relationships, culture, and architectures all hold great potential for remaining relatively stable.

As Collins and Porras showed in *Built to Last*,[7] those organizations that have sustained superior performance over decades and centuries have one thing in common: They exhibit an unwavering commitment to their core principles and values. Collins and Porras observed that more than 50% of the companies listed in *In Search of Excellence* were "excellent" when the book was written, but, less than two years later, they wouldn't have qualified according to the criteria of authors Thomas Peter and Robert Watterman.[8] Collins and Porras showed that principles kept organizations working in the long run. They also observed that excellence wasn't about having principles as management wallpaper for all to see but living them day to day. Especially important was adherence to these principles in times of difficulty, when short-term pressures could have led to short-term fixes but long-term pain, probably for someone else. The best companies didn't do this. The authors also found no correlation between the actual content of the principles themselves and long-term success. Sony's principles are different from GE, and both of them from 3M. As has been shown with commitment to the company's stakeholders, it is the living of the commitment that makes the difference.

---

[7]*See note 2 earlier in chapter.*

[8]In Search of Excellence: Lessons from America's Best-Run Companies, *Thomas J. Peters and Robert H. Waterman Jr., Harper & Rowe, New York, 1982*

As an example, one of my consulting clients has a principle named "mutuality." This principle states that a mutual benefit is a shared benefit, meaning that, in all relationships, both parties must be treated fairly for the long-term health of their organization. I knew of this principle when I first met this client because I saw it on the wall in a nice frame in the office lobby. I had assumed that it was a noble statement among other noble statements and thought no more of it until we agreed to put in place a global contract for our services. When I first sat down with the contract officer, I was prepared for the usual negotiation wherein I would have to argue for and defend my company's position on ownership and confidentiality on our intellectual assets. I fully expected to see such clauses for the client organization but was surprised to find that there was two-way acknowledgement of this important aspect of our relationship. Furthermore, the contract officer offered unsolicited, ongoing support to our organization if we felt that the mutuality principle wasn't being upheld. For more than 75 years, this company has been successful and continues to be successful, partly because of its strong relationships with all its stakeholders. It lives its principles.

This doesn't mean that principles and values are never stressed or violated, even in the best companies. It does mean that they are always there to provide consistent guidance and the right pull.

One thing that any lasting organization will want to establish for the long term is the nature of the relationships it has with its customers/consumers and other stakeholders. For these relationships to be stable, they must be built on trust. Trust simply means confidence that whatever commitment is made, it will be met according to the expressed, implied, or inferred conditions associated with it. It means making commitments relevant to the value perceived by the recipient and then doing what you said you would do. It's not hard to define, just hard to do when other pressures abound. For some relationships, it means keeping on doing what you are doing so well; for others, it means quickly changing what you do but still doing it efficiently, on time, politely, and so on. The model of trust that I believe explains the issue but doesn't lose the essence is one originally defined by Terry Winograd and Fernando Flores in their groundbreaking book *Understanding Computers and Cognition*.[9] I have adapted this model to more of a customer-relationship management view (see Figure 2.1). With this model, you can establish some stability of relationship management while the instances of the relationship can remain flexible. It assumes that each relationship has two prime types of participants: the *customer* and the *supplier*.

---

[9]Understanding Computers and Cognition: A New Foundation for Design, *Terry Winograd and Fernando Flores, Addison-Wesley, 1993*

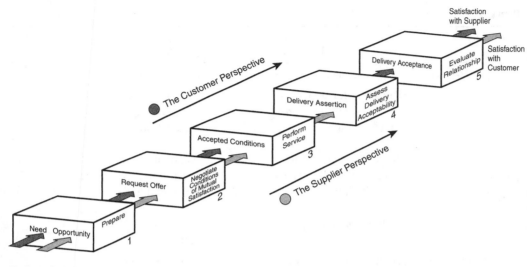

FIGURE 2.1

A model for managing customer relations.

This customer/supplier protocol, which works for any relationship or partnership, implies that the customer's criteria are paramount, and that determining and managing expectations throughout is most important. You can measure the strength and health of the relationship in terms of an asset that I will call *relationship equity*. The customer holds this equity in trust, in an "account" in the supplier's name. There's also a corresponding account for role reversal. There could be a high account balance in one, but a low balance in the other. For example, the customer might believe that the supplier provides incredible service and reliability and, as a result, the customer is always happy. On the other hand, the supplier might be disillusioned with the customer, who gets away with unreasonable demands and is very difficult to deal with.

How is the equity built and maintained? Table 2.2 explains actions taken and the debits and credits made to the accounts as the protocol is traversed.

TABLE 2.2   The Customer Supplier Protocol

Protocol Step	Customer	Supplier
Prepare	Identifies own need and determines whether and how to request service (who, what, when, where, why, how) based on previous history with or reputation of supplier	Identifies or perceives a customer need or opportunity and determines whether and how to offer service (who, what, when, where, why, how) based on previous history with or reputation of customer

TABLE 2.2   Continued

Protocol Step	Customer	Supplier
Negotiate	Makes request	Makes offer
	Rejects offer or accepts initial proposal subject to negotiation	Rejects request or accepts initial request subject to negotiation
	Negotiates terms and conditions AND agrees OR withdraws	Negotiates terms and conditions AND agrees OR withdraws
	Debits relationship equity	Debits relationship equity
Perform	Monitors progress of supplier according to negotiated terms and conditions	Delivers service
		Communicates with customer
	Debits or credits relationship equity	Proposes completion status
		Debits or credits relationship equity
Assess	Assesses the service and interaction with supplier	Monitors customer's assessment process
	Debits or credits relationship equity	Debits or credits relationship equity
Evaluate	Evaluates the supplier's performance	Evaluates the customer's performance
	Evaluates trust with regard to the relationship for consideration in future interactions	Evaluates trust with regard to the relationship for consideration in future interactions
	Debits or credits relationship equity	Debits or credits relationship equity

This trust/commitment cycle never ends. The relationship doesn't sleep. The equity built is spent when you ask someone to trust or when you enter any step in the process as well as request or agree to a change or if you withdraw from the situation. You can build up reserves through consistently keeping your promises over time, by doing what you said you would do. Relationship equity doesn't collect interest; without action, it erodes.

Every individual relationship must be thought of in these terms, and each instance or interaction must be managed to build equity as a measure of the important outcomes of the long-term objectives. Consequently, all processes should build in these steps, and all service deliverers and service recipients should be trained on this model as well as measured by it. It's the only stability possible as everything else about the business is changing.

This model is critical, businesses often ignore it in establishing partnerships and outsourcing. The corresponding agreements and workflows should incorporate this model while at the same time leaving flexible the specifics of the situation so that they can change.

As an example, I witnessed one manufacturing and service organization fall into the standard trap of mistakenly doing the job faster without building relationship equity and trust through consistent attention to the customer. The organization manufactured drink machines and supplied the drink mixes to be dispensed. Each client had the choice of a number of models and machine configurations, and the drinks could be changed at any time. Clients had good flexibility of choice and could change their mind about the coffees, teas, and soups of choice. This was a positive feature of the redesign to a mass-customizable product and service. The only problem encountered was that to "improve service," the organization set a target of delivering machines in less than 48 hours and evaluated itself on this measure rather than on understanding customer needs. Shortly after the new measurement targets were established, the reports of compliance to delivery standard came in very high. It appeared to be a job well done; however, customer satisfaction went down, not up. The real issue was that most customers wanted their machines to be delivered after water and electricity were configured for the site where the machine would be located. When machines were delivered early, they were often misplaced or broken because of improper temporary storage. The company rectified the situation by adding a simple question when the order is taken: "When will you be ready for the machine?" It then built its manufacturing and distribution schedule around customer-driven requirements. Trust went up, and business grew as a result.

Culture

Whenever the word *culture* is associated with a business process or organizational renewal, it usually has a negative connotation. Companies tacitly recognize that when their culture needs to change, the culture's inertia can become an impediment. If we look at it more positively, culture is an organization's basic way of doing and approaching things that can give great advantage because it's so hard to steal or replicate it quickly and smoothly. It can add stability, but it also can become a challenge when the organization decides to move away from a traditional value proposition. For example, companies with a track record of operational excellence typically struggle when moving toward a customer intimacy model. This is because the emphasis has always been on making the best product available and believing that this is what the customer should value. Instead, in a customer-intimate approach, the value might be more in how customers are treated than in the product's specific attributes. This requires a different set of behaviors and a change in staff beliefs that might have been built over decades.

Organizations should view this scenario as moving from one stable state to another. They should treat culture change as a serious aspect of transformation that adjusts human beliefs and behavior over a period of time and then stay the course. Culture change can't be a rapidly moving target; culture moves from one state to another infrequently. Without some overall cultural stability, chaos or paralysis is inevitable, as is a falling off of performance.

The culture change process must be tied to major process program transformation that seeks out those who aren't aware of the need to change and educates them. It looks for those who aren't capable of performing new jobs and trains them. It ferrets out those who aren't willing to give up traditional methods and changes their personal incentives.

Architecture

It seems like an oxymoron to refer to *flexible architecture* in a day of incredible transition on many fronts. At first thought, it's tempting to abandon all higher-level integration models because, traditionally, this has taken too long and has resulted in rigid definitions of target end states that are ignored because of later irrelevance. I would propose that many early attempts to do this were misguided because they didn't have adaptability as their prime requirement and measure. When this design objective is set, the rules change, and the resulting architectures actually help deliver reuse and speed of implementation, rather than constraining them.

The best way to get this point across can be through an example. This will be a banking example, but the situation might be frighteningly familiar to those in other industries.

A key driver in business banking today is the cost and speed of processing a payment and the ability to record the appropriate tracking information for consolidation of accounting and billing. One major international bank operating in more than 50 countries developed a number of different, yet redundant, payment-processing methods over time. This occurred because the various countries had already developed their own accounting methods, based on central banking regulations and local needs. Different processes, technologies, organizational structures, policies, regulations, stakeholders, and so on all drove the countries to maintain unique practices. The bank had to adopt each country's practices quickly to do business there. At best, there was some commonality of practices within regions comprising a number of countries.

At the same time, new forms of banking kept cropping up. In addition to branch banking, ATMs, kiosks, telephone, and Internet mechanisms arrived quickly, each bringing its own total solution and more redundancy and disintegration to the bank's operations.

Why did this happen? Simply because there was no common vision of the target state nor a roadmap of how to get there that would ensure easy, local individualized approaches. This has led to the scenario that places the bank at risk of losing its global customers. They want one way of doing business, anywhere and anytime, and each individual customer wants to be treated as one entity with one set of rules to manage its global financial assets.

When this bank came to deal with the ever-degrading relationship with its global customers, it concluded that several of its fundamental ways of working were flawed. For one thing, regardless of country, customer, and technology, a payment is a payment governed by international standards. Hence, payment processing should stand alone architecturally and be done once for all customers as a central, shared service.

Furthermore, all the different technologies are merely mass customization channels into the central mass production capability. Consequently, building new front ends and replacing old ones is easier if all interfaces to the back office are set up according to set rules, standards, and protocols. Without an agreement and strong commitment to an architecture that delivers better infrastructure, this would be impossible. The result isn't less flexibility; it's more.

The bank is now extending this model of common back-end mechanisms and rules to customer billing and reporting. It provides not only transaction control, but also a customer integration capability without kludging together unworkable disparate solutions internally.

Questioning Control

One difficult aspect within organizational change today involves control and decision-making authority. For the past couple of decades, companies have tried every trendy motivational model, but the key aspect behind many of them involves how much empowerment is given to the service providers and other workers. Many organizations have tried and abandoned excellence, team, or empowerment programs, finding that they were driving unfocused behavior and lacked cross-organizational cooperation. Our experience has been that empowerment works when staff are encouraged to deliver defined results for stakeholders and when they are measured against the outcomes for those stakeholders. However, staff must be able to determine how they contribute to the whole process of outcome delivery and to see the results. They must be personally able to do the work in the way it needs to be done. They must not be overly constrained. They must have some framework (typically provided by the process) within which they have freedom. As Erich Fromm wrote in the 1940s, "True freedom is not the absence of structure—letting employees go off and do whatever they want—but rather a clear structure that enables people to work within established boundaries in an autonomous and creative way."

Again, the appropriate answer lies between having no clear responsibility and wielding too much direct control. So what activities require tighter control, and which require looser monitoring?

Business Rules

As discussed in Ronald Ross's book *Business Rule Concepts*,[10] some policies, rules, and procedures can't be open to interpretation or subject to the arbitrary decision criteria of each individual, despite the customer pleas and staff desire to accommodate them. Regulatory requirements must be met, health and safety laws must be honored, financial calculations must be correct, and confidential information must not be shared. Tighter control is required to fulfill these "musts," especially if customers are navigating their own transactions or obtaining information through Internet channels. These types of rules must be adhered to with absolute rigor and therefore can often be better handled automatically. Humans don't need to get involved in the day to day. To do so just wastes a valuable resource, as well as the scarcest one—skilled humans.

If the workflow is well defined in a mass production environment and humans do the work, the workers are functioning in an industrial-revolution style of operation, where thinking and creativity is less valuable. Many people have claimed that many call centers fit this depiction and are essentially the new-age sweatshops with little dignity and pride in work. In this scenario, the staff members are just low-paid commodity resources like the factory workers of a hundred years ago. Fortunately, this isn't generally true. A more appropriate approach for this type of work might be a self-service model, wherein customers find their own solutions within the embedded rules of the software provided to them.

In other cases, motivated staff use their experience and expertise almost exclusively to get the job done. This is especially true in relationship management scenarios for smaller companies that have little in the way of formality.

In any case, it seems that, after understanding the nature of the expectations from stakeholders, ways of working can be hammered out that separate the "musts"—which can be automated or given to staff without discretion over their use—from the areas in which freedom is appropriate. This can free up scarce and experienced staff to focus on areas where their judgment can be focused on managing relationships or creating value in unstructured situations. This scenario requires that appropriate outcome-oriented measures be in place to evaluate the effectiveness of decisions and the health of the relationships being managed.

Organizations will have to decide on the degree of decision-making authority that makes sense, given their business and customer mix.

---

[10]*Business Rule Concepts: The New Mechanics of Business Information Systems, Ronald Ross, Business Rule Solutions, Inc., 1998*

Questioning Service Styles

Selecting appropriate service styles is closely tied to the previous considerations affecting responsibility and decision-making authority. Organizations can consider a wide range of styles of service at their interfaces with customers and other external or internal stakeholders. Furthermore, several of these approaches might be operating concurrently. For styles to be effective, many of the architectural arguments made earlier have to be in place; otherwise, an organization will just build up more redundancy of technologies and exacerbate a lack of integrity across multiple channels. In this vein, we must separate the interfaces with the outside world from the control, work distribution, and tracking that takes place and from the production work that must be done.

Based on the stakeholder types or segmentation, there are three major types of interfaces to service users:

- Intermediated front-line support
- Disintermediated self-service
- Automated exchange of information

Intermediated Front-Line Support

Intermediated front-line support implies a closer focus on relationship management, recognizing that different levels of service can be provided based on the segmentation of the value of those customers to the organization. The model typically strives to provide a single point of contact for either the entire relationship or, at worst, the transaction at hand. Figure 2.2 depicts this approach.

FIGURE 2.2
A human-to-human interface between service providers and service recipients.

Each stakeholder representative (for example, a major customer) deals with one company representative, who has full process (that is, results) accountability at the front line. This service provider is a trained, competent knowledge worker with access to all appropriate reference materials, information, tools, and decision-making authority affecting the stakeholder relationship. This is a full person-to-person relationship for situations that require knowledge to be put into action by someone who cares about the stakeholder relationship. The people conducting this work will have broader job definitions and should find the work enriching. A full suite of explicit knowledge access tools and access to others' experience of supports either end of the interaction.

Examples of this type of business solution can be found in sales- and customer-service–oriented business processes and any approaches requiring workers with special expertise. Technologies used to support these solutions typically embed knowledge in customer-relationship management, call-center, and help-desk software and keep this current with the latest lessons learned. These technologies often feature expert guidance systems, especially case-based reasoning and fuzzy-logic features. They sometimes use the results of data-mining exercises to update customer profiles and product-mix recommendations to the service provider. Typical costs for call-center transactions fall into the tens of dollars range.

Disintermediated Self-Service

In *disintermediated self-service*, each stakeholder (that is, the consumer) initiates or dispenses his or her own service through company-provided access mechanisms. These mechanisms are often automated and distributed according to predefined process protocols, and business terms and conditions that the partners had agreed on in advance. This allows service to be provided beyond the normal working hours of the service supplier. However, this human-to-machine relationship might require a human-to-human exception process in case of breakdown. Figure 2.3 depicts this approach.

FIGURE 2.3

A human-to-technology interface between service providers and service recipients.

Examples of this type of business solution can be found in business processes that focus on buying/ordering, information delivery, and explicit knowledge push or pull distribution. This solution requires the targeted stakeholders to be both comfortable with, and sufficiently competent in, helping themselves at a high level of quality.

Technologies used to support this approach embed business rules and workflows in online kiosks; Internet/intranet/extranet/portal software applications and databases; and computer/telephony integration solutions, which bring voice and data together. The provisioning of easy, yet significant, levels of just-in-time and just-enough training and help are implicit in the solution. Advanced solutions might also incorporate notification to a human service provider, who can offer assistance electronically to the user based on profiling of the user's actions.

Self-service solutions are typically an order of magnitude cheaper to operate. They also don't waste the scarce time of key human resources on the 80% of scenarios for which prior knowledge has been documented or embedded.

Automated Information Exchange

In automated exchange, each stakeholder (such as a supplier) receives service automatically with no direct involvement by either partner in the transaction. This is conducted according to predefined process protocols, terms, and conditions using interfacing information technologies. The knowledge of the company and its stakeholders are typically embedded as firm business rules in operational software. Automated exchange is best suited to situations that don't require interpretation, or those that simply pass information and reduce human drudgery. This explicit embedded relationship might also require a human-to-human exception process in case of breakdown. Figure 2.4 depicts this approach.

FIGURE 2.4

A technology-to-technology interface between service providers and service recipients.

Examples of automated exchange can be found in supply-chain management, just-in-time materials management, automated ordering and supply processes, pure data/information exchange, and other conditional event-driven situations that can occur based on a set of events, conditions, and rules.

In this case, technology helps execute the rules diligently. With critical technology, the knowledge gained from process design can be embedded easily and quickly into executable rules. More importantly, the technology must be able to change quickly when the rules change. Typical examples are EDI-type software, supply-chain applications, and push-oriented workflow environments. Any other custom-developed solutions that deal with routine information delivery to and from the outside world also qualify for consideration. Optimum development environments feature business rule engines/generators and object environments built on a reuse discipline.

In deciding which combination of stakeholder interface types to use, common sense as well as good analysis must prevail. Ask a few questions on behalf of your organization. Do you want to

- Provide service through human and/or automated means?
- Provide access to service where and when required?
- Provide access even if it is to those who are remote and mobile as well as those who are centralized or local?
- Extend the boundaries of your concern to make the customer's customer successful or your supplier's partners successful?
- Relate to customers directly (disintermediate)?
- Relate to customers completely (consolidate all actions associated with a customer's business event)?
- Have customer focus groups, knowledge, and feedback built in?

Some of your decisions will likely be safe ones. For example, there is little sense in using a self-service voice response system for a 911 call. Likewise, it's not necessary for a bank to stay open 24 hours a day to dispense cash when ATMs have become the norm. Other choices might not be so obvious, and timing might be more of a factor, rather than whether a style will prevail ultimately. Understand your customers and track their capabilities, expectations, and willingness to change.

Questioning Approaches to Work

All the previous questions significantly affect the way that work is done within the organization. Some of the prior choices will result in redistribution of work among employees and across business functions.

Moving Workloads to the Front of the Process

In general, work will move from the back end of the process to the front end. If the workflow within the process involves several people and organizations, this can have significant impact on the organizational structure and the roles of individuals involved. In many cases, whole jobs are affected or even eliminated, so how workflow is handled is important.

In a typical outdated scenario, a clerk receives mail-in, telephone, or in-person applications. The clerk checks the forms for completeness and sends them back for correction, if necessary. The initial check isn't for the suitability of the client but for the accuracy of the form's information. At that point, the acceptable forms are sent on to the next person, who conducts some more analysis to recommend acceptance of the client or transaction. Finally, a more skilled employee will look at the recommendation and give a yes/no decision. The decision is then passed back to another clerk, who will inform the client. The cycle can repeat if the client makes a change and resubmits.

Staying with the trend of substantive work happening earlier rather than later, the new approach might be to have the more skilled worker receive calls and do all the work with the support of appropriate information systems. There is no back and forth, and the job is concluded quickly, but it's done up front. Previously, the work might have involved several people in multiple departments. Now all the work will be done in one. It's more effective and efficient but has the price of having to deal with human change.

The previous example also begs the question regarding the front of the process. We define a process as starting with the first event that initiates action. Typically, this has been looked at as the first action from outside the organization. However, with today's extended value chains involving outside stakeholders and partners, it's prudent to question what really is "the front" and whether it should be redefined. Traditionally, a seaport terminal would define the ship-loading process as starting when the railcar arrived at the terminal. By changing the definition to the time that the shipper scheduled the railcar and shipment to leave their site, the terminal handler could be much better prepared for the shipment and the loading. A handler could also avoid surprises, corrective action, and expensive charges when ships couldn't depart at the expected start time because of missing shipments.

Eliminating Hand-Offs

Another workflow option is to eliminate as many hand-offs as possible. Traditional time-sensitive processes comprise three types of time: work time (or value-added time), transit time, and wait time, such as time in queues and time in inventory. It's not unusual to find that 80% or more of a process's total elapsed time is non-value added time. The major cause for this is the handing of work from one person to another. This key factor in time-to-market scenarios is also a key contributor to redundant work and quality problems. A general rule to correct this would be to eliminate as many hand-offs as possible—but within reason (for example, it wouldn't be practical for the 911 operator to come over and put out the fire).

Working in Parallel

When work time approaches total elapsed time as a result of squeezing out downtime, we must ask how we can reduce time to market even further. The answer is by conducting work in parallel, rather than sequentially. Many processes lend themselves to the parallel, or concurrent, approach. Having one piece of work in progress while others are being done is becoming commonplace. For example, during a hotel check-in, a credit check can be conducted while room availability is being reviewed, if the activities are launched in the right order. If the hotel staff did it right, both actions would have been done before the guest arrives. Restaurants that really work are masters of massive parallel processing in meal preparation. Construction companies handle many different projects at the same time using concurrent engineering techniques. No one needs this more than organizations that bring new products to market when being first is the key. Pharmaceutical companies, high-tech ventures, financial institutions, and telecom firms, to name a few, all can win by reducing R&D time by even a small amount with parallel processing.

Eradicating Low-Value–Added Work

In any of these processes, eradicating low-value–added tasks and redundancy is obviously valuable. This usually translates to eliminating unneeded checking and monitoring, consolidating roles, and making sure that the cost of doing the extra work is more than made up by the value created or the avoidance of noncompliance costs later. In this sense, tasks that bring in only an extra $10 of business for an extra $100 cost of trying to get the business clearly are suspect. Only by comparing the costs of a task to the value of its outcomes can we make the call to keep it or drop it. Risk is also a consideration because dropping a monitoring cost might end up as an environmental catastrophe.

Emphasizing Doing the Right Things Earlier

If they've done something wrong that must be corrected through downstream work, mature organizations will also realize the effort that must be put into avoidable rework and reconciliation. Appropriate guidance might not have been available when the work was initially performed, thus indicating a flaw in an earlier step or process. With the advent of knowledge-management practices, we are starting to realize that lessons learned and the best practices they suggest need to be made available and shared earlier than in the past. New emphasis is being given to more and earlier planning and prevention, as well as better shared access. By building these support systems into operational processes, advanced organizations encourage more flexibility in decision-making when appropriate.

Questioning Roles, Jobs, and Organizational Structures

A major cause of project failure is required changes in staff roles and jobs and where workers report within the organization. Inability to effect such changes will negate many good ideas in process renewal. If the process workflow can't be implemented in a structure that supports the outcomes of value to the process customer, we are wasting our time. In mapping work to people, job roles must cover from the trigger of an event through to the customer/stakeholders' outcomes and everything in between. Jobs should be whole, and the results and feedback from the affected stakeholders should be quick and obvious.

Complete responsibility requires knowledgeable staff, aligned with customers, for whom they have full accountability and control over results. This means broader job definitions as compared to previous practices. Roles and jobs are enriched with more meaning and typically more satisfaction associated with the responsibilities. Because of workload variations, staff can be more flexibly allocated to work, depending on the peaks and valleys of the situation. Staff, in this sense, must be seen—and see themselves—as taking responsibility for assigned or assumed roles, not as simply having narrowly focused positions. Workers are nodes in a delivery network, not boxes on an organization chart. They have more responsibility and empowerment within the process toward results. A simple example of this can be witnessed in service-oriented supermarket chains. At peak times when the checkout queues stretch to more than three customers, staff from various other departments are summoned to come to the front, open more lanes, and check out groceries until the peak is over. The staff can do this because the organization values flexibility and because workers have been trained to carry out multiple roles. They can also do it because their collective bargaining agreement was negotiated based on roles, not fixed positions.

These trends in broader job responsibility are being applied to management as well. New ideas beyond the typical management structures are being sought. Rather than align with traditional, hierarchical structures, management aligns with processes and outcomes. Managers don't get promoted away from those troublesome customers; they stay in the line of fire and handle the tougher situations or the more important customers. They are also rewarded on process outcomes associated with the organization's value proposition and the expectations of its stakeholders, as is their staff. They become supporter, trainer, coach, and consultant to their staff. They manage learning and knowledge sharing across teams. There are fewer levels of managers because they, too, are empowered to deliver results within the process framework.

Questioning Knowledge at Work

Knowledge management is a fundamental aspect found in many of the changes happening in progressive corporations. Consequently, advanced organizations are actively building in the concept of permanent training and retraining, and the management of learning and knowledge sharing as part of every process being renewed. From this perspective, corporation heads have realized that, although knowledge can be elusive and intangible, it's nonetheless a corporate asset required for adaptability and change. These organizations learn daily from their customers and supply chain partners because they have built processes consciously engage the organizations in learning. Keeping up with the customers is a necessity to maintain relevance and loyalty. Also, organizations know when to learn from other outside, as well as inside, sources and not just from customers, who don't always know what they don't know yet. These alternative sources of inspiration bring new ideas and are key to not getting stuck pursuing extensive refinements of marginal value when a new concept is called for.

A major factor in supporting these trends toward building intellectual capital is the collaboration of creative people. Work teams must be encouraged to collaborate regardless of the organizations to which their members belong. They must have team incentives, recognition, and rewards for sharing. The team learning that can take place can be in the context of the work to be done (for example, the process provides some organization), or around a subject of importance to the members as in communities of practice. Collaboration can be formal or informal. In either case, what collaborators know must be documented in a manner that can be communicated both upstream and downstream effectively and efficiently.

Questioning the Integration of Information

The last question that I will address is to what degree a corporation should integrate its information. Information is a corporate asset, but it also describes other corporate assets. The aim to have integrity and consistency of information isn't new. It has always made sense. Most organizations just have done a poor job of avoiding redundancy and thereby have created inconsistency and incredible workloads. Organizations with more than 25 sources of customer information are commonplace. Orders are scattered for the same supplier in tens of ordering systems. Individual locations and departments redo the same function with different automated solutions all the time. If we want to have information provisioned anywhere and anytime, and want it changed quickly with integrity, we have some serious questions to ask ourselves about our cross-functional commitments to one of our key corporate assets. We wouldn't manage our finances haphazardly in the way that we manage our information resources.

Integrated Access

Integrated access is vital to support front-line staff. With the introduction of single-point-of-contact service, staff can't function without knowing all they need to know. Integrated access enables self-help technologies that allow customers to provide their own service. Portals can be crippled or at least ineffective without it. If we can't capture information once at its source event, as a product of the work that identifies it, we will have to continue to build workarounds. Until we build new integrated solutions, we might have to clumsily pull together source data from multiple files and databases. If we do, the less-than-elegant gathering process should be transparent to the user, who needs to see only the result.

Process Status Information

Another requirement to consider is the degree of process-related status information needed. As we manage whole processes from front to back, especially business-to-consumer and business-to-business transactions and relationships, another type of information might be required. Many processes have a timed component and significant planning activity based on not being surprised. These require the ability to have or provide information about the progress toward delivery of results. That is, we might need to track and trace status in near real time to allow customers and suppliers to make appropriate decisions in the same time frame. Because our partners are using instant information to decide daily, we have to provide information access so they can conduct real-time analysis for fast response to their own pressures. Examples of superior performance in this realm can be found in organizations such as Federal Express and UPS, whose businesses are as much tracking and tracing as the actual delivery of goods. This trend of knowing where we are in a workflow is growing fast—even if it's not for tracking physical item movement but for gaining the information itself.

Summary

Clearly, organizations today are facing myriad societal, technical, environmental, economic, and political pressures in their attempts to survive and thrive. The number of choices facing them seems overwhelming. There appears to be no set of right or wrong answers other than to execute whatever choices they make extremely well. This chapter has outlined some of these options. Organizations have to sift through them carefully, come up with a set of decisions, and then do everything in their power to truly commit to their attainment, all the while gauging if the landscape is changing and the choice is still right for them. One thing is certain: By not making a choice, organizations default to a position that might be inappropriate and that puts them at risk. Before an organization embarks on a journey of process, organizational, human, or technological change, the questions in this chapter must be posed, answered, and communicated to all who might be affected or involved.

The next chapter will deal with the fundamental precepts that you need to understand to execute a program of change and day-to-day management within the organization based on processes. It will identify, define, and explain some important related concepts that should be commonly understood to consistently manage well. It will also establish a set of reusable principles for process-based change and process management.

Principles of Process Management

IN THIS CHAPTER

This chapter lays the foundation for the methods, techniques, and activities that make up the process of transforming an organization. I will build a basis that, once understood, will allow you to guide yourself through the confusing maze of options.

By taking an approach that relies heavily on a simple set of base principles, everyone involved in renewal work will be able to understand and communicate more clearly. You can make recommendations and decisions based on a set of commonly understood and consistent criteria. You can share and discuss rationale for change, as well as avoid the always dangerous approach of relying on thoughtless cookbooks that describe unequivocal steps to be followed, even when they are senseless or irrelevant. The entire method should become a useful guide that helps you exercise judgment more confidently.

This chapter has been partitioned into two sections. The first section defines concepts to help you understand the terms often used in process management. It will define the interaction among a number of closely aligned concepts, all of which should be exercised for businesses to function effectively and for change to become robust. The second section lists a set of guiding principles that have worked in thousands of situations. These principles are the essence of process management. When present and applied in an organization, these principles satisfy a set of critical factors for success. When absent or not applied, they highlight the increased business risk associated with a program of change.

Guiding Concepts

As I just mentioned, this section defines a number of very fundamental concepts and terms used throughout this book. It especially deals with the differentiation of the concepts

- Business
- Process
- Knowledge
- Rules

These ideas are all very powerful in their own right and are part of the search by architects and analysts to find the set of concepts which represents related, yet independent, business variables. Those variables can be isolated and changed independently to enable adaptability.

As we will see, this disentangling of concepts is a step in the maturing of organizational analysis, which has struggled with change when the concepts were intertwined and almost impossible to undo. Because we didn't know any better at the time, our business solutions exhibited a high degree of *dependence*. This caused many organizations that were previously successful in stable times to become hopelessly impotent when adapting to new business pressures and opportunities.

By managing some of these variables independently, as we learned to do with databases, we can change each relatively easily. This level of *interdependence* has been a step in the right direction. However, as happens in humans who successfully grow up, independence soon is replaced by a level of *interdependence,* wherein all factors stand alone but are connected in a set of known relationships. Any change in any one factor affects the others in the relationship, and that impact can be easily known. In this way, interdependence brings robustness and the ability to move more easily with the times. This is especially true when it comes to process modeling because, if the other variables are deeply embedded within the models, it is often necessary to change the entire process model. By defining such items as rules separately and cross-relating them to the process model, you can change the rule without changing the process design.

The same is true of the concepts examined next. It's vital that a business understand its processes, information, knowledge, and rules. We must make sure that we know the differences and the relationships among them to ensure that we don't see any one of them as the independent answer to all problems. We must work all of these concepts together synergistically to ensure that we understand their complex fit and can tweak any of them without having to change everything.

What Is a Business?

I define a *business* as any organization whose aim is to create results of value for someone who cares about those results. This is obviously a simple or, some might say, a simplistic view. But starting from the business's place in the world will help you understand how it must behave to serve its purpose.

Business as a Vehicle of Transformation

In simple terms, the purpose of any business entity is to act as a transformation mechanism. When appropriate events and conditions trigger action, customer requirements and consumable resources—such as raw materials, money, and information (see the left side of Figure 3.1)—are transformed into goods, services, and business outcomes for the customers' benefit (see the right side of Figure 3.1). These results can have a physical component, such as a tangible product, as well as an informational or knowledge-based one, such as a report, book, or expertise provided. Regardless of the nature of the delivered result, an emphasis on service and customer retention is the objective of most 21st century organizations.

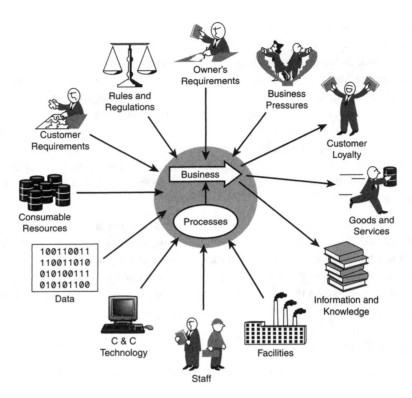

FIGURE 3.1

Understanding the business context and organizational capabilities.

At the same time that businesses are serving their customer and consumer markets, their performance is measured in terms of appropriate key performance indicators (KPIs) and evaluated against the requirements of the business owners and investors (see the top of Figure 3.1). Satisfying customers and owners concurrently while recognizing the multiple outside pressures and regulatory constraints is difficult, given the potential conflict among these guiding factors (again, refer to the top of Figure 3.1).

The business applies a number of reusable resources to enable this transformation (see the bottom of Figure 3.1). These capabilities include

- Cross-functional business processes. Interestingly, businesses might not recognize them as processes.
- Physical facilities. These include offices, factories, equipment, and tools.
- Computing and communications technology. These enable information flow, knowledge sharing, and communications.
- Human resources.

The traditional challenge of any business is to optimize results from competing courses of action, given performance objectives and scarcity of some resources. This isn't easy given the number of interdependent variables in play. It's made more difficult because the game is played on a business landscape that's changing rapidly. Different players might be playing by different rules and focusing on different time horizons. It's management's job in this environment to make the difficult decisions in a state of uncertainty and sometimes chaos.

Internal Versus External Perspectives

A fundamental obstacle in optimizing performance and flexibility is the often systemic conflict between those inside the organization and those outside it. This classic battle pits workforce performance measures and incentives against the true requirements of the market forces. The needs and wants of customers, consumers, suppliers, and shareholders will ultimately rule in any competitive business environment but might not be the focus of staff and managers.

The vertical structures of most organizations recognize and reward those who perform well against arbitrary, divisional targets. Unfortunately, these targets are often misaligned with external requirements, of which the organizations are often ignorant. The challenge is to align these two perspectives by segmenting programs of change and ultimately organizations into value-creating streams focused on and measured by outsiders, not insiders. To do this, all analysis and design need a process perspective. Process is the only way to segment a business that can be described in exactly the same terms as the business itself. A *process* is also a vehicle that delivers results valuable to those who care. That is why it must remain the primary way of segmenting change programs.

The Industrial Revolution

In focusing on managing the delivery of results to our customers and consumers, we are in a sense returning to the days before the Industrial Revolution, when work was performed completely in one place and time. Workers saw the results of what they did. Outcomes were clear, stakeholders weren't mysterious, and work processes had integrity. Craft workers did the whole job and took ownership of the results, not just small parts of it.

The advent of the Industrial Revolution in England in the late 18th century changed work significantly. Even though products and service had relatively long business cycles, everything had changed. Equipment availability and production capacity brought competitive advantage. However, financial capital was scarce because of the relatively expensive equipment and plant required.

A large pool of low-paid, uneducated laborers was clearly a commodity to be exploited. As usual, companies optimized based on their scarcest resource, and work methods were built around division of labor into repetitive simple tasks that could be easily taught. Human resources had no "value" reflected in accounting systems, which evolved to see only physical facilities as corporate assets on the balance sheet. A business's human resource, including middle management, was considered merely a labor overhead—strictly there to control work in a hierarchical structure.

This philosophy was central to many exponents of early industrial engineering and process re-engineering approaches. They saved money at the expense of staff knowledge because employee headcount reductions were simply exercises in accounting savings with no regard for the loss of knowledge or creativity assets. In the era that valued things over people, organizations measured themselves on such factors as Return on Assets (ROA) and Return on Investment (ROI). Internally, they focused on efficiency metrics such as ratios of physical outputs over physical inputs. Industrial engineering approaches worked because similar outputs existed across companies and could be compared over time.

Quality Management Period

In the 1970s, such respected teachers as W. Edwards Deming[1] and Philip Crosby[2] recognized that traditional industrial engineering approaches had outlived their usefulness. Even though the lifecycles of products and services were still long by today's standards, traditional mass production means were under question. The customer's role was starting to gain importance. Organizations realized that by meeting customer needs for better, faster, and cheaper results, they could gain in market share. This became most apparent when customers rejected the inferior offerings of traditional U.S. industries such as automobiles and steel. Offshore competition took away significant market share.

The shortening of business cycles—which required the capability to repeat success more frequently—exacerbated this trend. Also, the growth in the service aspects of business meant that product quality alone was no guarantee of keeping one's position in the marketplace. The messages of "Customer first" and "Continuous improvement" became the slogans of many organizations. However, most of them practiced their new approaches only in small groups within large organizations. Despite some performance improvements, there was still lots of room to do better, especially when it was clear that savings in production were mostly offset by increased expense in office and overhead positions.

During the 1970s and 1980s, plentiful financial capital poured in for equipment that had now become more of a commodity than a scarce resource. Everyone was on a level playing field when it came to physical assets. A skilled well-paid labor pool was growing steadily. Businesses also started to remove layers from their deep functional organizations. Businesses started implementing customer service in addition to efficiency measures.

---

[1] Out of the Crisis, *W. Edwards Deming, MIT Press, 1986*
[2] Quality Is Free: The Art of Making Quality Certain, *Philip B. Crosby, Mass Market Paperback, August 1992*

Despite the changing business landscape, bottom-line measures still focused on ROA and ROI. Human resources were still seen as having no residual value from a corporate financial perspective, unfortunately. Many organizations would live or sometimes die to regret this oversight.

Information Technology Revolution

In the 1990s with the advent of advanced information technology, we entered a knowledge-led revolution characterized by hyper rates of change. Business cycles became extremely short. Products and services were and still are constantly in flux. Mass production and continuous improvement approaches became totally insufficient for a business to thrive. Mass customization, individualization, personalization, one-to-one approaches, and permission marketing strategies started changing everything to a relationship-based business model. In this world, customer expectations skyrocketed and are still going higher, whereas loyalty is more fleeting.

Features of this new economy, within which we still find ourselves, are plentiful liquid capital and low-priced and universally accessible commodity equipment. More and more, the large pool of educated laborers available in the last few decades is becoming a scarce resource due to a rapidly growing increase in demand for them. This threatens to limit organizations' capability to grow and adapt. Within this ecosystem, human resources are investments to be leveraged.

To survive in this new world, the integration of tasks into full processes isn't an option—it's the only way to deliver results to the outside world. The people working in them, typically experience daily variation in fuller, more complex roles. They feel that they own more of the process within more "fuzzy," less structured organizations. Clearly, human capital is now critical for success even as we struggle to find ways to measure its value.

New measurement approaches are also creeping into complement traditional financial-based measures. Return on Management (ROM) approaches such as those developed by Paul Strassmann[3] are becoming more mainstream. ROM evaluates the effectiveness of the knowledge capital of what has traditionally been called *overhead* in corporations. Measures of staff competency, experience, retention, and loyalty are also being recognized, as are indicators of innovation. Many organizations have incorporated these concepts into a more comprehensive measurement system, often called a *balanced scorecard*[4] because it looks at multiple indicators of predictive organizational health, and not just at the end-of-game score.

[3] *"Measuring and Managing Knowledge Capital, Knowledge Executive Report," Paul Strassmann, June 1999*

[4] *"Having Trouble with Your Strategy? Then Map It," Robert S. Kaplan and David P. Norton, Harvard Business Review, September–October 2000, pages 167–176*

In balanced scorecard world, worker incentives focus more and more on collaboration to deliver stakeholder outcomes as part of a shared team reward in a total process and relationship.

These themes are commonly accepted, and all prognosticators emphasize the critical role of customers, cross-functional processes, and knowledgeable human resources.

This transition of the economy and society requires a new emphasis on professional practices to emphasize full processes and learning. These will be discussed next.

What Is a Business Process?

As has been described so far, there seems to be an awakening to the absolute necessity of managing along process lines. This becomes even more apparent when the nature of a process is examined.

A true *business process* starts with the first event that initiates a course of action. It isn't complete until the last aspect of the final outcome is satisfied from the point of view of the stakeholder who initiated the first event or triggered it. This outside-in perspective cuts across organizational structures, geographies, and technologies, and begs the question, "How do we know the criteria for satisfactory conclusion?" More importantly, "What relationship must we have with the stakeholder who initiates action?" In other words, "Who cares?"

A true process comprises all the things we do to provide someone who cares with what they expect to receive. It also contains all the actions we take when we fail to meet those expectations.

Within any true process, inputs of all types—such as raw materials, information, knowledge, commitments, and status—are transformed into outputs and results. This transformation occurs according to process guidance, such as policies, standards, procedures, rules, and individual knowledge. Reusable resources are employed to enable the change to happen. These resources can include facilities, equipment, technologies, and people.

From this perspective, any process clearly will contain logical and sometimes illogical steps, which usually cross professional functions and, often, organizational units. It's in this realm that you'll find the lion's share of misalignments because organizational and personal goals and incentives are frequently at odds with the organization's value proposition to the stakeholder who launched the process.

In a stakeholder-oriented process, you can easily find performance indicators and desired targets for future performance improvement. The process can have measurable objectives set and performance can be evaluated on an ongoing basis based on outcomes.

A final test of a process's completeness is whether the process delivers a clear product or service to an external stakeholder or another internal process.

What Is Business Process Management?

Business process management is itself a process that ensures continued improvement in an organization's performance. As with any process, business process management requires leadership and guidance. At times, this means taking a *radical-change perspective*, meaning that the fundamental tenets of the process are under re-examination and perhaps renewal. At other times, the process might undergo a cycle of continuous review and enhancement with minor adjustments being considered. At all times, the process's fit with other processes should be understood, examined, and challenged.

Processes are assets of an organization, much like people, facilities, and information. Well managed, they will pay off in terms of performance to the corporation. Processes, moreover, are somewhat special in that they are the vehicles that synchronize the other assets and aspects of change. They are the organizing framework for all the other components. If we don't have the answer to the question, "What should we do?" we can't justify our designs for change in other organizational capabilities. The process links the changes we make to the external business reasons for their existence because only processes can be measured in terms of business performance. They exist for no other purpose. Everything else is in place to make it possible to attain the processes' aim of achieving stakeholder results. The process management hexagon in Figure 3.2 depicts this concept.

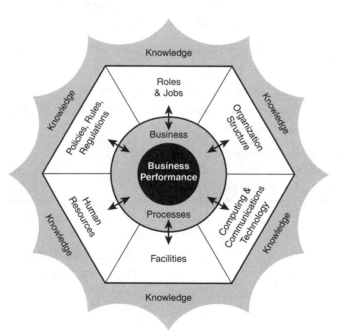

Figure 3.2

Process management hexagon.

Process management ensures that all other factors shown in Figure 3.2 are in sync to deliver performance. The work flow from input through transformation to output aligns with the desired results. The technology, people, and facilities enable the process to deliver repeatedly. The guidance of rules, roles, and organizational structure provides the controls to execute the process well. Knowledge and intellectual capital are embedded in a business's physical and technological assets and embodied in its human abilities. The hexagon in Figure 3.2 is always under stress. Process management is the never-ending journey that maintains the balance and keeps an organization pointed in the right direction.

What Is Knowledge?

Today, many businesses emphasize those processes that create knowledge in the form of new products and services or those that exploit created knowledge in the conduct of day-to-day activity. Thus, knowledge workers draw on their experience or their documented references more than ever before. *Knowledge* in business guides humans in making judgments, formulating decisions, and doing work. Knowledge in this sense provides context. It tells us who, what, when, where, why, and how to be most effective.

Implicit in this view of knowledge is the assumption of relevance to a business or a process objective. From this perspective, knowledge is different from information in that knowledge is the guide that helps us use data and information to attain results. *Information* is what's processed; *knowledge* is how and why information is processed.

It has become an accepted convention to divide knowledge into two major types: tacit and explicit.

- *Tacit knowledge* exists within a human being. It is *embodied*.
- *Explicit knowledge* has been articulated in an artifact of some type, rather than existing solely within a human being. It is *embedded*.

Table 3.1 outlines the advantages and disadvantages of each.

TABLE 3.1 Tacit Versus Explicit Knowledge

Advantages	*Disadvantages*
Tacit Knowledge	
The most powerful form of knowledge	Difficult to articulate formally
Drawn from real experience	Difficult to communicate and share
Includes insights, feelings, culture, and values	
Hard to steal or copy	
A source of creative advantage	

TABLE 3.1   Continued

Advantages	Disadvantages
Explicit Knowledge	
Can be articulated formally as pictures, models, and documents	Can become obsolete quickly; has a lag
Can be duplicated and transmitted easily	Easy to steal or copy
Can be processed and stored automatically	
Can be shared, copied, and imitated easily	

A survey of the popular dictionaries provides three main distinctions of the word knowledge: *recognition*, *guidance*, and *ability* (see Figure 3.3). Often, more than one of these is at play in a business dialog, transaction, or relationship, and the distinction of which meaning applies when in a business can be critical.

FIGURE 3.3
The three dimensions of knowledge.

Recognition

Recognition is the shallowest level of knowledge. Unless you can identify a problem, the application of knowledge won't occur because no action will ever be taken. Recognizing a problem with a customer relationship is a critical first step to resolving the problem or avoiding further problems. However, recognition by itself not sufficient. Many people will claim they "know," about a problem area, but what they know remains shallow compared to those who are knowledgeable in other dimensions.

Guidance

Guidance, or *referenceable knowledge* that tells you what to do, is the next dimension of knowledge. Guidance requires rich and deep sources with specific relevance so that an appropriate action can be taken. Without it, people might recognize a need or know how to do something but they would lack the specific context needed to do the right things correctly. Once a problem with a customer relationship is noted, it's imperative to find out more details, which then guides the appropriate response.

Ability

The third dimension of knowledge is the *ability* to accomplish some result that is of value to someone who cares. This know-how is obviously essential to the smooth functioning of an enterprise. Having this deepest form of knowledge often differentiates the enterprise from its competitors. Clearly, someone must be able to do what it takes to resolve a customer relationship problem, after it is recognized, and appropriate guidance is gained. Applying the three levels of knowledge enables a business to do the right things in the right way.

Applying Knowledge

By identifying the two types of knowledge and the three dimensions of knowledge, we can explore what knowledge is important to business. This can be represented as a two-by-three matrix, which I have named the Burlton Six Pack (see Figure 3.4).

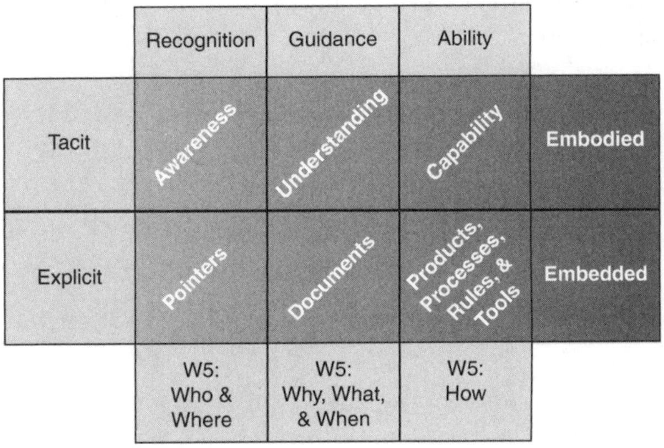

	Recognition	Guidance	Ability	
Tacit	Awareness	Understanding	Capability	Embodied
Explicit	Pointers	Documents	Products, Processes, Rules, & Tools	Embedded
	W5: Who & Where	W5: Why, What, & When	W5: How	

FIGURE 3.4
Burlton Knowledge Six Pack.

This scheme can be used to determine which set of alternatives form the best mix of solutions for a particular process problem. It also can be used as the basis for enabling software selection.

With today's emphasis on knowledge and intellectual capital, many questions are being asked about the value of such capital and how we can measure it. Again, process plays the key role. If we see knowledge as a guide embedded in an enabler to the processes we conduct, we can measure the value that the knowledge provides only in terms of the difference it makes in the process. Typically, this is done by examining process quality or the cost of nonconformance— that is, the cost of lost opportunity to do better due to better knowledge. This can appear as the total downstream cost of not having that knowledge available, costs of extra work, customer dissatisfaction, repairs or corrections, lost staff, and so on.

It can also be measured as the cost of the lost opportunity that would have been realized if the knowledge had been accessible immediately, rather than later. For now, let's say that we improve the "flow" with what we "know."

What Is Knowledge Management?

Knowledge management (KM) is the set of professional practices that improves an organization's human resources capabilities and enhances the organization's ability to share what employees know. KM is a set of processes that delivers capability to others in order to meet the organization's objectives.

Knowledge in business can be seen to have a life cycle of its own, as shown in Figure 3.5:

1. Knowledge must be *created* either within or outside the organization. Ideas evolve in iterative tacit and explicit loops until the knowledge is ready for distribution to those outside the creating group.

2. Knowledge can then be *stored* somewhere, either tacitly or explicitly, so that it's accessible for others to find and use.

3. Those who need the specific knowledge must *find out* where it is by searching in the right places and/or by asking the right people.

4. Once the knowledge source is found, the user will then go through the act of actually *acquiring* it—that is, gaining personal knowledge from other humans or documented sources.

5. Once acquired, the knowledge can be put to *use* toward some productive purpose.

6. As a result of having applied the knowledge, perhaps repeatedly, the user will *learn* what worked well and what didn't. This learning can then be significant input into further iterations of the knowledge creation and distribution process.

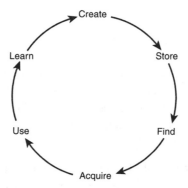

FIGURE 3.5
The knowledge life cycle.

Learning contributes highly to the effective management of this cycle. Without the learning component, the cycle is devoid of knowledge. It merely becomes an information delivery strategy, disconnected from the leverage of more effective human experience. Applying the delivered knowledge to operating the business (finding, acquiring, and using) will have some initial value, but the delivered knowledge will be immediately out-of-date unless it's continuously renewed with the latest lessons learned (learning, creating, and storing).

Knowledge management processes oversee this cycle for optimal performance across all aspects of the Burlton Six Pack (see Figure 3.6).

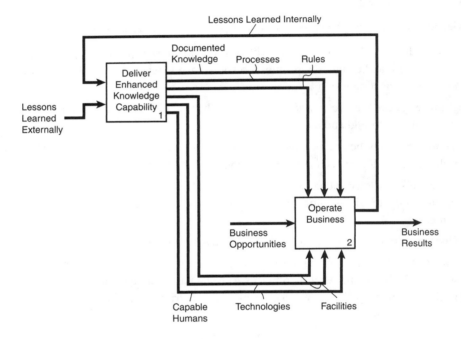

FIGURE 3.6

The knowledge creation and exploitation process.

The objective of knowledge management processes is to make this cycle more effective as well as more efficient. This implies that corporate knowledge must be made available in readily accessible forms, such as documents, processes, and rules. These could be embedded in human resources, in information technologies, or in the design of facilities. In this way, the embedded knowledge can be reused and continually evaluated for effectiveness and improvement.

Improving the knowledge management lifecycle is critical to organizational success; without it, overall business performance will suffer. Getting the best knowledge through the cycle quickly before it ages is a major goal within intellect-based, fast-paced companies.

This challenge applies at the individual, workgroup, company-wide, and intercompany levels. Each wider level offers a greater degree of leverage and improved business results but also brings with it a set of more difficult issues, as long-standing ways of doing things must be overcome.

Knowledge management creates and maintains the optimum environment to make this happen. It closes the process feedback loop, which continuously converts tacit knowledge, based on experience, into explicit knowledge for wider communication. This explicit knowledge turns back into tacit knowledge again through inference, experience, and learning.

Improving the sharing of knowledge, then, delivers better guidance and more effective enablers to the business process at hand. This pays off when applied to individual workers, communities of practice, and corporate-wide knowledge creation.

Individual knowledge enhancement is key to developing a flexible and adaptable work force, whose members can provide better service and help others learn in an environment of rapid change. *Communities of practice*—people with a common interest and bond associated with a knowledge topic or way of working—generate knowledge that can be shared if it is harnessed and communicated.

Corporate knowledge creation processes help bring new products and services to market faster.

An organization's individual, community, and corporate levels all deliver capability in a learning environment, enabling the organization's other processes to function. It should be no surprise that leading organizations emphasize these knowledge creation processes today as their only sustainable advantage.

What Are Business Rules?

A subset of our knowledge can be represented as *business rules*. Rules are constraints on human behavior or business system behavior, normally derived from legislation, regulations, or policy and expressed in the form of a declarative sentence. We can leverage our knowledge of best practices and lessons learned repeatedly by consistently applying the same rule under the same conditions. Normally embedded in technology or documents, rules represent what we know in a consistent structure that allows easy, broad sharing. Rules provide a consistent expression of business requirements. Rules, like knowledge, provide guidance to business processes.

Business rules consist of terms, facts, and rules:

- *Terms* simply identify the business concepts we use through a noun or noun phrase, such as *customer*, *payment*, *order*, and *credit*. Clearly, if business partners and staff don't have a common understanding of terms, business will be hard to transact. Terms are the most stable of business concepts. They change less often than facts and rules.

- *Facts* describe relationships among terms—how business concepts connect to one another. Facts are expressed as a verb or verb phrase that connects terms, such as "Customers place orders and make payments for them using credit." Knowledge of these connections is clearly essential for running a business. Facts change less often than rules.

- *Rules* constrain terms and facts. An instance of a rule is a truth statement governing a fact usually involving *must* (constraint) or *should* (guideline). A sample rule might be, "Customers who have outstanding payments older than 90 days must not be granted credit for new orders." "Must" rules can be automated and shared quickly. Humans can interpret "should" rules according to their individual knowledge and experience.

A rule is "a statement which accomplishes any of the following—defines a phrase (term), relates terms (facts), constrains populations of facts (constraints), calculates a new piece of information by applying mathematical formulas to known information (mathematical derivation), deduces a new piece of information by applying logical formulas to known information (inference), (or) initiates an action (action enablers)."[5]

If written strictly in business language, each rule can stand alone and does not need to be embedded deeply in procedures, workflows, and software logic. In this way, rules can be changed more easily than any of these other hosts. They also leave behind a more stable set of processes and technologies that are also easier to change when the rules are separated from the hosts. As a significant advantage, businesses can identify, normalize, and manage standalone rules as reusable assets, applicable across business processes, documents, and technologies.

By putting in place shared rules, a businesses can achieve independence of variables and significant advantage in adaptability and change. They can expect tremendous productivity breakthroughs as well as integrity similar to that achieved when software developers separated normalized data from logic.

What Is Business Rule Management?

Business rule management, like process and data management, attempts to see rules as assets that can be reused in many situations. As organizations require more integrity of execution across multiple channels and functions, they must have integrity of rules within and across processes or relationships with their stakeholders will suffer.

Business rule management captures, reconciles, publishes, and makes an organization aware of the business's rules. It aims for rule independence. It attempts to shorten the time and effort required from identifying the need to change a rule to making the new rule accessible to all enablers. This area will mushroom in the coming years as organizations begin to understand the need for complete process management and for integrity and ease of change.

---

5 *"One More Obsession," Barbara von Halle, DBNewsletter, May/June 1997, pages 3–4*

The 10 Principles of Process Management

Implicit in the preceding discussion are a number of fundamental principles that must be honored in order to deliver business results to customers and to satisfy the needs of the organization's other stakeholders. These principles underlie the methods of business operation and change. Understanding and living according to these principles will get managers and practitioners alike through some tough debates about managing processes. Without the principles, teams can easily get lost and distracted from the intent of the journey.

The 10 principles are

1. Business change must be performance driven.
2. Business change must be stakeholder based.
3. Business change decisions must be traceable to the stakeholder criteria.
4. The business must be segmented along business process lines to synchronize change.
5. Business processes must be managed holistically.
6. Process renewal initiatives must inspire shared insight.
7. Process renewal initiatives must be conducted from the outside in.
8. Process renewal initiatives must be conducted in an iterative, time-boxed approach.
9. Business change is all about people.
10. Business change is a journey, not a destination.

Principle 1: Business Change Must Be Performance Driven

This principle deals with the question, "How can we evaluate what we are doing and how well we are doing it?"

All change must be based on business performance measurement. All the things we do, we should do for a reason, and measurement allows us to know if we are acting consistently with the reason. This principle in no way says what the right measurement indicators should be. Every industry is different, and every company has its own strategy for which a variety of indicators are possible. Nonetheless, it's vital that each organization choose wisely; the old adage, "You get what you measure," seems true for all organizations.

Clearly, profit and market share will be important performance indicators for automobile companies; customer satisfaction and retention for services firms; share price and staff loyalty for dot-coms. Government will have different drivers than the private sector, and monopolies will have different drivers than free-market firms. All, however, must know their aim in life and set a scorecard to evaluate how they're doing.

Traditionally, competitive organizations have used physical asset-based measures or investor-based measures, which I have likened to hearing last night's final score without seeing the football game. Although we know that all teams go out to win and, in the long term, a team must win or its management and coaches will be fired, just having the final score after the fact does little to help our understanding of the whole game. We don't know if it was a good game for our team or not. We don't know if it was exciting and if our fans were happy, or perhaps not because we should have done better. We don't know if our strategy worked, or if it was abandoned part way through. We don't know what the team should probably do differently in the next game. We only know the result.

Similarly, in business, most of us need other feedback to know what's working. A high stock price or good return on assets is nice, but how can we contribute to it with what we do every day? Earlier, I talked about evaluating human resources and intellectual capital as measured by return on management. However, this too can disconnect us from what we must do as far as many of our staff are concerned. As in sports, we need predictive measures, not just after-the-fact reports, to see the total picture. Constructing a connected measurement system is critical for us to break down overall targets into what people do every day.

A popular response to this has been the "balanced scorecard" approach, which tries to put in place a set of measures that aren't oriented just to the financial bottom line. Measures of all major components of success are required, including customer satisfaction and loyalty, innovation, knowledge and people, customers, suppliers, processes, as well as the financial side of the organization. From this perspective, the measurement-oriented approach doesn't have to be just financial numbers but can also include outsider perceptions. This means that all organizations, regardless of business mission, can find their own set of performance metrics from which all decisions regarding processes can be derived and linked to each other.

This concept is normally referred to as *traceability*. Traceability simply means that everything we do, and every decision we make under ideal circumstances, relates through a set of linked performance measures to the organization's scorecard.

After performance measurement factors are determined, the organization sets some performance targets. There may be inherent conflict among the targets. Meeting targeted measures associated with customer acquisition, such as achieving rapid market share growth, could be in direct opposition to the requirement to delight our customers. Attaining good satisfaction levels and delivering higher profits by reducing costs may be fundamentally at odds, especially if we also are striving for no headcount growth at the same time. Likewise, improving speed may fly in the face of our quality improvement initiative. Cost reduction can also be a killer of customer satisfaction, depending how it's done. Management must send clear messages on strategy and priority and not rely just on wishes and targets. Remember, hope is not a strategy. Both hope *and* business strategies are needed.

The bottom line for any business improvement is that well-thought-out, targeted measurements will inspire and track progress and ensure that we allocate our scarce human and financial resources to things that matter most.

Principle 2: Business Change Must Be Stakeholder Based

This principle asks, "Who cares about what we are doing and how well we are doing it? What do they care about?"

This principle continues the thought process surrounding traceability started in the first principle, but from the perspective of those other organizations and people that surround the organization in focus—its stakeholders. A stakeholder is anyone or any group that's affected by, has a vested interest in, or can influence the organization's performance in some way.

Clearly some stakeholders are more important than others when it comes to the organization's success, and this will change over time. This principle recognizes that the organization doesn't exist only for its own purposes—it must serve a larger community than itself. Stakeholders provide context for the business—its own ecosystem.

Stakeholder needs and expectations are the prime drivers of the balanced scorecard and also help determine what that scorecard should be.

Stakeholders can be classified into a number of broad and deep types. Typical generic categories are

- Customers and consumers
- Owners
- Staff
- Suppliers
- Community
- The enterprise itself

These categories will vary wildly for different companies and significantly from industry to industry.

Often, significant overlaps in classification result in confusion. For example, many organizations have customers or suppliers who are also their competitors. How should the competitor be classified? Also, what's good for the customer might be not so good for the staff or might violate legal and regulatory community rules. Again, a balance must be struck.

In most organizations, one level of stakeholder type is insufficient, especially when we look at what certain parts of the organization do and whom they deal with. *Customer segmentation* is a well-developed function in many sales-oriented companies. It's the basis for marketing campaigns, sales organization design, and incentive schemes. Segmentation is used less, however, as a driver and organizer of business change initiatives and process management, an area where it holds great potential. Likewise, we can segment or structure the other stakeholder types, such as staff or suppliers, into hierarchical categories, from general types to more specific sub-types.

Types should be segmented according to their different requirements and the difference in the way that they are to be treated. For example, telecommunications companies treat residential customers differently from multinational business customers. If there's no difference in treatment required, further segmentation might not be required.

To analyze a stakeholder segment, we should know the current state of our relationship with that segment and what would we want it to be in the future. The gap between these two states will drive our needs for change. The future state view will provide a set of evaluation criteria for change from the current reality.

From the current state, we should determine where we are with each type and sub-type that warrants distinction. This evaluation includes knowing the following about each stakeholder type:

- Our principles and values as they affect the type
- Key performance indicators (KPIs) and actual performance measurements
- Interactions from and to the stakeholder type including
    Business events/outcomes
    Flows of work, material, data, knowledge, and commitments
    Health of current interactions
- Health of the overall relationship

For the future state, we should know where we need to be at the end of the planning horizon with each type and sub-type that warrants distinction. This projection should cover

- Principles and values
- Expectations and relationship vision
- Key performance indicators (KPIs) and performance targets
- Interactions from and to the stakeholder type including
    Business events/outcomes
    Flows of work, material, data, knowledge, and commitments
- Critical success factors

The stakeholder criteria will depend on the stakeholders' actual needs, but this will be balanced with the organization's desires.

The degree of importance placed on each stakeholder type will also depend on the value proposition that the organization chooses for itself. If the organization sees itself first and foremost as a customer/consumer service excellence company, it will focus heavily on the customer segmentation and customer criteria. If it sees itself as primarily an excellent manufacturer, it will focus more on suppliers and distributors, and its customer orientation will be toward quality of product more than service at all costs. If it sees itself as an innovator above all else, the organization will have a different mix of staff and community stakeholders than the others and might depend on channel partners to get products and services to market.

Another factor in the stakeholder analysis will be the organization's philosophy toward its prime mission. This is especially a key factor in today's drive toward e-businesses. Many organizations have come and gone—some by design and others, not. Organizations that see themselves as built to last will have a totally different perspective from those that plan to take advantage of their intellectual property or capability in the short term and flip the firm to others purely for immediate financial gain.

Executives with an incentive to haul in lots of stock options in the short term might de-emphasize staff criteria for market share or growth. In any case, the organization must come up with a set of criteria based on balancing the outsiders' needs and expectations that can be measured to make decisions now and to prioritize later. These stakeholder evaluation criteria reflect the value added by their relationship with the organization.

Principle 3: Business Change Decisions Must Be Traceable to the Stakeholder Criteria

Principle 3 tackles with the question, "Why should we make the choices we make?"

This principle is almost self-evident and doesn't require a lot of explanation. However, that doesn't mean it's common practice. As a matter of fact, it's often ignored or abused. Personal and political agendas more often form the basis for proposals, recommendations, and approvals of courses of actions than criteria derived from outcomes of value to our stakeholders. The key question is, "What's the reason or justification for a particular decision? Is it business or personal?"

The challenge is to obtain accepted criteria before we enter into choosing among business options, even small ones, and to use those criteria instead of the personal drivers of powerful players. Conflicting personal, political drivers among decision makers can devastate a sound decision-making process. When those drivers are also misaligned to the organization's mission, vision, and values and to its stakeholders' expectations, we cannot expect to optimize results, and disaster is always possible. Change initiatives that waste millions of dollars can be found in almost all organizations of size. The root cause is almost always poor decision making, or, some would say, poor management due to the factors described here.

Again, insist on agreement to the future state stakeholder criteria that will determine your course of action; then and only then, select that course.

This simple philosophy of tracing business change decisions to stakeholder criteria is consistent with many popular strategies for personal and professional success. Stephen Covey's second habit of highly successful people states, "Begin with the end in mind."[6] Sports psychologist Terry Orlick[7] claims that the first thing any competitive athlete must have is a clear picture of what success is. Visualization of that end state drives the behavior to get there. If you don't know or care about where you are going, any behavior will suffice.

To actually put this principle into practice, management must consciously and visibly agree on the criteria first and then publish them. Management must also empower those working on change to work creatively within those parameters.

An example is the up-front agreement necessary in the process-renewal projects I have handled for various businesses. I always fight hard to get the commitment that we will use the stakeholder criteria to reach a solution. We all agree not to discuss or even try to think about any organizational structure already in place. This is hard to manage, but, if I don't get this commitment, it usually means that managers are thinking more about the drivers of direct relevance to them personally and currently. These current personal drivers seldom align within the team or with the best interests of external stakeholders.

Principle 3 should be practiced in numerous situations. In deciding on design options for every aspect of the process management hexagon (refer to Figure 3.2), we should use the stakeholder criteria. In making scoping decisions, in selecting among alternatives in business cases, in allocating resources to work requirements, in communication and human change management, and many other business practices, it will serve you well.

Principle 4: The Business Must Be Segmented Along Business Process Lines to Synchronize Change

Based on the earlier discussion in this chapter, it's natural to view *process* as the prime segmentation strategy internal to organizations and—more and more frequently—among organizations. As business cycles of products and services shrink timewise, management structures with overly

---

[6]The 7 Habits of Highly Effective People: Powerful Lessons in Personal Change, *Stephen R. Covey, Simon & Schuster, New York, 1989, pages 96–144*

[7]*"Embracing Your Potential: Steps to self-discovery, balance, and success in sports, work and life," Terry Orlick, Human Kinetics, 1998, pages 66–75*

rigid organizational boundaries and planning mechanisms are too slow to respond. They don't anticipate changes well enough to lead the market.

Also, a customer or supplier clicks on a mouse while on a Web site, with the expectation of quick, efficient, and effective results.

In both scenarios, seamless cross-functional integration is mandatory. Restructuring functional units alone won't do it. Focusing on people skills and empowerment also won't do it by itself; such approaches are aimless. A technological basis for organizing the delivery of results is likewise misdirected because technology will automate only what we want it to. Despite wider-focusing technologies, such as enterprise resource planning and customer relationship management, businesses require results-oriented structures.

Only process can stake the claim of achieving enterprise-wide integration because, by definition, a process starts with the first triggering event that initiates action and doesn't end until the results of value are delivered to the appropriate stakeholders. This event/outcome pairing defines the processes that we have. All other structures should be put in place solely to serve the event-to-outcome process and therefore to deliver added value to stakeholders.

This strategy implies that in deciding how to invest in change, prioritizing along process lines is requisite. In this way, processes organize strategy and become a key link in the traceability chain between business/stakeholder criteria and the day-to-day actions of all the people in the value chain.

Aggregated around events for stakeholders, process definitions become more stable. The first event will define the start of the process, and the last outcome, its end. Other events and outcomes can appear in the interim, but they are still part of the same process. For example, when a customer clicks on a Web site to order a product, he launches the "Fulfill order process." The process isn't complete until satisfactory delivery has occurred, and payment has been received. Other events along the way can include receipt of an inquiry regarding status of shipment, invoicing, receipt of payment, and so on. Other types of events to consider include

- Arrival events, such as "Order phone rings"
- Scheduled events, such as "Invoice creation at 6:00AM every day"
- Conditional events, such as an alert warning "Out of stock condition"

Each event will or should generate an appropriate business response. Process analysis doesn't rest until all actions are complete. In event/outcome analysis, the organization is treated as a black box, and we don't look inside. Looking internally in the process will only confuse us—we'll get to that later. In order for you to manage processes, they must be defined as independent activities. However, in their performance, it's clear that they are interdependent.

In identifying processes that need to be renewed to resolve a problem, start with those event/outcome pairings that involve the customers and consumers affected by the problem. These processes are referred to as *core processes*. Look at the customer/consumer life cycle, which starts with the first interaction or awareness that this stakeholder has with the organization and proceeds to the last interaction in that relationship. This would span everything from marketing through to, in worst case, losing the customer, or, in best case, delivery of the completed product or service. From the core processes, we can derive the processes that deliver guidance to them (*guiding processes*) and those that deliver reusable enablers to them (*enabling processes*). These processes should themselves be defined, taking into account events and outcomes but from the perspective of other stakeholders.

Especially important is the need to see the core processes as customers of the guiding and enabling processes. In this way, value creation can be traced from the processes traditionally seen as overhead. Processes such as hiring staff, developing systems and guidelines, and so forth exist only to support the business objectives that are the target of the core processes. They should be measured primarily by the impact they have on the core processes, such as their impact on operational capacity. Their internal measures of efficiency, such as headcount and expense, are irrelevant in this situation.

By segmenting the business along process-value added lines, we have a clear framework for organizing and prioritizing change and for measuring the impact of our efforts in terms that the business executives can understand.

Principle 5: Business Processes Must Be Managed Holistically

One traditional pitfall associated with business change is an inability to deliver and sustain benefits. In process-oriented change, the problem can be exacerbated if the proponents of change can't find appropriate champions. These sponsors must take a full-process perspective—that is, one that delivers on behalf of external stakeholders, and not just for internal functional managers.

Typically, anyone in a position to act is also typically responsible for only a portion of the day-to-day process and might not have the interest, knowledge, or motivation to take the whole process into account. This person seldom has the authority to act on behalf of the full process. Consequently, it's becoming more and more prevalent to appoint a full *process owner*, sometimes referred to as a *process steward*, for each process of the organization.

The process owner acts as advocate on behalf of the process, taking responsibility for the process's performance for stakeholders. The process owner works not only to deliver improvements in process projects but also to remain in the role subsequent to completion of these projects. This means staying on top of process and stakeholder performance metrics and reviewing current performance against the best in the business. It also means assessing the work methods and other guides and enablers for the process, as defined in the process hexagon (refer to Figure 3.2). The process owner is always looking for an edge and evaluating the risk of not adapting. He ensures that feedback mechanisms exist to gather lessons learned and that knowledge from the latest experience and practices is distributed.

Primarily, the process owner makes certain that the process continues to perform to requirements for its stakeholders, and he takes corrective or anticipatory action as needed to either continuously improve or to introduce radical change. The objective is similar to that of total quality management, although the process owner's focus is wider and spans organizational control boundaries. Process owners must be effective even though they might have no direct control over the resources involved in the execution and management of the daily work being performed.

There are several structural approaches to achieve the goals of process management. One is full-process organization, in which all workers in the process report to the process owner, who controls all staff and is accountable for all results. This avoids the problem of internal organizational behavior and incentives that are misaligned with desired outcomes. This is the utopia for process ownership and results-oriented performance management.

In this model, well-designed natural organizational units send finished products and services to one another. Process teams manage all work from business event through to business outcome. This approach upholds a very strong "customer" orientation and accountability for results. Feedback and information are shared broadly. The model is fully traceable, both process-wise and people-wise.

It's can be very hard to transition from other models of hierarchical management to a process-organized approach because multiple processes might have to move simultaneously. Such a change clearly requires incredibly strong top management leadership. One way of making this happen is to implement a single point-of-contact for service to stakeholders. This one-stop-shopping approach widens the point of contact's job to be fully aligned with the activities in the process; the individual's performance measurement is simply tied to stakeholder value added. Clearly, this also has a significant organizational impact.

Another organizational option is a mixed function-and-process approach wherein day-to-day control rests with functional line management, but monitoring and improvement responsibility goes to process owners. These might be dedicated process owners who have a very small staff and rely on advocacy and influence. They might also be line managers who also are responsible for certain processes. Process owners, then, can have a cross-functional responsibility without the direct ability to change what people do. In this case, their success lies in their ability to influence those who do have direct control. These could be the line managers or the managers of the line managers.

The critical mechanism that must be in place for ongoing process management to be effective is a forum within which processes are discussed their performance vetted, and the incentive for process outcomes shared among all involved managers. Typically, every senior manager not only has a line but also has at least one process to report against in the forum and to act on. The managers' personal evaluations must rest on their reports and their success, and they must take reporting and follow-up seriously. Top management must also be decisive about the consequences of not supporting the approach.

Staff involved in the day-to-day process also must see feedback on the ultimate results of the process. They must have incentives to support overall stakeholder value creation and not to do just what's convenient for themselves.

Principle 6: Process Renewal Initiatives Must Inspire Shared Insight

Process renewal relies heavily on gathering information, gaining understanding, and arriving at innovative approaches and designs for change. In many organizations, approaches to change have mirrored the now classic debate in any knowledge management discussion group: What form of knowledge is most appropriate to understand and communicate the nature of change needed? Should this be done explicitly through documents and models or tacitly through low-tech meetings and discussions? Experience has shown that using either approach exclusively is risky.

It's hard to argue against the fact that one learns best by being in the work environment itself. This type of knowledge allows one to internalize the subtleties of "being there." It's also true that working closely with "knowers" rapidly accelerates the learning curve. In small areas of an organization, this type of learning is manageable because everyone can identify the area's knowers and trusts them as credible sources of process information. This type of knowledge is hard to steal but sometimes hard to change.

As its organizational focus grows, a business requires more formal approaches to identify, connect, and share what's known as well as to realize the identities and trustworthiness of its knowers. It's also usually impractical to learn everything required first hand in the timeframes required by modern change. Hence, accessible knowledge artifacts, often in the form of explicit documents, hold great importance to help bridge the knowledge chasm between "knower" and "solution stakeholder."

The quantum jumps in knowledge experienced by society and the associated historical leaps in quality of life can be traced to the availability of breakthrough distribution mechanisms and media associated with explicit knowledge artifacts. The advent of language, writing, paper, scribes, printing presses, copy machines, and electronic media have all provided a great acceleration in the amount of both tacit *and* explicit knowledge available to members of society.

With the advent of each, a leap forward in the human condition ensued. There's reason to believe that the current breakthrough enabled by electronically networked distribution of such artifacts will also lead us to similar levels of tacit knowledge enhancement, due to the democratization of access to explicit knowledge.

The prime lesson that we can learn from the past lies in how tacit and explicit knowledge interact with one another in a never-ending learning process. Today's challenge is no different, with the exception of the speed with which the learning must occur.

The TTEE knowledge discovery model (see Figure 3.7) deals with all types of knowledge conversion—tacit to tacit, tacit to explicit, explicit to explicit, and explicit to tacit—in a series of iterations or learning cycles. This model has a distinct R&D flavor and is being adopted by companies that want quality products and services to enter the market quickly in a competitive environment. This approach manages a creative and collaborative process of deeply embodied knowledge discovery resulting in the deepest form of knowledge embedding—that is, knowledge is embedded into our process definitions. In their analysis of successful Japanese companies, Ikujiro Nonaka and Hirotaka Takeuchi support the iterative creativity of the TTEE model.[8]

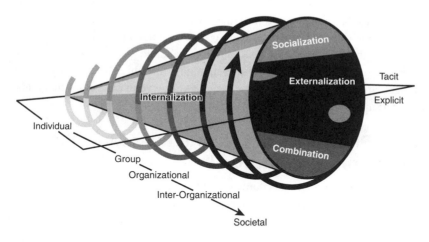

FIGURE 3.7
The knowledge discovery model.

Examples of this business solution can be found in many internal company processes that create artifacts for other parts of the organization to use, including process design.

---

[8]The Knowledge-Creating Company: How Japanese Companies Create the Dynamics of Innovation, *Ikujiro Nonaka and Hirotaka Takeuchi, Oxford University Press, 1995*

In doing this work, it's important to be cautious about too much emphasis on the models themselves. They are only one aspect of the deliverable. The other is arrival at a common understanding of the situation and its potential for improvement.

> **NOTE**
>
> Models and documentation are only abstractions of the real world and not comprehensive in their reach. Not everything can be explicitly modeled or documented in pictures and words. Some things are tacit and must be explained in other terms. Metaphors, scenarios, and verbal examples are often more useful than written, technical reports to assure common learning and validation, which are necessary conditions for any change to proceed. If we just focus on models, we will never bring to the surface what we are unaware of.

Recognition of the value of sharing insight, not just documents, is reflected in the methods discussed later in this book. A number of activities will uncover what we know, so that it can be shared across a group in workshops. These workshops will create artifacts or records of the agreements and ideas, but more importantly they will embody a deeper tacit understanding of what's important to allow better decision making and common commitment. In many cases, a discussion of strengths and weaknesses will be more valuable than the charts created. Especially regarding strategy and architecture, there are no right answers, only a better sense of how to judge. Not everything can be objective. Don't leave out activities that embody trust, commitment, and understanding in the participants.

Principle 7: Process Renewal Initiatives Must Be Conducted from the Outside In

In any change initiative, it's easy to become overwhelmed with the daunting task to be accomplished. There are myriad concepts to master, all of which are in play concurrently and all of which interact with one another. If we try to deal with too much at once, we will never finish the job; instead, we will fall prey to "analysis paralysis." Each step of the way will require a strong ability to focus on the work at hand with the confidence that we will get to the other aspects later when the time is right.

Managing multiple levels of detail or going to an overly complex level is the biggest risk. It won't be possible to understand and communicate that understanding when looking too soon at 500 flow boxes with decision points throughout. Everything we do should be understood and validated at its own level, starting at the top box and then working down. At each level, the objects we are analyzing must be looked at only with regard to their own context before any decomposition occurs.

Processes and organizations should employ the black-box approach. For example, we will look at the organization-in-focus and how it interacts with its external stakeholders before we analyze the processes of that organization. We will then identify each process for that organization and select the priority ones to examine further. We'll examine each chosen process in turn to see how it works with regard to its external stakeholders and other related, internal processes. We will break down each process into its next level of activities, and each of those will be examined. In this way, we'll keep analysis and design at an appropriate level of detail. We won't spend unnecessary time analyzing work that won't even exist later. We will focus on the *key* aspects, not *all* aspects. We will understand the drivers and have the insight needed before moving on. The context will provide meaning at each and every level of detail or decomposition. The details will come if and when they are needed.

Principle 8: Process Renewal Initiatives Must Be Conducted in an Iterative, Time-Boxed Approach

The arguments in Principle 7 call for a top-down approach to conducting change. The arguments in Principle 6 call for a discovery approach that fosters learning. Principle 8 extends these two ideas into an approach that encourages you to learn, create something, review it, and plan the next cycle of the same. It assumes that people don't know everything in advance and that they must create an environment wherein they can figure things out and articulate them incrementally. This iterative approach can be found in knowledge creation processes,[9] in prototyping of technology,[10] and in research-oriented activities. It assumes that you will get it wrong before you get it right and that you will know the result of a change only when you try it. It also assumes that we need to attempt changes first at a fairly high level of abstraction before we get too detailed.

This concept isn't new, but, more recently, those applying the concept have proven the benefit of doing only a time-fixed amount of work before reviews occur. This is often referred to as *time boxing*.

Time boxing dictates that the activity schedule is preset and the amount of work performed varies according to what can be done within the timeframe. For example, a schedule might say, "Each Tuesday afternoon from 1:00 to 5:00, we will review what we have learned in the past week with the key participants in the process in order to validate our findings." Such a statement ensures that the team will not get too deep too soon, too far off track without correction, and will be able to gain gradual commitment toward the deliverables from the participants. It

---

[9]*See note 8 previously in chapter.*

[10]Application Prototyping: A Requirements Definition Strategy for the '80s, *Bernard H. Boar, John Wiley & Sons, 1984*

also solves one of the biggest problems in process-oriented and other change situations—that is, scheduling the participants, especially management, for key reviews. In this approach, everyone schedules weeks and months of reviews and other workshops in advance with no surprises and no excuses.

Each time-boxed cycle includes major types of activity: knowledge gathering, analysis, reconciliation and packaging of findings, and results validation.

When gathering knowledge, the previously described approach of starting at the top and decomposing downward into detail is a key tactic. Of all the components at any level, only the important ones should be investigated. What's important should be determined by the impact of that activity on the desired outcomes of the overall process, by the frequency of its execution, by the degree of problems encountered, by the amount of inconsistency in its methods, and so on. Those gathering knowledge should recognize that the 80/20 rule is in full play. This rule suggests that 80% of the effort in a process is consumed in 20% of the activities, that 80% of the problems are caused by 20% of the process, and so on. The session are fixed in time and therefore must be limited in scope. Even if the participants gain only 50% of the critical understanding at any level at each iteration, the knowledge gained with each iteration will add up quickly, as seen in Table 3.2.

TABLE 3.2   The Value of Timeboxing and Iteration

Iteration Number	Outstanding Knowledge Gained	Incremental Knowledge Gained	Cumulative Knowledge Gained
1	50%	50%	50%
2	50%	25%	75%
3	50%	12.5%	87.5%
4	50%	6.25%	93.75%

It appears that there's little value studying things to death when an incremental approach will get us there. Experience bears this out. It also confirms commitment to the findings is also built incrementally. However, it's important that the right knowledge be pursued—that is, relevant knowledge to the task at hand as defined by the stakeholder criteria. Whatever is to be dealt with at any level or number of iteration must be prioritized according to those criteria and other factors that tell us where to drill and where to stop. In this way, the analysis and design might be lumpy. In other words, some parts of the process under review are known in detail because it's important to know at that level, whereas other parts are known at a broader, higher level only (see Figure 3.8). Note that although there are different levels of detail at different points, the process remains connected without breaks from left to right. This prioritization should occur as part of the review or validation session at the end of each iteration, when we seek consensus on what we got right, what we didn't get right, what we missed, and what priority we should look at next. We've found that a simple ABC ranking is sufficient, wherein we can be confident that we will get to the A's by next time but the C's won't be addressed now. (They might become A's in later iterations.)

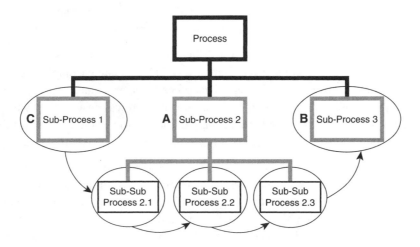

FIGURE 3.8

Process prioritization and decomposition.

Not all work can be at the lowest level of detail nor needs to be. If four levels of decomposition are pursued and each level has five subprocess components, there would be 5, 25, 125, and 625 chunks of detail to investigate, respectively. To avoid this, prioritization is a must. Certain overly detail-oriented staff should be kept away from this type of work. We are analyzing and developing processes, not procedures.

This type of rapid-fire work can put tremendous pressure on team members, who are now living a series of short-term deadlines. Perfectionists will have a difficult time with this. What's needed are good listeners, who can develop trust and respect, and good presenters who will explain but never defend their findings. They must not take changes personally; they must be comfortable in revealing their incomplete, incorrect work products and see the changes to them as a positive. Likewise, those who tend to dominate or push their own solutions are inappropriate for this work.

Principle 9: Business Change Is All About People

At a seminar I facilitated a few years ago in Toronto, a participant came up to me and said that she had found the two days extremely valuable. When I asked her why, she told me that she came to find out "Where do we do human change management?" She said she was leaving knowing that, "Human change isn't something you do; it's everything you do." That phrasing of the message has stayed with me ever since. It's absolutely true.

Chapters 6 through 8 explain in detail how to support decisions that have been made and the people who make them. Many steps in managing change are there for no good reason other than decision support. Intellectually, you could argue that many steps are unnecessary or a waste of time and effort. Sadly, you are right, *if* you don't consider the human element.

Change initiatives are often used simply as ways of creating a document—a specification for a system, for example. Instead, you must see them as a vehicle of more encompassing transformation. You aren't just converting technology, data, procedures, or organizations; you are converting people into enthusiastic supporters and participants who will provide you with a competitive edge that can't be matched. This is one reason that you should encourage the analysis of existing processes. This analysis fosters understanding and communication.

To do this, a number of factors become paramount. In addition to your communications strategy, you must support changes with appropriate roles and responsibilities, organizational structures, empowerment within accountability, aligned performance incentives, and recognition as well as personal growth opportunities. During transition, the staff must feel that an appropriate level of trustworthy communication is happening. They should feel a sense of contribution as a result of their participation.

Principle 10: Business Change Is a Journey, Not a Destination

A major distinguishing feature between process management and the wave of business process re-engineering (BPR) efforts that swept past us in the early and mid-1990s is their approaches to continuity of effort. BPR emphasized radical change of business processes and everything that touched them in a big-bang, "break-all-the-eggs" approach but did little to uphold the notion of supporting the ongoing management of the implemented change or the ongoing implementation of change. It assumed that the solution would have stability in a stable marketplace. Perhaps for these reasons, as well as human resistance to the inhumane approaches sometimes taken, BPR took its share of criticism and failed to deliver the anticipated results more often than not.

Two major business factors must be taken into account today:

- We don't have time to get it right, so whatever we do will have to adjust as we learn in the marketplace.
- Whatever we do, no matter how right, will be short-lived and have to change anyway.

Consequently, classic BPR philosophies won't work. Instead, we must build adaptable solutions and keep our eye on what is changing to be able to adapt in the future. This essentially means that we will never arrive at the Nirvana of stability but will always be getting there.

We must recognize that, at any point in time, our stakeholders will have a set of requirements that are in flux. The balance among these requirements will change as each of the stakeholders' contributions to us change. This will make some stakeholders more important to us than others. For example, when no one is buying, the customer relationship seems more important, and, when few skilled resources can be found, staff relationships become more valued.

The ebb and flow of stakeholder and market evolution means that processes must be managed, even when they aren't undergoing radical change. Without process ownership, ongoing measurement, benchmarking, and constant attention to stakeholders of all types, we will fall behind through attrition. Change is required even if we simply want to maintain our current position.

If change is a journey, it's important to pay attention to all the principles that precede this one all the time. Notice especially that seeking perfection before action is suicide. Doing something small now and learning are more valuable than getting a bigger process right later. Whatever we do, we must be prepared to do it again better on the next go around.

Building learning feedback and knowledge distribution into processes is mandatory. Constantly gaining tacit insight before designing is key. Designing for change is essential. Acting fast isn't a risk if we are prepared to pay attention to outcomes and adjust accordingly.

Summary

This chapter has laid the foundation for the framework methodology of managing organizational and human change. By defining and describing the main concepts of business, process, knowledge, and rules, I have attempted to ensure a common language. Participants in all initiatives must understand these concepts consistently.

I have also laid out 10 critical principles for managing processes. These principles address risk factors that need to be examined in any transformation design. If these risk factors are ignored, the chance of success will be reduced, possibly to a very low level.

The following chapter will provide some examples of companies with good track records of managing along process lines. All experienced a major organizational transformation, and all now manage their processes as a matter of course.

New-Age Company Experiences

IN THIS CHAPTER

This chapter will tell three different stories. Each is a success story in its own right, with quite varying characteristics and solution designs. The organizations involved all had similar technologies and ideas available to them but chose differing paths. They all did and continue to do some things the same, however. All the companies were and still are deeply committed to their stakeholders and chose work and organizational designs based on what was best for their stakeholders. Also, they are all performance driven and measure their outcomes rigorously. Lastly, each organization designed and continues to run its business along business process lines. From the initiating trigger to the final outcome, everything in each firm is connected.

The first case subject is The Morningstar Packing Company. In terms of human organizational models and true flatness of structure, Morningstar is indeed unique and hard to copy. The second is Stanford University's Financial Aid Office, which now offers excellent one-stop shopping to students, having transformed itself from a functionally organized (*silo-based*) model of service. The last is Rexall.com, which went from a paper-based multilevel marketing company to a combination of e-business and traditional distribution approach (*clicks-and-mortar*) business model while managing to keep its channel strategy intact.

You can learn something from each of them.

The Morningstar Packing Company

The Morningstar Packing Company in California is a very focused organization that manufactures tomato paste and related products. I have included it as an example of a very mature and innovative organization that handles its staff in a remarkably simple way. Nowhere have I seen an organization with such a high degree of employee—or "colleague," as Morningstar calls them—empowerment and such a strong alignment to business process outcomes.

About Morningstar

Morningstar is the largest producer of tomato paste in the United States, with approximately a 30% market share. It wastes very little of its raw material and sells byproducts as cattle feed. It has strong, quality management; it delivers a product of consistent color and thickness and with other quality attributes important to customers.

Morningstar produces more than 750 million pounds of paste annually, running a 24-hour-a-day operation for approximately three to four months of the year. It does this with approximately 90 full-time and more than 500 seasonal colleagues in plant operations.

Chris Rufer started Morningstar in 1970 as a small California trucking company. In 1990, working with tomato growers, Chris started a tomato processing business at one site.

Today, Morningstar controls much of its supply chain, with three processing facilities in addition to its trucking operation and a harvesting subsidiary, developed recently in cooperation with growers. Morningstar has the two most productive and efficient tomato paste processing sites in the world.

Morningstar has always been a pioneer, introducing industry-changing ideas such as the "bag-in-a-box" concept that optimizes storage and transportation and a harvesting technology that tripled picking productivity.

With the *commoditization*, or lack of differentiation, of all food products, industry costs and pressures to gain more efficiency continue to mount for Morningstar. Also, after prices are negotiated and set with suppliers according to statewide pricing structures, they can't be renegotiated. These pressures recently drove out one of Morningstar's competitors. Morningstar acquired some of the defunct business's facilities to process its own products into generic, bulk consumer products to sell to institutions. This is a new market for them.

Strategic Intent

Morningstar's stated mission is "to produce tomato products that consistently achieve the product and service expectations of our customers in a cost effective and environmentally friendly manner."

Its value proposition is clearly one of operational excellence in manufacturing. It's not primarily about customer intimacy or product innovation, even though Morningstar does a good job in these areas also.

The company has a strong vision that takes into account high levels of performance for customers and itself, a self-managed and process-oriented organization, innovation in the use of enabling technology, and happiness for all stakeholders, including its staff, which it refers to as *colleagues*.

Its ultimate key performance indicator (KPI) is Return On Investment. As you will see, everything else Morningstar does in all processes is strongly aligned and can be traced to the objective of optimizing this measure.

Colleague Principles

Morningstar is a highly principled organization. It not only publishes its principles—it clearly lives them every day. Some aspects of its principles follow:

- Its mission is everyone's "boss," not another person. No supervisors are needed because colleagues know what they are doing and why.
- Everyone must visibly commit to both individual goals and teamwork and maintain integrity.
- Personal responsibility and initiative to self-management is the baseline for all work.

- Tolerance and respect for individual differences are required at all times.

- Communication among colleagues must be direct, and conflicts must be resolved immediately.

- Colleagues must care about their mission, their outside contacts, and one another and proactively share information that will be of value.

- Colleagues should "Do what is right. Live, speak and endeavor to find the truth."

These principles aren't just wall charts; in fact, you won't find them on the Morningstar walls. But they are well understood and form the foundation for colleague behavior and process performance every day.

Stakeholders

Morningstar treats its stakeholders seriously and has strong relationships with each. Its customers include

- Those who purchase paste to make and distribute tomato consumer products such as juices, soups, ketchup, and sauces

- Customers for the non-paste waste that can't be used for human consumption but is a food for livestock

- Institutional customers for bulk-packaged, tomato-based consumer products, including military organizations, schools, and restaurant chains

Morningstar doesn't sell consumer products directly to consumers.

Its other stakeholders include

- Tomato growers
- Suppliers of packing materials
- Energy suppliers
- Suppliers of plant and equipment maintenance
- A trucking company (part of the company family)
- Harvesters (part of the company family)
- The California Tomato Growers Association, which negotiates prices and premium levels on behalf of all growers in the state
- State of California regulatory and environmental agencies
- Colleagues, full-time and seasonal
- The owner

Processes

Because Morningstar has no wall chart of process architecture, I can't repeat it here. Nonetheless, its processes are clear to the colleagues who work there. My understanding is that the following are some of the key ones:

- Plan business. Morningstar visits many other businesses for best practices comparison and does a lot of research. It also supports a friendly rivalry between sister factories, while encouraging strong sharing between them.
- Negotiate industry prices and premium levels.
- Prepare a packing plan.
- Develop an acquisition plan, for the various types of tomatoes and timings.
- Develop a growing plan with growers. Determine the types and volumes of tomatoes each grower will have ready in each planned harvesting week.
- Arrange the harvesting and loading.
- Harvest the fruit.
- Transport the fruit to the factory site.
- Grade the arriving fruit. A state agency runs grading stations on site.
- Process the product. Make the paste or other product.
- Distribute the finished product to customers.
- Monitor the weather and growing conditions and maintain production plans.
- Monitor environmental and safety compliance.
- Provide colleagues.
- Provide facilities.
- Provide information technologies.

Technologies and Facilities

Morningstar's technologies are primarily its state-of-the-art processing facilities. Its aseptic processing plant is monitored completely online through real-time feedback networks that link into its control room. Other facilities and technologies include its high productivity harvesting machines and various vehicles, a gravity feed process, and a closed-loop water management system. Offices are in the same building that house the factory operations.

Information technology doesn't predominate. Morningstar uses some basic business management software and some database management systems applications. Colleague KPI reports are produced centrally and distributed back to colleagues for self-initiated action. The building of a personal feedback dashboard is underway. With growth into new areas such as bulk consumer products for institutions, the company has recognized the need for a more architected approach. Nonetheless, information technology is clearly just an enabler, and not the reason, for Morningstar's success.

Organizational Structure and Colleague Management

This area truly distinguishes Morningstar from any other organization that I've seen. It has little in the way of traditional, formal reporting relationships. This doesn't mean that roles aren't well defined; they are very well known to all, just not in an overly rigid way. An organizational chart doesn't exist in the traditional sense. Morningstar's structure is completely flat, with no levels or layers, just roles and responsibilities. In fact, the non–core-process colleagues believe strongly that, in effect, they report to the core process workers. They see their job as supporting production.

Mission-driven and performance-based colleague self-management clearly works for Morningstar. Even among seasonal workers, there is a return rate of more than 90%. These workers are well treated. They value their seasonal health insurance, collegial work environment, better-than-average pay, and a work process with no bosses.

Colleague Letter of Understanding

That there are no bosses doesn't mean that everyone simply does what they want without direction or incentives. Each colleague must negotiate and sign a colleague letter of understanding that covers the commitments that he will make to other colleagues. The letter documents the individual colleague's

- Acceptance of total personal responsibility for vision, overall mission, principles, his own commercial mission, and specific personal processes/activities within his awareness
- Degree of freedom and decision-making authority
- Performance indicators (all other colleague measures are aligned contributors to the Morningstar mission and ROI)
- Short-term and long-term goals
- Rights and responsibilities to share information and knowledge
- Requirements for resources
- Personal improvement and knowledge enhancement goals("perfect world" and personal goals levels are set)
- Compensation and benefits
- Conditions of periodic letter-of-understanding renewal
- Business philosophy

This "letter" is taken to other colleagues in each colleague's "Ring of Responsibility" to be reviewed, discussed, modified, and signed by all colleagues with whom the colleague interacts in his peer group.

On an ongoing basis, individual progress against KPIs is monitored and tied into compensation reviews, which are also done by peer colleagues. Everyone and every area are graphed, and results are made available to the peer group. Subsequently, the peer group adjusts base compensation. Any significant changes are made based on peer recommendations to the owner.

Hiring proposals come from peer groups, and then they hire new colleagues themselves, using prevailing industry wage data provided by office colleagues. New staff goes through a rigorous orientation on the work culture and methods.

Colleagues' "Rings of Responsibility" are totally results oriented. Each ring has full process stewardship in action, even though it's not named as such. All Morningstar processes are linked and focused on the results of value to Morningstar and all its stakeholders. In addition to core workplace teams, there are enterprise colleague groups for organization-wide aspects such as IT and facilities. Large changes happen through tactical alliances of colleagues with an enterprise group. If a capital project must be conducted, a capital project proposal is prepared and presented to the owner.

This environment was put in place from day one by the owner. There was no transformation from an old model, just an organic evolution of the original concept.

Morningstar Summary

Morningstar is the best example that I've seen of a mature process-managed company. Nowhere else have I witnessed or even heard of a company that's so driven to manage its relationships in such a natural way—totally process-empowered and a great place to work.

Stanford University's Financial Aid Office

Providing financial aid to students is a critical issue for Stanford University because the university is proud of its academic and athletic achievements. To maintain its national leadership and reputation, Stanford has to continue to attract the world's top students despite the high cost of tuition, books, and lodging. This cost amounted to more than $30,000 annually per student when revision of the financial aid office started in 1995, and is higher now. This case will focus on the transformation that the office went through, and the results achieved by moving to a process-organized approach.

About the Financial Aid Office

The mission of Stanford's Financial Aid Office (FAO) is "to assess the financial needs of incoming, matriculated, and graduate students, and to package appropriate support." It also administers scholarship funds, work study, and federally regulated loan programs and grants. Its vision is to do this fairly, quickly, and efficiently for students and their families.

Going into the change initiative, the FAO staff faced work overload all year round. All experts in one aspect of the service to students, these capable financial aid professionals became potential bottlenecks in the delivery of student solutions through no fault of their own. Vacation and personal time was almost impossible to schedule. Many students were treated as exceptions, and the quality of the aid package was considered paramount, regardless of time or impact on staff or students. Students and their families faced frustration and delay.

The lack of integrated information and lack of trust in the student data compounded all these problems. As at other universities, nonexistent information, redundancy, lack of integrity, inaccessibility of student and aid files and information, and inadequate management information were not unusual. Also, all university offices and programs—including the FAO—were facing budget reductions, despite the costs of accelerating regulatory changes.

In this tough environment, the FAO had to change its approach while living with existing hard-to-manage, sequential, drawn-out, and fragmented processes that were exception oriented for applicants. Because of rework and poor supporting mechanisms, the overworked staff couldn't avoid peak bottlenecks and queues. The risk-averse behavior of the FAO staff was understandable, given the situation. This attitude made dealing with the FAO difficult for the customers—that is, the students—who often didn't know where to go or what to do. There was no clear accountability for each student's case. As a result, loans and grants were often late, and temporary loans had to be arranged to get students through semester startup until they got their funds.

Clearly, this had to change.

Stakeholders

The FAO started its journey to change by understanding what was important to those who had a stake in the FAO processes. The FAO's customers were

- Students
- Families

External stakeholders of the financial aid office were

- Lenders
- Donors
- Other schools

- Federal and state regulators
- Loan guarantors

Internal university stakeholders were

- The Admissions office
- The Bursar office
- The Registrar office
- The Controller
- Schools within the Stanford academic structure
- Other departments
- The athletic department
- The FAO staff

Based on an analysis of these relationships, performance-based criteria were established to assess options for the FAO change initiative. These criteria were used to choose among different alternatives of process, organizational, and technological change. The best option would be the one that meets the most criteria most completely. Table 4.1 shows the criteria used.

TABLE 4.1 Criteria for Evaluating Competing Process Design Options

Project Perspective	Criteria
Level of service to students and families	Speed of turnaround from aid request to funds at the Bursar office
	Accuracy of aid amount
	Availability of information regarding aid in general
	Availability of information regarding personal aid status
	Student perception of the new process
Effectiveness and efficiency within Stanford	Speed of turnaround from aid request to funds at the Bursar office
	Amount of rework and repeat work
	Appropriate compliance levels achieved
	Overall cost of ongoing operation to Stanford

TABLE 4.1   Continued

Project Perspective	*Criteria*
Satisfaction of the FAO staff	Ability to conduct standard approach while accommodating exceptions
	Overall workload
	Variety of interesting work and motivation level
	Supportiveness of new approach
	Reasonable workloads and personal effects on staff
	Perception of solution by valued staff
Change project cost and risk	Support by IT systems
	Overall cost to Stanford
	Effect on capital funding levels

Processes

Based on examining the stakeholders' needs, the processes of the FAO were determined:

Core Processes

- Provide application documents
- Advise/counsel students and parents
- Provide financial aid (involves following steps):
    - Collect applications/information
    - Analyze need and award aid
    - Process loans
    - Process student jobs
    - Process grants
    - Process outside awards
    - Process institutional aid for graduate students

- Administer work study for graduate students
- Process short-term loans
- Provide financial aid transcripts

Guiding Processes

- Analyze/interpret and implement regulations and policies
- Manage funds
- Produce external reports

Enabling Processes

- Provide administrative support
- Provide training and access to reference materials
- Maintain job listings
- Provide HR support
- Provide IT support

Proposed changes focused on the set of core processes. The main solution principle adopted was a single-point-of-contact student service model managed by "student-focused" teams supported with integrated information. The solution would define technology requirements and implement some significant non–technology-based improvements.

The FAO staff members were highly educated, with a large percentage being graduates of the university. Because each staff member was responsible for a small portion of the overall aid package, there was little challenge to their jobs, other than completing a huge workload consisting of many repetitive, manual, and redundant steps. The "one-stop-shopping" student/case management strategy featured a much higher delegation of responsibility and accountability for service results.

With the process change, generalist roles now predominate in which each staff member can perform a wide variety of activities. Specialist roles provide support, coaching, training, and advice. Some generalists also take responsibility for an aspect of specialization to support all FAO student service advisors. Some experts, such as federal loan professionals, are full-time.

Through a team-based structure, incentives and rewards are shared, and information and knowledge sharing have become natural. Workloads are more balanced, and some work processes such as temporary loan provisioning, tracking, and repayment have almost disappeared as compared to former levels. Prevention of unnecessary work is emphasized rather than corrective action.

The one-stop-shopping process solution also provides more flexibility in response to outside changes. The mechanisms—processes, job designs, organizational structures, systems infrastructure, applications, physical facilities, policies and procedures, and culture—can manage students, cases, and aid programs of any type, not just those governed by today's regulations or a set of specific applications. The capacity to manage change and implement a "learning organization" was put in place. Staff members are trained to handle the student's human situation, not just regulations and case files.

The university's process renewal team sought out maneuverable automation support to manage the workflow, and not just data. Automation with built-in policies, rules, regulations and training was the goal, although the automation choices at the time weren't as robust as would have been preferred. This automation made time for and commitment to regular re-education of staff possible.

Project Approach

Training and awareness sessions for the staff and the management team were conducted to kick off the project. The process architecture was produced, and the alignment of process with technology was examined, although an unproven version of a software package had already been picked. This would prove to be a constraining issue later, especially because this was Stanford's first administrative exposure to distributed technology.

The existing core processes were analyzed, modeled, and understood. At the start of the project, significant resistance to change arose. To overcome a large portion of this resistance, staff members were involved extensively in the project from beginning to end. Contests were held to identify process changes that would decrease workloads, and emphasis was placed on choosing suggestions from the line staff.

The office identified quick wins, and introduced many to realize significant savings right away. Quick wins alone improved productivity by more than 10% and eliminated significant overtime within the first year. The new process was designed, and an organizational approach proposed. The models of the new processes were developed.

Some techniques were very useful. The process architecture based on customer analysis and event outcome pairings was used repeatedly to define interactions and workflows. Management and staff workshops helped with consensus and understanding. Timeboxed, cross-functional process-modeling techniques were applied to great benefit.

A number of workshops were held for outside stakeholders to gain their input into the change process. A cross-sectional group of students were asked to represent the concerns of their peers, and their ideas were incorporated into the final solution. Other offices within the university affected by the changes to the FAO participated in meetings to determine how their interactions with the FAO could be made smoother and more automated.

The biggest challenge arose from the selection of a software package before process redesign. The expectations of the process team were often met with lack of capability or expensive change controls from the vendor. Also, the existing network and university software applications weren't designed to work with the new software yet.

Management feared the impact of change on their jobs and positions. Months were spent redefining the organizational structure and writing new job descriptions, with careful emphasis placed on each person's expanding responsibilities and authority. Two new approaches helped significantly reduce the staff's former lack of acceptance:

- Meetings were held without management present, and grievances were aired and presented to management in a non-personal forum.
- Management introduced its principles of change to the whole office at a full FAO meeting with no restrictions placed on the concerns that could be raised.

Technologies and Facilities

Business process automation software was involved in the FAO changes, but the new technology environment wasn't fully integrated with existing technologies. It interfaced with many existing applications, including the package that provided an integrated student aid database, new LAN capabilities, and new processors (clients and servers).

The selected software had some significant automation gaps, particularly in the processing of guaranteed loans. To overcome these gaps, the FAO worked closely with a large private-sector guarantor to incorporate the guarantor's automated systems into the overall technology solution. This significantly reduced the amount of manual effort required to process loans.

The financial aid office space was also reconfigured to allow service to students to be less sequential. By eliminating walls and opening up the workspace, teams could work together more easily.

Organizational Structure and Team Approach

As mentioned, the organization design for student-focused teams was innovative. Figure 4.1 shows the teams within the Financial Aid Office's structure.

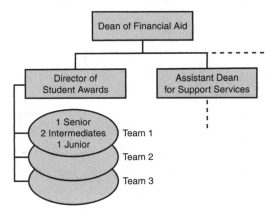

FIGURE 4.1

Stanford University Financial Aid Office organization.

Each team of four staff members takes responsibility for a set of students. The senior, most experienced member of a student servicing team takes responsibility for the most complex student cases. These cases involve loans, grants, and other circumstances that require the most extensive knowledge. The two intermediate team members handle the normal cases. They have some experience but not as much as the senior does. The junior team member is learning to handle the wide range of services that the FAO provides. Juniors typically deal with simple student requirements. Each is the primary contact with specific students, but other team members can pick up work in case of temporary absence or loss of another team member. This is full-service and process management. The student services director is the process owner, who keeps the teams working holistically and student focused.

Stanford Summary

This solution took two years to roll out, due in large part to the changes required in the computing environment and organizational changes. Many of the quick wins that provided the staff with additional time for training on the new processes and systems are still in place.

Using teams composed of generalists eliminated many bottlenecks in the processing of aid packages while providing the necessary challenge to the staff members. Including the line staff in the development of the new processes did much to smooth the transition to the new way of performing work, and many resistant staff members became the biggest supporters as their roles expanded and their responsibilities grew.

The FAO's performance has improved dramatically, but it required changes to all aspects on the wheel of change: the processes, organizational structure, roles and jobs, facilities, computing and communications environment, human resources, and policies and rules. What began as an automated system implementation became a restructuring of the entire way the FAO conducted business. For each step of the way, emphasis was placed on allowing easy participation for the FAO's primary stakeholders (the students and their parents).

The key lessons learned in conducting this initiative are

- Design your processes before ordering or specifying software packages.
- You need very top-level active support, as Stanford had, to make change work because it's too easy to fall back and abandon the tough changes.
- You must deliver savings along the way to pay for the extra time and cost of changing.
- Human change management is more than 50% of the work. Soliciting the input of the line staff at each step in the project does much to gain their support for the change effort.
- Highly educated, intelligent staff must be challenged with a variety of non-repetitive tasks. Being responsible for the entire process, rather than just a small portion of the process, is one way of providing the additional needed challenge and level of responsibility.

- The Business Context and Architect and Align phase deliverables are essential to help all other phases.

- Change takes time, and it's hard work.

- You need a methodology to guide your work. As the complexity of the change expands, and the number of guides and enablers that must simultaneously undergo transformation increases, the more important the methodology becomes.

Rexall.com

Rexall.com is the online business model offered by Rexall Showcase International, part of the highly successful Rexall Sundown (RSI) family of nutritional product companies based in Florida. The Rexall name has a very high brand recognition and level of trust due to its 100-year-old reputation in the drug store business.

Rexall Showcase International's business model is to sell through a multi-level marketing approach. This division of RSI has been in operation for more than 10 years, providing for the highest quality nutritional products and winning numerous awards from the leading independent quality audit firms. Through Rexall.com, it offers more than 120 unique formulations for exclusive distribution by distributors that it calls *independent business owners (IBOs)*. Its product lines include patented formulas, proprietary blends, exclusive ingredients, and innovative delivery systems.

RSI and Rexall Showcase International have undergone remarkable changes in the past two years and have managed to more than weather the transition. During these changes, RSI thrived as a result of its resilience. In 1999 and 2000, RSI acquired a number of complementary companies.

In January 2000, RSI announced the immediate launch of Rexall.com, a rebirth of Rexall Showcase International as an e-business featuring the redesign of virtually all the business processes within Rexall Showcase. Despite some expected hiccups in transforming some of the longer serving distributors to the new business models, the transition has succeeded remarkably. The resilient Rexall.com made progress during the acquisition of RSI by Royal Numico to form one of the largest nutritional companies in the world. Headquartered in the Netherlands, Royal Numico is also a 100-year-old nutritional products company. Even after the Royal Numico acquisition, Rexall.com joined forces with Enrich, another network marketing company. This was a lot of change in a short period of time that could have been difficult for any organization to manage. Rexall.com has managed it well.

Salomon Smith Barney[1] studied the top direct-selling companies in the industry, and found that "Rexall.com is the clear leader with respect to helping its distributors effectively market their dot-com business." According to the report, Rexall.com's Web site is "well-thought-out in terms of layout and ease of use," its "categories are clearly defined and sub categorized," and it provides detailed product info in a user-friendly manner that "distinguishes Rexall.com from other network marketing sites."

The report discusses the challenges many "pure" Internet companies are facing as they reach the pivotal point of having to become profitable or close up shop. It goes on to say, "With an emphasis placed on the leveraging of existing business relationships, personalized customer service and the lure of owing a dot-com business, the online direct-selling industry will be the next successful phase of the 'click and mortar' evolution."

Before the Dot-Com Launch

Before the birth of Rexall.com, Rexall Showcase International was known as just Rexall and already had an impressive track record. The organization was a clear leader in its business model in the nutritional business. It used traditional multilevel marketing, but did it well. Distributors recruited other distributors, who were expected to sell to customers and build their own networks. The model was very collegial and supportive across the network of distributors because the compensation plan—the most generous plan in the industry—encouraged up to six levels of distributors; those in the upper line of the network would receive compensation based on sales. Also, distributors at any level could outperform those above them (their *upline*), so more than just the early entrants into the business made significant income. This encouraged strong upward and downward knowledge sharing and support from those with experience.

The operational model was primarily paper based. Distributor sign-up was done manually with forms, as was product ordering. Transactions took place through the Rexall telephone call center. Rexall trained its distributors through scheduled conference calls and the purchase of audio and videotapes. New distributor recruitment followed a well-defined, one-on-one, scripted procedure augmented by audiotape testimonials and local group meetings. "Team building" guidebooks were sold for distribution to serious prospects. The roles of the first level distributors and others in the chain were clear in the recruiting and training process. The process required a lot of support and coordination and it was learned through the mentoring of the upline distributors.

Product knowledge was harder to acquire, especially when new products were launched, unless a distributor attended the conference that announced the product. But Rexall provided excellent materials describing each product; distributors could purchase the materials to pass on to their customers.

---

1 "Salomon Smith Barney Equity Research Report—Internet-Direct Selling," June 21, 2000

Rexall's successes were based on the trust factor between distributor and customers and among distributors. This was a good model for the 20th century, but Rexall's leadership knew that the model wasn't scalable into the 21st century. Because of outside pricing pressures and the slowness of the recruiting and sales processes, Rexall's way of doing business wasn't viable in the long term, so its executives decided to change it dramatically.

After the Dot-Com Launch

Because the entire landscape of business was changing with the advent of the Internet and the e-commerce activity it generated, Rexall decided to take a huge leap with the introduction of Rexall.com. However, rather than go direct and cut out its distributor channel, it decided to blend the advantages of personal distributor relationships with e-commerce and let each do what it was best at doing. Its distributors were renamed independent business owners (IBOs).

Creating the IBO program became more than just a new Internet strategy for a brick-and-mortar company—it became a complete reinvention of the entire business model. In President and Chief Operating Officer David J. Schofield's announcement, he stated, "Rexall.com provides the only 'all-inclusive' Internet model within our industry and will allow our Independent Business Owners to sell Rexall Showcase International products to their customers and to prospect, recruit, train, communicate, support and interact with their customers and business builders much more effectively. We also have made other fundamental changes in our business model to stimulate consumer consumption of our unique products, as well as reducing the cost to join our business, which we feel will make us much more competitive within the marketplace."[2]

Let's look at some of the main characteristics of Rexall.com's comprehensive approach to its new processes.

Mission

Rexall.com's mission is "to provide the best online business opportunity while offering consumers quality products and personalized service." Its business model is built on "fairness and integrity and is structured to benefit everyone we touch."

Rexall believes that the most successful e-commerce companies will be those that provide competitively priced, high-quality products along with personalized service. It saw the strength of the thousands of Independent Business Owners, who each have an incentive to provide positive, personalized services to their customers, as compared to the business stakeholders of a traditional e-commerce company.

[2]*Rexall Showcase International press release, Boca Raton, Fla., January 26, 2000*

Clearly, Rexall has a "customer intimacy" value proposition, if you consider that its customers are IBOs as well as the purchasers and users of its products. Its solution is designed clearly with all stakeholders in mind.

Values

Rexall has also made sure that its traditional value system didn't change dramatically. It has emphasized certain aspects because of fears that it might have abandoned its personal relationship approach by developing a Web-based solution. It has remained committed to being easy to do business with, to having top quality products with a money-back guarantee, and to being accessible and providing support.

In the move to an Internet-supported process model, it has added a few more principles, such as a permission approach that fires IBOs for spamming and a commitment to safety and security of transactions. The company has also pledged that information gathered over the Internet will never be sold, traded, rented, or disclosed without permission.

Stakeholders

For the purposes of this study, I will confine myself to the stakeholders who were the target of the transformation: the customers who use the nutritional products and the IBOs who create the demand for the products and acquire new IBOs. Naturally, the IBOs themselves will also be product customers.

Rexall.com Product Customers

As noted, the customers are treated along permission marketing lines, whereby they won't be aggressively sold to unless they choose to be. This approach encourages them to build relationships rather than just buy products.

Rexall.com offers a fully automated storefront for self-service usage that allows customers to manage their own orders and gain their own knowledge. Through the storefront or by phone, if they prefer, customers have the following features available to them:

- Newsletters outlining health tips and nutritional research, should they choose to register for them. The price is giving up their anonymity.
- Information about Rexall.com-patented products and trial results.
- The ability to access specific health interest or product Web sites for more knowledge.
- The ability to purchase directly from Rexall.com online or by phone, exclusive products blended to suit specific health goals, such as cardiovascular disease prevention or cholesterol reduction.
- The ability to place recurring orders to be shipped automatically according to the customers' preferred schedule.

- The capability to track order delivery.
- A money-back guarantee.

IBOs

Clearly for Rexall.com, the success of this new concept depends on each IBO striving to build a reputation for his company that helps protect the integrity of the overall Rexall business. To ensure this, leading Rexall distributors—who were intimately involved with the development of the Rexall.com model—designed an IBO creed to guide actions and enhance success. Rexall and other IBOs honor and enforce this creed in no uncertain terms. Rexall.com encourages potential IBOs who can't support the creed to not sign up. Those who do aspire to work this way can benefit from a set of Rexall.com services that make their jobs easier. With these services in place, IBOs can be more focused on the processes of recruiting other IBOs and getting customers to buy products. A lot of the time they would have spent previously on operational issues such as ordering products and signing up new IBOs can now be done directly on a self-service basis.

Some of the valuable capabilities available to IBOs from Rexall.com are

- A portfolio of exclusive products that the parent company doesn't offer through other channels or subsidiaries.
- Access to a wide and deep online knowledge base previously available only from other upline distributors.
- Significant training materials in every aspect of how to conduct business online as well as through phone access, local meetings, and national conferences.
- An Internet basics glossary and online usage training for IBOs.
- Information about e-business relationship management best practices and reusable components for incorporation into IBO sites (available through the Rexall.com Web site).
- Strong human support from their upline IBOs and access to Rexall customer service reps, who can help with product and business knowledge.
- A comprehensive set of marketing tools such as
  - Slide presentations
  - E-mail templates
  - Sales strategies
  - Reusable print and Web advertising materials
  - A personalized storefront and recruiting Web site design and modification tools
  - Business cards, letterhead, and envelopes
  - Offline marketing tools and guidance

4

NEW-AGE
COMPANY
EXPERIENCES

- Online tracking of many relevant factors such as
  - The volume of an IBO's own sales as well as those of IBOs below her in her own organization (her *downline*)
  - Compensation levels earned
  - Specific orders' status
  - IBO Web site traffic and tracking of prospects
  - Notification of potential customer and IBO references for expressions of interest
  - Automatic connection of customer purchases to IBO accounts and of downline IBOs for automatic compensation calculation
- Rexall technology such as
  - Access to all tools to build Web sites and storefronts
  - Hosting of Web sites
- Clear compensation plan.
- Low financial investment.

Process Development

In rolling out the changes for the new business model across tens of thousands of IBOs, the key to Rexall.com's success was the up-front time it spent developing its processes with IBO representatives. Every possible event trigger was meticulously thought out, from a wide range of different customer types and potential IBOs as well as from IBOs with varying levels of upline and downline connections. This happened before the technology was designed in detail or developed. Part of the strength of the Rexall.com business model is its simplicity. Perhaps the biggest challenge was to draw out all the knowledge in the heads of many senior, experienced stakeholders and to incorporate it into process design and knowledge bases.

Clearly the IBOs are involved with many processes:

Customer-Related Processes

- Make customers aware of the Rexall products
- Educate customers
- Fulfill and track orders

IBO-Related Processes

- Make potential IBOs aware of the business opportunity
- Educate potential IBOs

- Sign up IBOs
- Develop tools and technologies for marketing and service delivery
- Start up IBOs
- Train IBOs
- Monitor business activity
- Manage relationships with customers, upline IBOs, and downline IBOs

Rexall.com is also involved with several processes when it comes to its customer and IBOs:

- Develop products
- Manage legal and regulatory issues
- Manufacture products
- Fulfill orders
- Provide customer service
- Provide IBO service
- Enable IBOs
- Manage relationships with IBOs
- Learn and distribute knowledge
- Provide technology capability
- Produce marketing materials for both online and offline promotions
- Manage technology infrastructure
- Operate facilities

Transformation Program for Adaptability

The discussion in this case study has focused very much on a rapidly changing business environment, the massive impact on business models that technology can have, the critical role of a stakeholder-based approach, and the importance of getting the processes right. As with any situation, other aspects of change can also come into play. By examining the Process Renewal Hexagon repeated here in Figure 4.2, you will see that other aspects of transformation had to be dealt with also.

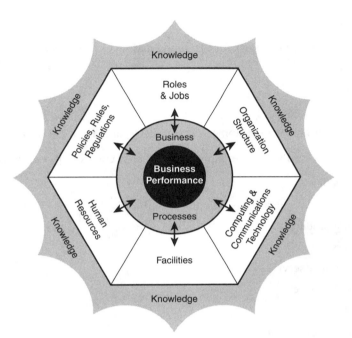

FIGURE 4.2

The Process Management Hexagon.

Business Performance

Along with Rexall.com's new model came a new pricing strategy. Across the board, prices were slashed by more than 30%. Some were reduced by more than 50%. This clearly would have an impact on Rexall's profit margins in the short term, that would be made up only if volume would grow. Also, the business performance of successful distributors would be severely affected because their compensation is based on the volume of sales in their downline. This latter issue lead to a compensation plan review but also to the departure of some longer-term distributors. Nonetheless, Rexall deemed that, because of market conditions and pressures, prices had to drop, or the alternatives would have been worse.

Process Changes

As discussed earlier, many processes were changed. The ones affecting IBOS and customers were the most dramatically different from past processes. Many others within RSI weren't affected much. The impact on product development, manufacturing, and even order fulfillment was limited. The process changes that were instituted supported the new financial model of business performance and new business models.

Policies and Rules

A significant number of policies and rules were clearly blown away and replaced. The IBO compensation plan changed more than once during design and throughout the rollout period. The effect on country operations and business practices in countries such as Canada and Japan varied from effects in the United States. The need to be responsive and have self-service processes changed some older policies that would otherwise have slowed down the new processes.

Roles and Jobs

The IBO's prime role didn't change, but her responsibilities varied dramatically from the past. Furthermore, the customer and prospective IBO now would take on some of the roles that the distributor previously would have done for them. Some IBOs with no technology skills initially expressed fear and doubt over the changes.

Organizational Structure

Because the compensation plan changed, there was a one-time opportunity for IBOs to reconfigure their own downline teams to optimize their return. This, however, wasn't a substantive change in most cases and generally didn't make up for the revenue drop because of lowered prices.

Technology

Technology changes were consequential as has been discussed earlier. The Internet's technology potential and the growth of computer access in the target market made it possible to conceive of the new business model. However, the technology specification was finished only after the joint Rexall/distributor team determined the process and rules changes.

Facilities

There was little impact on facilities. This isn't always the case.

Humans

For some people, the change brought by Rexall.com was welcomed. The technologically literate had been clamoring for an e-business solution to ease the mundane tasks of finding, signing up, and educating new IBOs. Selling online helped reduce the stigma of traditional network marketing for many potential recruits. Those used to Internet marketing models welcomed the change.

However, a large proportion of pre–dot-com Rexall distributors were above the age of 45, and many had never touched a computer before. As a result, Rexall spent significant time and effort in designing the technology solution for ease of use. It also held a number of workshops for the basic training of how to use a computer and the Internet for existing distributors. Without this attention to the basic human capabilities, the uptake would have been much less. There were some who didn't choose to go with the new approach, but many successfully made the transition.

The problem with the change in the compensation plan has been noted already. Rexall introduced the changed processes and technologies at the same time it dropped prices dramatically. The company admits that it didn't handle this part of the transformation as well as it could have. Some IBOs with wide and deep teams lost half their income. To Rexall.com's credit, it did adjust the plans later to try to alleviate the damage. However, new compensation plans that make it harder to achieve what successful practitioners had become used to are often judged negatively. New participants will accept it more easily. As Rexall.com discovered, sometimes the market realities must drive the change despite the impact on some human resources.

Rexall.com Summary

The design of the solution and the initial rollout took less than a year. After initial rollout, ongoing evolution of most aspects of the solution continued, with larger changes coming in the first months that followed. The solution is still evolving today.

Rexall.com is an example of what an organization can do to manage significant change when it has the commitment and a senior management that champions the change. Rexall.com didn't do everything perfectly, but it also didn't wait forever to act. By thinking through all aspects of the Process Management Hexagon and introducing the synchronized changes together, Rexall.com learned a lot just by being in the marketplace and not just speculating about it. Rexall also wasn't afraid to admit its mistakes, change ideas as it went forward, and evolve functionality over time. It understood that there would be casualties in the ranks of its IBOs but knew that the revised model would attract new customers as well as IBOs who wouldn't have joined otherwise. the company knew that to not change would have been the worse thing it could do.

Summary

The three cases in this chapter all depicted a number of attributes of the ideal transformation. None of the subjects has transformed itself perfectly, but none of them are resting on their laurels, either. Each continues to manage its processes and to improve. By looking at all of them and adopting some of the lessons learned, you can realize similar benefits.

Chapter 5, "The Process Management Framework," will describe the work that must be done to realize the improvements you seek. It will describe the phases and critical factors that must be managed to realize stakeholder-driven and process-based change across all aspects of the Process Management Hexagon.

The Process Management Framework

IN THIS CHAPTER

The challenge in any organization that wants to improve its performance is to come up with an approach in which everyone has confidence. Personal preferences always compete against consistency of techniques throughout an organization. For that reason, organizations employ many methods of working, derived from many sources, and each method has some merit. Arguments over exactly which to use often reflects power struggles more than genuine methodological debates. In many cases, change agents make up their own methods based on what they hope will work. These often reflect a bias from a particular professional viewpoint.

For example, methodologies from information technology organizations usually focus on processes as a way to fulfill system requirements. These methods often shortchange the other aspects of transformation, such as culture and structure. On the other hand, approaches from human resource professionals are great at dealing with roles, jobs, and competencies, but usually fall short when it comes to facilities and technologies. HR staffers are often caught up in organizational structure thinking rather than cross-functional perspectives. The general framework described in this chapter attempts to provide guidance that can be used organization-wide because it takes a business, rather than a functional, perspective. It's designed to accommodate a wide range of professional requirements and to align them with one another.

Another challenge to coming up with an accepted, reusable approach is the belief that anything too formal will take too long, especially given the perceived enormous pressure to change. Many fear that developing and implementing formalized methods takes too much time from too many people and takes too long to get a result. The "just-do-it" advocates miss the point that doing the wrong things fast is never a good business option. Their desire to reach a quick conclusion actually provides a strong case for reuse and good planning that associates the scarcest human and financial resources only with the most important things for the business. Using the formalized methods of the Process Management Framework doesn't waste resources in false starts, rework, and delivering poor results to people and organizations that notice.

The approach that I've taken to the Process Management Framework is to produce a set of guidelines based on best practices in the profession of business change and management. You won't find any component of the framework that is considered revolutionary; it's just good sense. Its value comes from logically putting together concepts so that they maintain alignment and traceability to business objectives.

The Process Management Framework is designed to be performance driven. It can be used comprehensively or partially, depending on how complex your initiative is. It scales up and down to initiatives and organizations of all sizes if used with common sense. It has several entry points. You don't have to start from the beginning and go all the way through to the end, although you would probably benefit if you did. The framework's components and techniques can be modified to accommodate approaches that have proven to work in your organization. It's a guideline, not a cookbook to be followed without question.

Process Management Principles

This Process Management Framework has been built on the 10 business change management principles described in Chapter 3. They are repeated here:

1. Business change must be performance driven.
2. Business change must be stakeholder based.
3. Business change decisions must be traceable to the stakeholder criteria.
4. The business must be segmented along business process lines to synchronize change.
5. Business processes must be managed holistically.
6. Process renewal initiatives must inspire shared insight.
7. Process renewal initiatives must be conducted from the outside in.
8. Process renewal initiatives must be conducted in an iterative, time-boxed approach.
9. Business change is all about people.
10. Business change is a journey, not a destination.

Framework Description

Based on these principles, the Process Management Framework is intended to be a flexible and reusable guideline that works with other professional approaches. It won't magically work alone, however. It requires that good practices be applied in other areas. Some of the most directly relevant practices are project management, risk management, and human change management. All of these are present all the time during the execution of the Process Management Framework. They don't occur at points in the framework, but they continuously evolve during all phases and steps that are conducted. Each management practice is addressed in its own chapter (Chapters 6 through 8).

The framework isn't intended to be a static document. It should evolve based on its use. The lessons learned based on using the framework should be applied in the updates of the phases, steps, deliverables, techniques, and roles. The framework must mature along with the organization that uses it; otherwise, it will fall out of favor and not be valuable.

The framework encompasses eight major types of activities directed at improved business performance. These logical groupings of activities will be referred to as the *phases* of the framework. Each phase accomplishes a specific purpose. The framework progresses through several modes as the phases unfold. Modes change and take on different perspectives. Figure 5.1 depicts the modes and the phases as a set of clouds rising to higher and higher levels of performance.

5

THE PROCESS MANAGEMENT FRAMEWORK

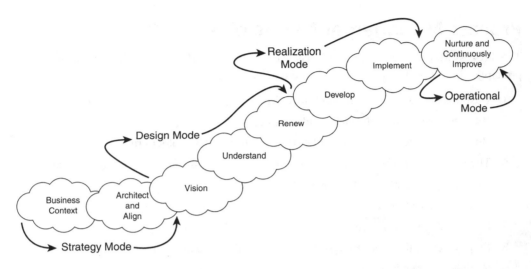

FIGURE 5.1

The Process Management Framework's modes and phases.

The initial mode is one of focusing on strategy. This comprises the Business Context phase and the Architect and Align phase. The steps of the Business Context phase provide an understanding of the business environment and the enterprise's strategic intent; during this phase, the organization defines the requirements of the business's stakeholders for business performance success. In the Architect and Align phase, an organization identifies its processes and aligns the priority ones to its other enterprise assets, such as people and technologies. The steps of the Architect and Align phase lay out an integrated program of change. In this Strategy mode, a portion of the enterprise or the whole thing will be examined to set the appropriate direction required for a set of processes and projects.

Subsequently, process management moves into a Design mode for a process-in-focus. This mode contains the Vision, Understand, and Renew phases. The Design mode is oriented around the definition of what must be built.

In the Vision phase, an organization defines the scope and success criteria for a project. It also plans the approach for the project and produces a business case for change. It develops a communication strategy for the affected stakeholders and starts to execute it.

In the Understand phase, an organization gathers information about an existing process and finds opportunities to improve the process. This phase provides the basis for communicating the rationale for changes to stakeholders with vested interests.

During the Renew phase, an organization produces its new approach for conducting the process in focus. It delivers validated models and test cases for later use. It produces a release-oriented transformation strategy for development and implementation.

Next, the mode switches to realizing the design. The Realization mode contains the Develop and Implement phases. During the Develop phase, an organization produces all its process guides and enablers and other capabilities. It prepares facilities and technologies for implementation.

The Implement phase gets everyone ready for the rollout of process and other aligned changes, subsequent to a full business test or pilot.

Everything isn't necessarily delivered at once during the Realization mode. An organization is more likely to release versions of any particular solution and to roll them out over time.

The last mode, the Operational mode, is the actual running of business processes day to day. Its only phase, Nurture and Continuously Improve, isn't trivial. Its major contribution from a process management viewpoint is the ongoing assessment and improvement of the processes in place. Results and observations from the Nurture and Continuously Improve phase are significant contributors to the next round of strategy formulation.

If taken seriously, the whole cycle is never ending. The organization will continue to climb to higher levels of performance.

The Framework as a Process of Discovery and Learning

The Process Management Hexagon was introduced in Chapter 3, "Principles of Process Management," as the basis for how work is conducted in the framework. Figure 5.2 shows the hexagon again. It emphasizes that a business is made up of processes that deliver performance and value at the center. The hexagon also depicts the necessary interrelationships of process with policies/rules, jobs, organization, technology, facilities, and people. It also shows that, without knowledge, none of these would be supportable.

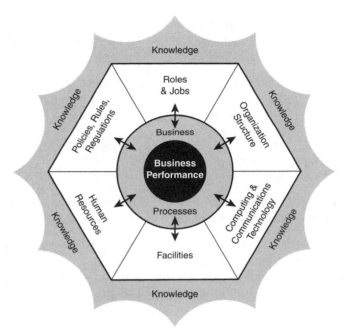

FIGURE 5.2

The Process Management Hexagon.

The hexagon is the basis for addressing all the work in each phase. In every mode and phase, those involved will look at all the segments of the hexagon and deal with them from their particular perspective. Each phase focuses on enabling more effective and efficient processes that will deliver improved performance for the organization's customers and stakeholders. The emphasis will vary from phase to phase and will depend on the specific project's nature; however, all segments of the hexagon must be addressed. Figure 5.3 graphically shows the iterative nature of the phases regarding each hexagon segment.

Each of the eight phases deals with both the existing situation (Current State) as well as the situation envisioned for the future (Future State). Each will evolve the understanding of the current state and add specifics to the design for what is yet to come. Because both states can be understood in balance at every turn, each state will add to the knowledge of the true requirements for a successful migration. In any journey, we must know where we are currently and decide where we want to go in the future; otherwise, all the maps and models in the world won't help. Addressing both perspectives throughout will help us maintain our course and allow for insight to be gained, learning to occur, and corrections to be made.

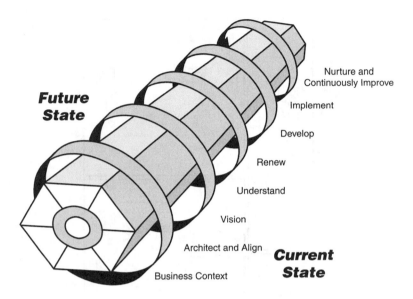

FIGURE 5.3

The framework as a process of discovery and learning.

None of the phases attempts to deliver perfect knowledge before moving on to the next. Instead, each adds to what has preceded it. The approach advocated and described is an iterative one that attempts to avoid paralysis through too much analysis. It strives to exploit both operations of the human brain: the analytic and the conceptual thinking styles. This evolutionary approach to revolutionary change is designed to gain buy-in and eliminate objections as it proceeds. Building commitment to the solution is constantly addressed through successively zeroing in on the logical results.

Framework Traceability

The first principle of process management is that business change must be performance driven. This implies that all actions must be traceable back to the business reasons for the change. Figure 5.4 shows the relationships that the major capabilities must have with one another. You should always strive to connect from any concept on the page to the others. If you can't trace to the others, you run a high risk of poor results. The Process Management Framework has been designed to support this traceability.

> **NOTE**
>
> Figure 5.4 shows a simplified form of the framework's traceability. In the following section, each phase is shown in much more detail. The purpose of the overall view is to show how the pieces fit together.

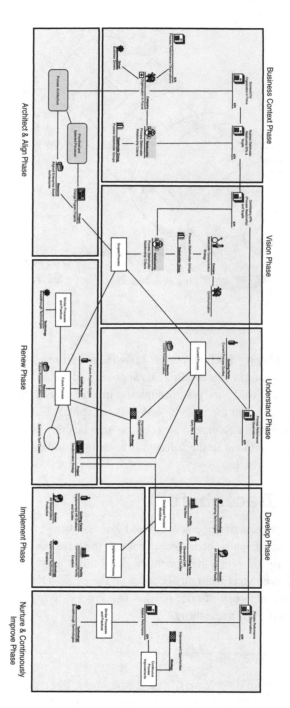

FIGURE 5.4

Traceability across the Process Management Framework phases.

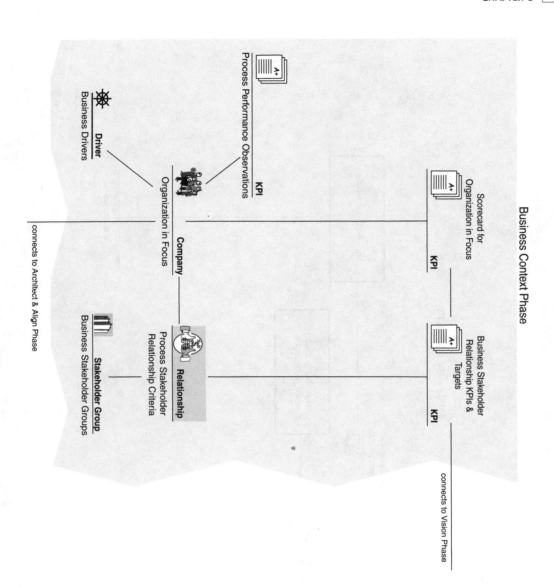

FIGURE 5.4

Continued, showing the Business Context Phase.

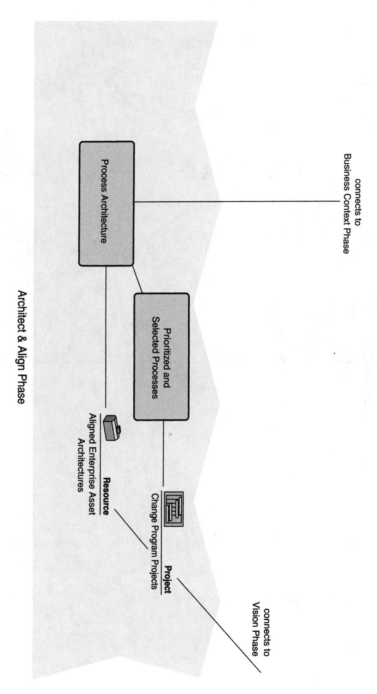

FIGURE 5.4

Continued, showing the Architect & Align Phase.

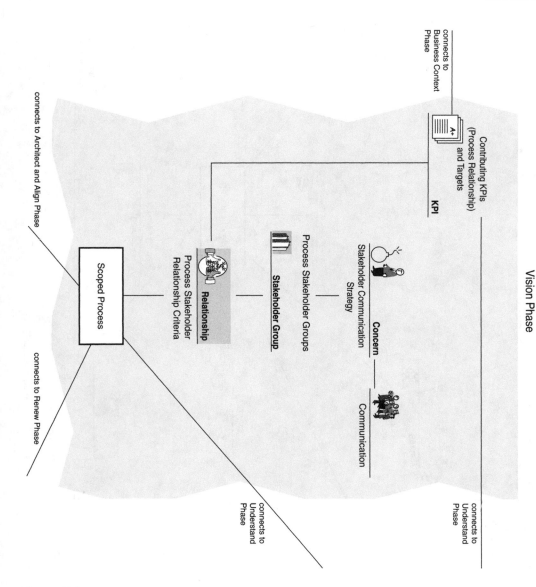

FIGURE 5.4

Continued, showing the Vision Phase.

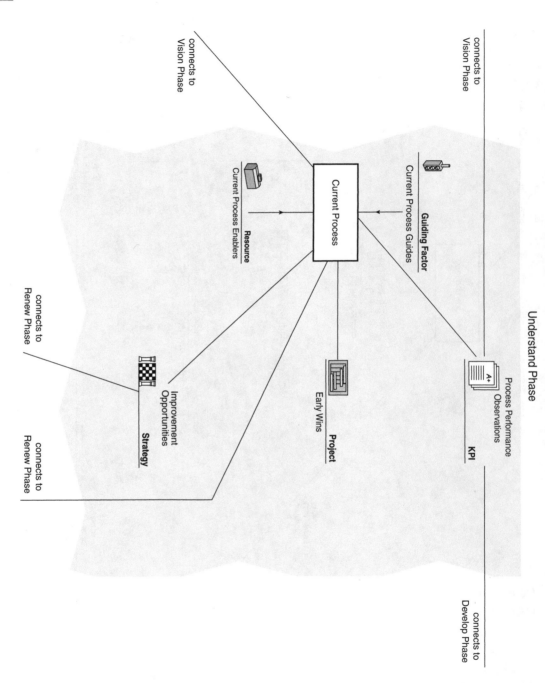

FIGURE 5.4

Continued, showing the Understand Phase.

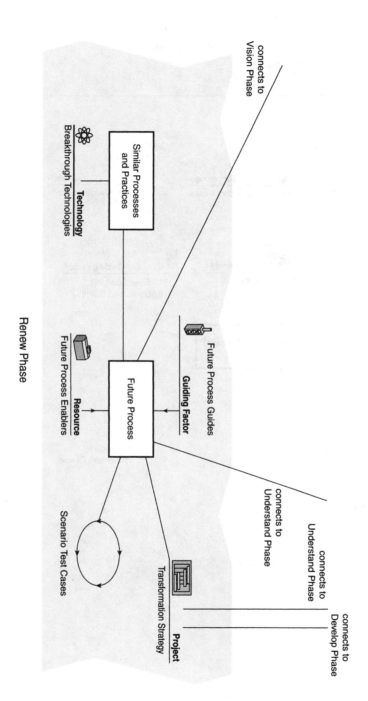

FIGURE 5.4

Continued, showing the Renew Phase.

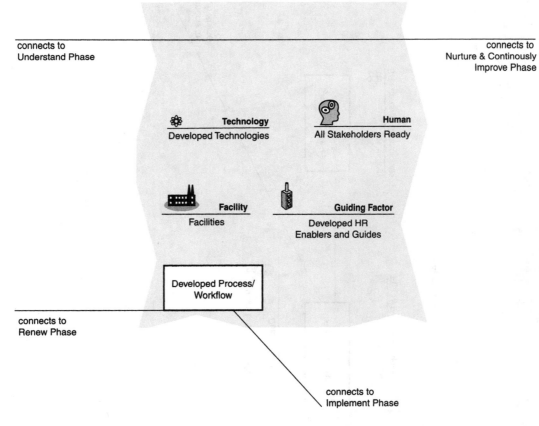

FIGURE 5.4

Continued, showing the Develop Phase.

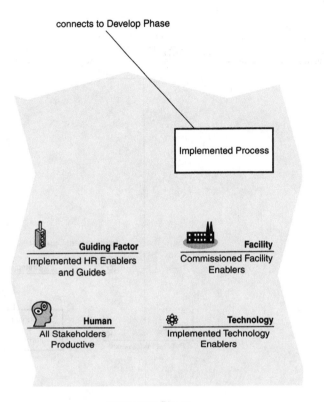

connects to Develop Phase

Implemented Process

Guiding Factor
Implemented HR Enablers
and Guides

Facility
Commissioned Facility
Enablers

Human
All Stakeholders
Productive

Technology
Implemented Technology
Enablers

Implement Phase

FIGURE 5.4
Continued, showing the Implement Phase.

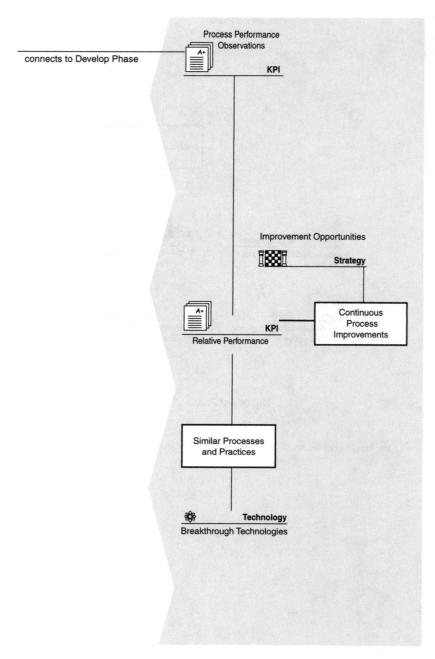

Nurture & Continuously Improve Phase

FIGURE 5.4

Continued, showing the final phase: Nurture & Continuously Improve.

In the Business Context phase, the Organization-in-Focus examines its current performance measures and pays attention to the business drivers in its environment. It also sets some direction as part of its strategy planning. As part of this, the organization establishes its measurement scorecard so that it can monitor all leading and lagging indicators of business performance. It also determines who its stakeholders are and what's important to them. This helps establish healthy relationships and loyalty and ultimately long-term success against the scorecard. A set of criteria is established to assess options for change and priorities for resource allocation.

In the Architect and Align phase, business processes are mapped as a process architecture, which is then cross-referenced to other organization-wide architectures for other assets such as facilities, technologies, and human resources. These architectures are assessed using the stakeholder criteria, and a top set of priority processes is identified for change, along with the associated related impacts on other asset architectures. These priorities are documented as part of a justified program plan for change that lists a set of project initiatives to introduce the new capabilities.

Each initiative to deliver improved business performance through process renewal is scoped as part of the Vision phase. The stakeholders of the chosen process are identified and their need of this process is documented to set the evaluation criteria for later selecting and designing best-fit solutions. The process's contribution to overall performance improvement is established through the link to the scorecard. On business case justification, the issues and concerns that the affected stakeholders might have are identified, a change management strategy is established, and initial communication starts.

The Understand phase is then launched to discover the strengths and weaknesses of the existing ways of working. Process maps are developed, and each process's guides and enablers are analyzed. The process is measured in more detail and reported on. Analysis finds opportunities for some early focused solutions to be built quickly, and they are implemented. Also, more complex and comprehensive needs for change are detailed and submitted for consideration during the Renew phase.

As the Understand phase gets going, the Renew phase is launching research into other organizations that have had success with process changes similar to the one under review for the Organization-in-Focus. Researchers look for breakthrough technologies that it could allow the process-in-focus to function more productively. These ideas, along with the findings from the Understand phase, are brought together to develop new process concepts and process models as well as new guides and enablers. These are then assessed or validated using test cases comprising alternative business process scenarios. These will also be used later to test the solution components as they are developed.

The net result of the Understand and Renew phases is a cost-justified transformation strategy. This also launches the Develop phase, during which the organization builds or acquires the reusable capability needed to function in the new process world. Needed process-related guidance, including rules and procedures, is created. The organization also readies its facilities and equipment, technologies, human and organizational capability, and knowledge-transfer mechanisms for the change. Those working in the Develop phase don't wait to hand over their deliverables until they are all done. They work in sync with processes already at the Implement phase to deliver regular releases of functionality to the business. During the Implement phase, the organization tests the business feasibility in pilots and rolls out solutions after preparing its people for the change to come.

After all is in place, the ongoing Nurture and Continuously Improve phase kicks in. During this phase, the organization continues to perform many of the activities that were performed in the renewal project but on a more limited scale. It assesses its performance regularly using stakeholder feedback and more formal metrics that are now part of the regular performance-reporting scorecard. It continues to examine opportunities for improvement based on these and considers the results of ongoing benchmarking. The continuously improving organization searches for inspiration from the outside world. When major gaps become apparent or predictable, it starts whole change again.

These phases are described in more detail in the following sections.

Defining the Business Context for Change

The purpose of the Business Context phase is to ensure that a common understanding of the business landscape is held by all key decision-makers. It answers the question, "What criteria will your organization use to decide among competing options for change?" It provides a balanced set of commonly accepted decision-making criteria for change based on business drivers and business stakeholder requirements. It strives to ensure that members of the organization gain shared insight about the stakeholders who ultimately determine the future success of the enterprise. It doesn't aim for depth; it strives to ensure breadth and fit of perspectives.

Results

The major consolidated deliverable from this phase is a Business Context Report, which summarizes the current and future states of the relationships during the planning horizon. It starts by defining business drivers and ends by establishing evaluation criteria based on the defined drivers. It summarizes the current performance of the Organization-in-Focus and examines its current and anticipated business pressures as well as its capabilities. The report documents stakeholders' needs and expectations and compares them to current performance. It establishes criteria based on stakeholder expectations to be used to set later business priorities for change.

Concepts Handled

Figure 5.5 depicts the concepts dealt with in the Business Context phase.

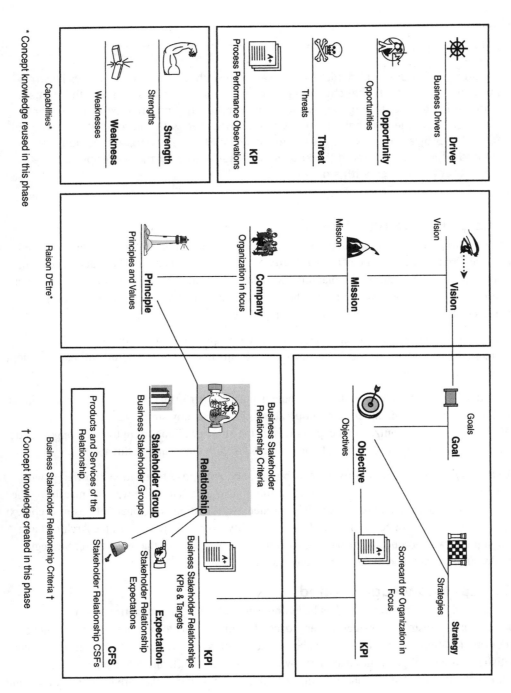

FIGURE 5.5

Framework concepts in the Business Context phase.

> **NOTE**
>
> Figures 5.5 through 5.12 depict the framework's eight phases. These figures illustrate a number of concepts that should already be known to the business. For these, there should be documentation, perhaps disjoint and hard to find, that exists already or a number of people who have the knowledge associated with the concepts. Marked in the figures by an asterisk (*), these concepts should be reviewed, understood, and reused. Then you can create the knowledge associated with the newer phase concepts that are marked with a dagger (†).

Concept Knowledge Reused

The most important set of existing concepts in the Business Context phase is that associated with the Organization-in-Focus *raison d'etre*, or reasons for existence. The organization's mission should be stable during the planning horizon, as should its principles, values, and vision. These statements of purpose define the business and are the core around which all other aspects of the business are centered. They should exist.

It's obviously imperative that an organization listen to signals from the outside world. These business drivers will affect the strategies and programs that the organization will have to adopt to remain responsive.

Of course, it is important to understand today's business performance and to anticipate what it will be in the near term under current operations. Likewise, any strategy formulation depends on the state of the organization's capabilities. If the strategy aligns strengths with opportunities, it is a different response than if it aligns weaknesses with environment threats.

A strategy based on existing drivers, capabilities, and enterprise foundation knowledge will provide a number of goals and objectives. It might also establish some ways of measuring the progress toward goals and objectives. This strategy formulation component of business context creates support for concepts in later phases. In reality, some of the work in the Architect and Align phase will produce contributions back to the strategic plans that exist there. Strategy guides architecture, and architecture guides strategy.

Concept Knowledge Created

By taking the existing work that has been done and validating it, you can start to develop a process-based business management approach. The first step is to find out who cares about your organization and what they care about. The intent is to develop a set of criteria that, when satisfied, would delight your customers, owners, suppliers, staff, and other stakeholders. Ultimately, this is what you are in business to do, so you better make sure everyone knows and agrees what success would look like.

Identifying the stakeholder groups is clearly the start. This alone often brings clarity to the way business is discussed within the organization. A common understanding of stakeholder categories and sub-types provides a framework for all. Some aspects of this might be reusable for marketing or customer segmentation strategies or for human resource categorizations.

The next concept to understand is that of the relationship because it's what you must manage well; it's your processes that do that. The first questions regarding the organization/stakeholder relationship are, "How well are our products and services working today for our stakeholders? Are they contributing toward a healthy relationship?" Based on the answers, you can determine the degree of the gap that exists between what exists now and what stakeholders want and need.

Then you should examine the stated principles and values of the organization for compliance with that witnessed in the stakeholders' experience. You must have principles that you honor. These principles and values start to form the set of stakeholder-based decision criteria.

These criteria are built from the expectations that the stakeholders will have for your organization at the end of the planning horizon. They are also contributed to by the expectations that you will have of stakeholders because a relationship is a mutual affair. You must make sure that the expectations of your customers do not conflict with what your staff will require from you. This can be a tricky balancing act.

The next puzzle piece is to determine how to evaluate whether the relationship requirements are being met. By associating a set of key performance indicators (KPIs) with each relationship, you can define a balanced measurement system to be assessed continually. But perhaps even more valuable, you can get answers to the question of how much change is required in each metric to meet the requirements of the relationship principles and expectations within defined timeframes.

For the relationship to succeed in terms of performance, you must work out a set of Critical Success factors (CSFs), which must go well or be in place to be able to meet KPI targets and stakeholder expectations.

When rationalized across the set of stakeholders, the total set of knowledge created in the Business Context phase comprises the evaluation criteria to be used to prioritize change and build a program of process-based transformation. Processes exist to serve stakeholders. If you don't know what's important to your relationship with them, you can't optimize your business.

Steps

The following steps are recommended to populate the concepts of the Business Context phase. They are described in detail in Chapter 10, "Discovering the Context for Business Change":

1. Validate the mission.

2. Analyze the business drivers.

3. Classify the stakeholder types.

4. Document current interactions and health.

5. Document principles and values.

6. Envision the future and set expectations.

7. Produce key performance indicators (KPIs) and targets.

8. Determine critical success factors.

Architecting Processes and Aligning Business Strategies

The purpose of the Architect and Align phase is to identify the relationships among business processes, technologies, facilities, human resources, and business strategy. An organization maps this information to the results of the Business Context phase to produce priorities for a program of change. The processes are defined based on stakeholder service and interaction lines. The program of change is aligned to the business strategy and to all architectural components.

Results

The major consolidated deliverable from the Architect and Align phase, a Business Architecture Report, summarizes the phase results. It starts with the definition of a common set of business processes and ends with a program of change that prioritizes the processes and other architectures. A key component will be the process migration strategy, a ranked list complete with the rationale of the processes that seem to hold greatest potential for enabling change in business performance, as well as a description of the potential ramifications. The process architecture also links to the overall architectures of other organizational assets.

The net result is a migration strategy organized by process, which shows the alignment of recommended changes to organization, technology, facility, and human architectures. These process changes will deliver the greatest degree of business performance improvements.

Concepts Handled

Figure 5.6 depicts the concepts dealt with in the Architect and Align phase.

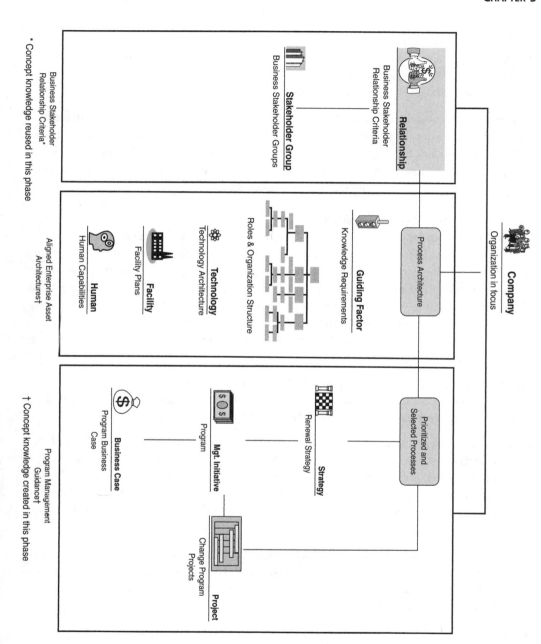

FIGURE 5.6

Framework concepts in the Architect and Align phase.

Concept Knowledge Reused

The knowledge gained and associated with the many concepts just discovered in the Business Context phase will be reused in conducting architectural analysis. The business stakeholder relationship criteria are especially important.

From each business stakeholder group, you can identify the events and outcomes and, therefore, the processes for the process architecture. From the criteria, principles, expectations, key performance indicator targets, and critical success factors for each, you can prioritize which processes should be dealt with first. Understanding these is required to create the new knowledge required for architecture and program management.

Concept Knowledge Created

The first set of knowledge to be created in this phase will concern the concepts of enterprise asset architectures. These represent the reusable assets of the organization that provide leverage with their repeated application. Starting with the process architecture creation from the stakeholder interactions and applying the stakeholder criteria, a prioritized list of business areas can be defined. This initial set of focus areas then provides the basis for assessing the fit of knowledge types needed to support them. The processes and knowledge then allow a more focused determination of which technologies have the greatest potential for leveraging business performance improvement potential.

The most appropriate strategy for organizational alignment is determined to make the process, knowledge, and technology solutions most viable. Facility options are also addressed, especially ones that affect the potential relocation of staff to new sites, cities, or countries.

Finally, within asset architecture, the requirements of human resources are examined, and the fit with current capacities as well as skills and competencies is investigated. The architecture alignment is iterated until all components fall in sync with one another, and a set of architectures with integrity is produced. The architectures guide the organization in producing and managing a program of change that rolls out the benefits envisioned in the architectures and stakeholder expectations.

An overall strategy can be developed that synchronizes the dependencies among the total set of changes that must be produced. As it is a strategy, it must be adaptable enough to be re-examined regularly to accommodate marketplace variations. By examining the high-level costs, benefits, and risks in a business case, the overall program can be justified, funded, and provided resources.

Specific projects will be initiated and rolled out within a shorter planning horizon. Each process-oriented project goes through the subsequent Process Management Framework phases, starting with the Vision phase. Others might deal with only infrastructure and can proceed directly to the Develop phase.

The net result of the Architect and Align phase is a changeable, manageable program, based on business stakeholder needs and a process organization. Program components are fully traceable to business drivers, and decisions regarding resourcing can be made.

Steps

The following steps are recommended to populate the concepts of the Architect and Align phase. They are described in detail in Chapter 11, "Configuring Business Processes and Aligning Other Strategies":

1. Identify business processes.
2. Match processes to criteria and prioritize.
3. Identify information and knowledge needs.
4. Identify strategic technologies.
5. Identify facility requirements.
6. Determine organization strategy.
7. Determine human capabilities.
8. Determine alignment opportunities and constraints.

Creating the Vision for Change

The purpose of the Vision phase is to determine and confirm the future state performance requirements of the process to be renewed and to define the scope of the process and other variable characteristics to be analyzed as part of the project. In this phase, an organization strives to ensure that the right project is being conducted and that everyone associated with it knows the criteria for success and agrees. Based on this common agreement, the process renewal team gains resource commitment and approval to proceed with the initiative for the chosen process. The Vision phase can be the launching point in the framework for organizations that choose to accept the risk of not conducting Business Context or Architect and Align activities. (An organization might take this shortcut if it wants to conduct only standalone process projects.)

Results

During the Vision phase, an organization produces deliverables that define the stakeholders for the process, their expectations for the future, the ways of measuring their performance, and the target levels of performance improvement. It clearly defines the inclusions and exclusions of the scope and determines an approach and business case justification. Change management and communications strategies are delivered, and a project plan to define the details of the next two phases, Understand and Renew, is produced.

Concepts Handled

Figure 5.7 depicts the concepts dealt with in the Vision phase.

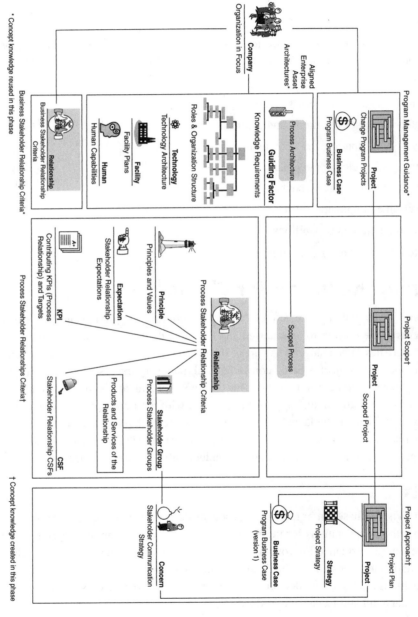

FIGURE 5.7

Framework concepts in the Vision phase.

Concept Knowledge Reused

Knowledge regarding concepts gathered or developed in the previous two phases are leveraged in the Vision phase. If this prior knowledge is readily accessible, this phase will be aligned and much easier to conduct. Many organizations, however, start here. If you decide to skip the previous two phases, be sure to spend a little extra effort at this point to gather some background information that will launch the project on the right trajectory.

From the Business Context phase, the information describing the overall business stakeholder relationship criteria will accelerate the stakeholder analysis for the specific process to follow. You can reuse many of the stakeholders' interactions, principles, expectations, performance targets, and critical success factors at the process level. You can derive such metrics from them.

You should also understand the aligned set of architectures ascertained in the Architect and Align phase because they will either enable or constrain some aspects of the particular process project to be defined in the Vision phase. You can determine many of the interfaces between the chosen scope and other excluded areas of change by knowing these existing architectural models.

The business case and project definition from the program management guidance developed in the Architect and Align phase will help you build your initial project business case and plan.

Concept Knowledge Created

Starting with the results of previous phases, you can more easily develop your criteria, scope, and approach for the process renewal project.

Your first step should be to identify the external and internal stakeholders for the process selected. Then you can determine the things that you want them to care about by developing the criteria that affects their future performance. To establish the vision for future success, these criteria should include relevant enterprise principles, expectations for the future state, performance targets for the new process, and critical success factors to be met.

You should also be strong in setting the boundaries of analysis, design, and implementation to establish the project scope. Process inclusions and exclusions are key for estimating your plan and resourcing your team as well as for later project control. Other aspects of scope, such as locations, types of information, and policies, must also be addressed and commonly understood in no uncertain terms.

Based on the process stakeholder relationship criteria and the project scope, you can develop your approach to running your process renewal project. This should include considerations for project, risk, and human change management. You should define the steps you will conduct and deliverables you will produce and the resources and timeframes needed to complete the work.

Be sure to develop a strategy and plan for communicating with stakeholders, based on your anticipation of their objections and concerns. This takes resource time and focus.

Consolidate the project strategy, business case, and communications approach in a plan used in the upcoming two phases (Understand and Renew). Make sure that the plan is accepted and the resources are committed according to the program management guidance if you have it.

Steps

The following steps are recommended to populate the concepts of this phase. They are described in detail in Chapter 12, "Charting the Course of Change":

1. Select the renewal processes and identify stakeholders.
2. Formulate a process vision.
3. Identify performance improvement targets.
4. Define project scope.
5. Develop project strategy.
6. Develop an initial business case.
7. Develop communication and human change strategy.
8. Finalize a project plan.

Understanding the Existing Process

The purpose of the Understand phase is to gain a sufficient understanding of the current situation so that a baseline for change can be established. In this phase, an organization documents and validates its current reality and defines its improvement priorities. It isn't the purpose of this phase to deliver detailed perfect knowledge—just enough to be confident to move into solution creation.

Results

During the Understand phase, an organization seeks to deliver a common understanding of what the existing process actually does so that the right improvements can be made and perceptions managed. It measures actual performance levels and documents what works well and not so well today. Based on this, it determines the required changes and implements some immediate improvements where feasible.

Concepts Handled

Figure 5.8 depicts the concepts dealt with the Understand phase.

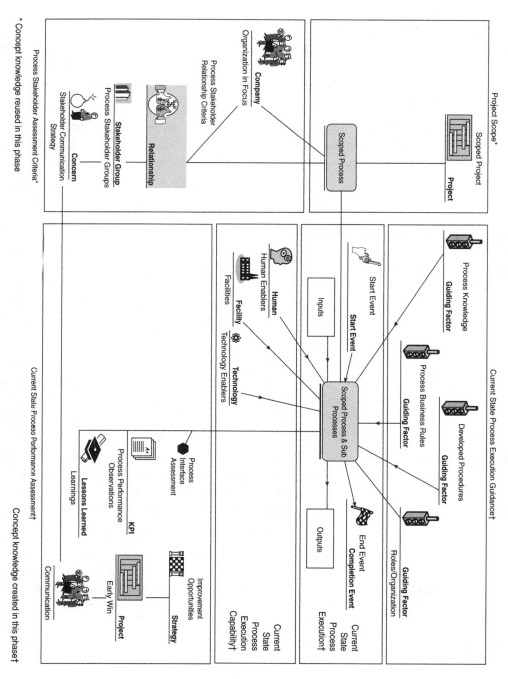

FIGURE 5.8

Framework concepts in the Understand phase.

Concept Knowledge Reused

The knowledge gained in the Vision phase will apply directly in the Understand phase. Without this basis, the work here will be a disaster. I can guarantee that it will wander aimlessly and be fraught with politicking and confusion. Aspects of the relationship criteria and scoping are especially important.

The interactions and flows between the process-in-focus and its stakeholders actually define the process's outcomes. The principles, expectations, performance targets, and future CSFs are all reference points of comparison to assess the current state's gaps in effectiveness and efficiency.

The stakeholder group's concerns must be responded to all the way through the Understand phase via a well-executed communication program.

Concept Knowledge Created

Starting with an understanding of the results of the Vision phase and a validation of the scope produced there, you should first focus on attaining a good definition of the current state process execution. In other words, get a clear understanding of what triggers each activity in the process and what inputs are available when it occurs. Also look at the outputs created and define the closing event that indicates the process activity's completion. This must be what actually goes on, not what people would like you to believe.

While looking at the input-process-output flow, also discover what's used to guide the current state execution. Find the actual types of knowledge used, whether tacit or explicit, available or hard to find. Identify the actual rules applied to the work's decision-making. Review procedures to see how frequently they are followed. Look at the roles and responsibilities of those doing the work and document the organizational units that they report to.

Examine the reusable current state capabilities and the enterprise assets. Look at the humans doing the work. Examine the technologies automating information management or providing embedded knowledge access or rules execution. Walk through the facilities and equipment used to conduct non–information-oriented tasks as well as those required to support knowledge workers.

Throughout the Understand phase, as you delve into the process in more depth, ask lots of questions. Investigate how well each interfacing step, input, guide, output, and enabler contributes toward the objectives of the process today and also how well it would meet the process stakeholder relationship criteria for the future. Measure the current process observations against the key performance indicators defined and evaluate the gap in the performance expected in the future.

Search hard for lessons learned about what's poor, good, and great practice from those who currently do the work and also understand the need to change. From these lessons, identify improvement opportunities. Some will be long term and require full process redesign in the

Renew phase; others will be attainable in the short term. These quick wins will require a low effort and will face little resistance. Implement them as fast as you can.

Take all your understanding, findings, and opportunities and develop regular communications for the stakeholders according to the schedule and frequency of the communication strategy. Communicate them early and often to help staff navigate the change journey. You will regret it later if you don't.

Steps

The following steps are recommended to populate the concepts of this phase (they are described in detail in Chapter 13, "Understanding the Existing Situation"):

1. Confirm scope and boundaries.
2. Map existing process understanding.
3. Measure process performance.
4. Determine root causes.
5. Identify improvement priorities.
6. Implement early wins.

Renewing the Process Design

The Renew phase's purpose is to design or redesign the process, its guides, and its enablers to meet the stakeholders' visionary requirements. It also ensures that the solution will work and has merit from a business perspective.

Results

In the Renew phase, an organization redesigns its business process to meet the stretch goals, accomplish the process vision, and test the design for viability. It develops new concepts and delivers validated models of them. It ensures the feasibility of changes and provides models to coordinate subsequent phases. The major deliverable from the Renew phase is a transformation strategy for the delivery of all the asset capability required to make the solution a success. This strategy delivers process models for later development and test cases for later usage. It also delivers an approved, updated business case with much more confidence and less risk than might have existed in previous phases.

Concepts Handled

Figure 5.9 depicts the concepts dealt with in the Renew phase.

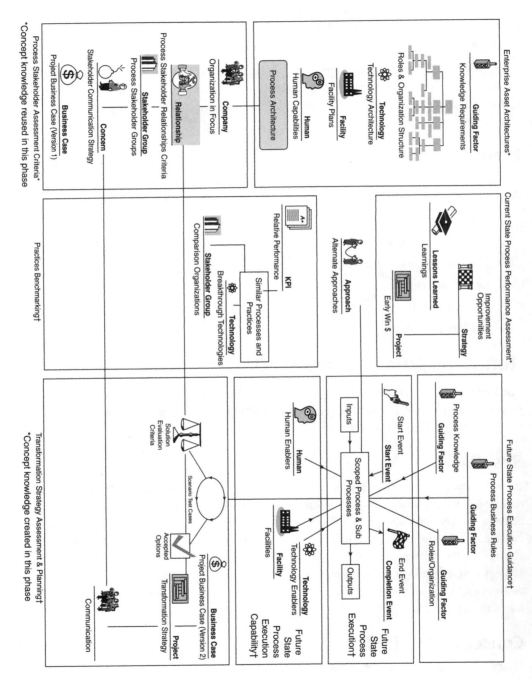

FIGURE 5.9

Framework concepts in the Renew phase.

Concept Knowledge Reused

The wide variety of knowledge gained in the phases that have preceded the Renew phase is valuable in designing the future state of the business process. All of it can be reused here to create innovative and feasible solutions.

The enterprise asset architectures provide a lot of insight and guidance toward ensuring a fit with other solutions that might already be in place or are planned. They ensure feasibility later at implementation time. They also provide the guiding principles for general and detailed design. If you refer to these architectures at this point, you will avoid a lot of rework later during the Develop and Implement phases.

The process relationship assessment criteria will continue to serve you well. They will provide the functional criteria for evaluating the number of options that will be available as a result of redesign. If you meet the needs of the stakeholders as you defined them in the Vision phase, you will have the basis for communicating the value of the change as part of the concerns-based communications in this phase. You will also be able to establish the business case update with less resistance.

Use the current state performance assessment results to establish some design principles that will drive or guide the design for the future state process solution. The lessons learned, and improvement priorities will be a great sanity check to be sure that spectacular new solutions don't ignore the problems of the past by re-creating them. You will have to re-examine the early wins that should be in some form of rollout by now. Some will survive major redesign; others will be temporary. Know the difference.

Concept Knowledge Created

After using what you've learned from the past phases, it's time to look for other inspiration to help trigger new approaches. The benchmarking of practices is a proven way to do this. By identifying other organizations that have solved process issues similar to what you are facing, you can learn what they did differently and how they implemented their solutions. You can learn about the technologies employed and, perhaps, other breakthroughs in the innovative use of enablers. You can also discover some of the measurements used to justify the solution. Performance gaps between what they are doing and what you are accomplishing provide evidence to all that the need is genuine. It also bolsters confidence that you, too, can make the transition.

From the architectures, stakeholder criteria, current state assessment, and practices benchmarking, you can create a small set of alternative approaches. By using creative thinking and brainstorming approaches, you can synthesize a few solutions to examine further in this phase.

You can model these alternatives with the same modeling techniques used to capture the current state. Defining the future state process execution, future state guidance, and future state capabilities will allow you to ensure that they will work. You will also be able to describe practices realized in a model better than if they are just a few vague concepts. Be sure, however, not to get lost in too much detail. You will be able to add detail later in the Develop phase. Although you looked at procedure in the current state, it's premature to develop to that level yet.

Validating the current state was easy because all you had to do was get the incumbents together and walk through what they actually did. You can't do that with something not built yet. You have to find another way to reduce the risk. Try using the process-scenario approach that takes a number of different types of stakeholders with different conditions and situations and walks them through the process to see if it works. Role-play the situations under extreme and normal circumstances. Use these as the basis for building mock-up prototypes and for building automated mathematical simulations to test performance assumptions.

To evaluate your alternatives, you must ensure that the evaluation criteria are agreed on before designing solutions. These will be built based on the stakeholder criteria for functional compliance, and on cost, benefit, and business risk criteria for financial feasibility. Make sure that you recognize the criteria up front in this phase. It's a valuable part of assessing and planning the transformation strategy.

In addition to the evaluation criteria and scenarios, transformation planning requires two other concepts to be instantiated. You should dust off the first version of the business case developed in the Vision phase and update it with the details now available. Especially focus on the better knowledge that you now should have regarding costs, benefits, and risks. From this you should develop the transformation strategy using whatever you've learned in earlier phases as well as in Renew.

Be sure not to let up on the communication to curious and concerned stakeholders of all types. The transformation strategy will go nowhere without it.

Steps

The following steps are recommended to populate the concepts of this phase. They are described in detail in Chapter 14, "Designing the Renewed Process":

1. Benchmark processes and trends.
2. Gain enabler knowledge.
3. Finalize evaluation criteria.
4. Rethink the approach.
5. Model the renewed process.
6. Demonstrate/validate the renewed process.
7. Update the business case for development.
8. Develop a transformation strategy.

Developing Enablers and Support Mechanisms

The purpose of the Develop phase is to develop in detail all components for all releases of the business process solution. During this phase, an organization will build or change all the supporting mechanisms required for the new process to work according to stakeholder requirements.

Results

In the Develop phase, an organization develops and constructs the infrastructures for facilities, technology, and human core competencies. It also defines or redefines policies and rules, jobs, and organizational structures, and realigns HR incentives. It develops and tests all technologies, hardware, software, and networks. The training capability is also made ready.

Concepts Handled

Figure 5.10 depicts the concepts dealt with in the Develop phase.

Concept Knowledge Reused

The whole point of the Develop phase is to bring to life all the ideas created in previous phases. All the work done previously occurred only so that you could be in this position.

The future state solution design gives you the requirements, definition, or basis for producing a lot of related deliverables in different professional areas. It depicts what the process workflow will be, what information and knowledge will be needed, what triggering events are in play, and what responses will be required. You can tell what technologies are required and what they have to do, what people will be responsible for, and how they should be organized. You can relate the business rules to their process of usage.

This design is the basis for training materials and ongoing knowledge distribution that you'll use to build the infrastructures needed for technology and facilities and also to educate staff and other stakeholders about the way of doing business. You can also use them to ensure that the other deliverables of this phase are consistent with a set of design principles and interface standards. In this way, the results of other initiatives underway or to come will fit.

When you enter the Develop phase, you need the guidance of the stakeholder criteria used in all phases and the transformation strategy produced in the Renew phase. Test all deliverables as well as the overall solution using the scenario test cases. Use these also as the basis for training cases and reference material examples. Don't forget that stakeholder concerns must still be managed as they change, and the communication strategy must be exercised frequently.

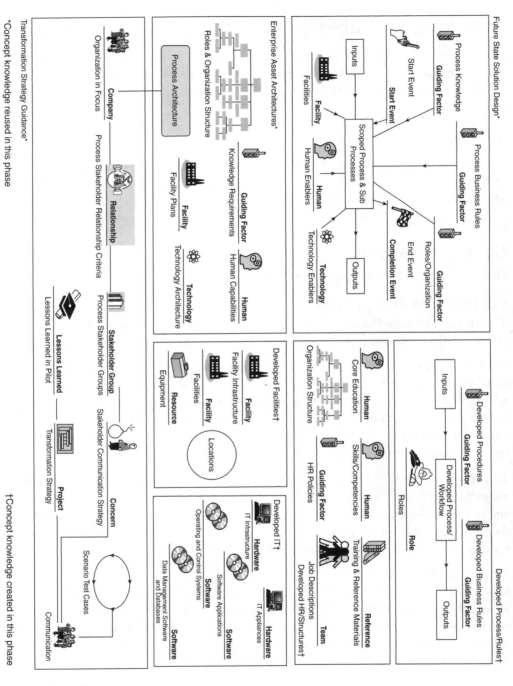

FIGURE 5.10

Framework concepts in the Develop phase.

Concept Knowledge Created

Based on the great work that you've done to date in coming up with a better way of working, you now have the opportunity to build that better way. Because you have a transformation strategy and a process solution design, you can do a lot of the building concurrently. Be sure, however, to manage the synchronicity for fit and avoid miscommunications.

Develop the process to its required level of detail, covering the roles that people will have to assume. Also develop and gain approval for the detailed business rules required and write procedures if you have to. Don't embed the rules if you can avoid it.

Develop the guidance that will affect the human resources involved with conducting and managing the work. You might have to develop new job descriptions, skills, competency definitions, and organizational models. Likewise, human resource policies might have to be updated. You might also have to build knowledge transfer enablers, such as education programs and specific training courses in whatever media you will use.

Facilities take time to arrange and build, so start as soon as you are confident of the solution's match to needs. Physical infrastructures are especially time-consuming to get going, and delays can prevent you from meeting your planned dates. Specialized equipment can cause you headaches to acquire, especially if you have to navigate a convoluted purchasing process. Some equipment and facilities can be inextricably linked to technology and information flow if you are building real-time controls into production facilities and have to link business and production systems and data together.

Information technology isn't unlike facilities and equipment in its potential complexity. Start early to build IT infrastructures such as networks, operating and control systems, and data management integration capabilities. You don't have to know the details of your applications to do some of this. You can test the connectivity of information appliances (such as handheld devices into the wireless network) before you write code.

You can choose to buy commercial, off-the-shelf software or build your own solutions. The requirements will be more confidently known because of the future state solution design built around complete processes with integrity. Use the scenarios and process maps to make sure that the vendors and your developers show you complete scenarios, and not just partial or functional views of their offerings.

All of this will give you an integrated solution ready for testing or rollout to the business. If it is just for one release of the solution, the Develop phase could go on for some time until all releases are complete.

Steps

The following steps are recommended to populate the concepts of the Develop phase. They are described in detail in Chapter 15, "Developing Capability for the Renewed Process":

1. Build physical infrastructures.
2. Provide human core capabilities.
3. Build computing infrastructure.
4. Develop processes, procedures, and rules.
5. Redefine jobs.
6. Design organizational changes.
7. Update human resources policies.
8. Develop/integrate technology and systems.
9. Develop training capability.

Implementing the Change

The framework's Implement phase prepares all stakeholders who will be affected by the implemented solution in some way. It's also releases versions of the integrated solution according to the transformation strategy.

Results

During the Implement phase, an organization puts in place all the changes necessary to achieve initial performance improvement and to continue to improve. It delivers the early and ongoing results by running trials and pilot tests, educating key stakeholders, and rolling out the solution in a series of releases.

Concepts Handled

Figure 5.11 depicts the concepts dealt with in the Implement phase.

Concept Knowledge Reused

Going into the Implement phase, you will have many capabilities developed and ready for exploitation. Everything that you've worked for is ready to go live or at least ready for live testing. Make sure that no developments have lagged behind because failure can result from any one of the factors that's supposed to have been completed by now.

Your processes and rules will have been tested in scenario walkthroughs. Workflows will be stable using defined new roles.

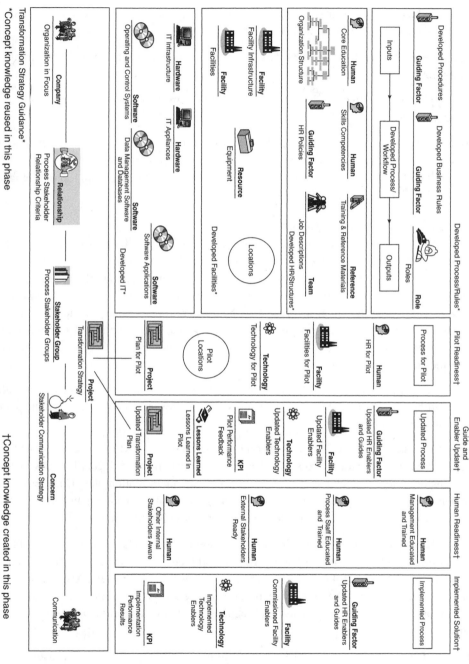

FIGURE 5.11

Framework concepts in the Implement phase.

Your HR guidance, enablers, and structures will have been established and communicated. They will be ready to be rolled out and used.

Your facilities and equipment will be ready for the pilot and ultimately ready for full implementation in existing and new locations.

Your IT applications, networks, databases, and other systems technology will be tested and ready for pilot testing and full rollout.

The transformation strategy guidance will tell you what to do, when to do it, and where to do it. It should also be clear as to who will be responsible. At this point, old concerns might have been dealt with but new ones will arise from anywhere and anyone. Keep on top of it, and never stop listening and communicating.

Concept Knowledge Created

The first set of knowledge to be produced is the readiness for the pilot project, where full business testing will take place for the first time. You have to be sure to tune the process to the pilot location's peculiarities after you pick the trial site. You must prepare the managers and staff to be ready to give it a fair trial. Make sure that they are trained. You are testing the materials also. Make sure that other involved stakeholders are trained on aspects that affect them. Also make sure that the facilities are ready and work before starting up a trial with real customers. For all of this, the first thing to do is prepare a comprehensive (in scope, if not depth) plan for the conduct of the pilot project.

As a result of the pilot test, you will have learned a lot. Some things you will be happy with, and other things you will want to change. Many of the guides and enablers will require some minor or major updates.

Your pilot will have provided you with experiences, lessons, and performance measures that will guide the changes you have to make. These changes should be reflected in a new version of the transformation strategy and a much more specific transformation plan. Changes or refinements to the process workflow, rules, technologies, facilities, and human enablers will be required and will have to be sent back to the Develop phase for attention.

After updates are made and the specific transformation plan is produced, make sure that all staff and other stakeholders involved in the rollout and ongoing operation are trained and capable. This includes managers, knowledge workers, customers, and suppliers. Also, make sure that all other stakeholders who aren't directly affected—such as the public, shareholders, community groups, environmental agencies, and regulators—don't experience surprises. The humans must be ready to roll.

When implementation is deemed finished, you will have a set of performance measures against your KPIs and will know how you've done. The technology, facilities, and people will all be settled in.

Steps

The following steps are recommended to populate the concepts of the Implement phase. They are described in detail in Chapter 16, "Implementing and Rolling Out the Business Solution":

1. Prepare for business testing.
2. Complete business tests and pilots.
3. Update deliverables.
4. Educate management.
5. Develop rollout plans.
6. Train staff.
7. Develop and run marketing programs.
8. Roll out changes.

Operating the Process and Continuing to Improve

The purpose of Nurture and Continuously Improve phase is to continue to find opportunities for improvement based on experience, new enablers, and enhanced knowledge. In this phase, you strive to ensure that the new process is operated and enhanced as a whole process regardless of organizational structure.

Results

In the Nurture and Continuously Improve phase, an organization obtains feedback regarding the implemented process solution by continuing to measure the process performance according to the KPIs defined in the project. The organization also searches for opportunities to do better based on experience, changing conditions, and knowledge sharing.

Concepts Handled

Figure 5.12 depicts the concepts dealt with in the Nurture and Continuously Improve phase.

Concept Knowledge Reused

The Nurture and Continuously Improve phase is unlike the other framework phases in that it isn't usually time-bound. It's an ongoing activity until the need for a major renewal is apparent, at which time the whole Process Management Framework cycle starts up again. This phase is the ongoing execution of the process and its day-to-day management as a process by the process owner. As such, it uses all the capability that the renewal project will have delivered. The implemented solution, process, facilities, technologies, and human enablers are the baseline on which the business will run and the subject of continuing assessment for improvement.

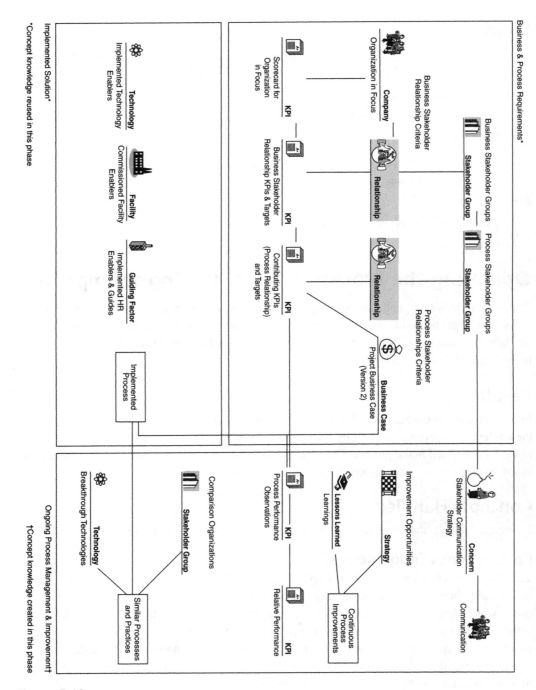

FIGURE 5.12

Framework concepts in the Nurture and Continuously Improve phase.

What you learned about the business in the framework phases to date will be very relevant and must always be kept in mind. You must be sure that the participants in the day-to-day don't lose sight of why the solution was implemented. You must continue to manage the required relationships and keep them healthy. You also should follow up the project's business case to be sure that the anticipated benefits are being realized. Publicize your successes to help in later efforts.

Concept Knowledge Created

The business and process requirements that drove the renewal project must be fresh in your mind during the Nurture and Continuously Improve phase. You must also pay attention to the actual results as reported by the newly instituted measurement system. The chain of contributing measurements against the defined KPI scorecard will become a key component of your management dashboard and for assessing the process's health as well as its need for enhancement. These actuals-mapped-against-expectations are invaluable tools, but they assume that nothing has changed in the business and process stakeholders' criteria. This assumption can be dangerous. Clearly, then, you must continue to reassess the relationship criteria of the business and process stakeholders, as well as the company's evolving strategies and plans, to understand if any gaps are starting to emerge in processes and capabilities. In short, keep the work that you did in the Business Context, Architect and Align, and Vision phases current.

Based on this, you need to continue to improve the whole process, not just isolated parts of it. As mentioned, use the results of observed measurements to find areas to be enhanced. You should also continue to benchmark your processes against other organizations' processes, especially if they are outperforming you. Also examine the opportunity that new and emerging technologies might bring as they mature.

The participants in the process also gain a great deal of knowledge as they do their work. You can gather a lot of this knowledge and share it with the other participants in a knowledge-managed environment. You can also use it to find improvements in your process as you go forward.

Especially in a process-managed environment, never forget that people need to know what's going on. Communication that emphasizes process, stakeholder, and traceability to the business mission is needed to gradually change the organization's culture.

Steps

The following steps are recommended to populate the concepts of the Nurture and Continuously Improve phase. They describe the essential aspects of the process manager's job:

1. Stabilize the solution.
2. Measure performance.
3. Conduct a post-implementation review.

4. Make adjustments.

5. Find opportunities for improvement.

6. Adopt the solution.

Scaling the Process Renewal Framework

The framework described generally in this chapter and in detail in Chapters 10 through 16 is comprehensive. From project to project, its use will vary, sometimes significantly. The framework is designed to scale for use on small or large projects. For small local initiatives that aim at improving a focused aspect of the business, you can omit some steps and cover others more extensively. For enterprise-wide initiatives, most of what's described might be required, and some areas might need more in-depth analysis. You will have to judge, but be confident that you understand the intent of each phase and step and can communicate the result with confidence. Keep in mind a number of factors regarding scalability, as described in Table 5.1.

TABLE 5.1   Factors for Framework Use

Large	*Small*
Degree of Performance Improvement Required	
Use all phases and steps and conduct Vision and Renew in careful detail. Understand must be done, focusing on breadth, not depth. Human impact deliverables and activities must be a priority.	Fast-track the project and do Vision broadly, not deeply. Emphasize Understand and early wins. Scale back on depth of Renew.
Number of Processes Involved	
Focus on Business Context and Architect and Align to develop an overall program strategy.	Conduct Architect and Align for fit of chosen process, not for program planning. Focus on phases after Architect and Align.
Breadth of Scope	
Use all phases in detail, especially Vision, Understand, and Renew.	Focus on Understand and Renew with a fast-tracked Vision.
Risks/Cost	
Use all phases in detail and implement go/no-go reviews at checkpoints.	Fast-track but communicate to stakeholders.

TABLE 5.1 Continued

Large	Small
Degree of Technological Change	
Use all phases in detail, especially Vision and Renew. Emphasize stakeholder awareness, education, and training.	Focus on workflows. Involve current process staff extensively.
Human Impact	
Use all phases in detail but emphasize Vision and Understand. Communication and participation of staff must be built in all the way through.	Focus on the process flow. Communicate and listen but reduce the frequency.
Management Commitment and Involvement	
Use all phases but reduce the depth of some deliverables that would normally be produced just for managers.	For larger projects, build in more checkpoints and project off-ramps that managers must approve. Produce deliverables just for them before proceeding.

You must be cautious; the framework isn't a recipe to be followed without thinking. You also shouldn't use it inappropriately. It isn't a hammer either. You will have to think.

Related Professional Practices

Keep in mind that the framework focuses on process management. It also integrates the overall management of business change. It isn't a systems development methodology. It doesn't show how policies and business rules should be documented. It won't guide you through job design or organization development. It won't develop training courses for you. It won't tell you how to draw blueprints for the new building that you might need.

It will, however, make it easier to do all of these more quickly and to a higher quality level. You will invoke the methods of each area of professional practice under the umbrella of the Develop phase. Figure 5.13 shows a simplified example for the system development area. Treating the framework as an extension to information systems development can become a fatal mistake. These methods are separate yet tightly dependent on one another, passing critical knowledge among themselves. The Process Management Framework shown across the top interacts with the information systems development phases shown at the bottom. A number of deliverables flow back and forth, but the two professional practice areas aren't parts of one another. They are complementary. The same is true of the other professional areas built as part of the Develop phase.

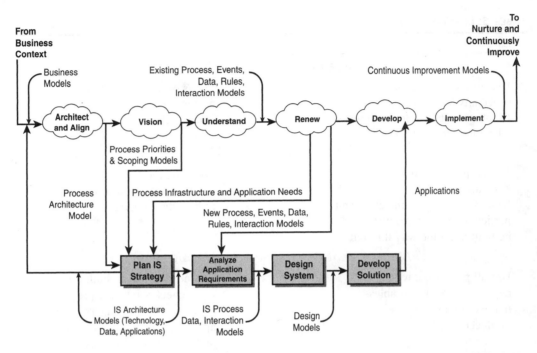

FIGURE 5.13
The relationship between process management methods and information systems development.

Summary

This chapter has introduced the Process Management Framework. It's an approach to deliver process-oriented business change and improved business performance for the organization's stakeholders.

Through the eight well-defined phases of the framework, an organization can look at an overall business area and produce a program of process-based change. The framework helps the organization design new process solutions, and then realize the design by developing and implementing the solutions. It also provides an environment for ongoing improvement as a result of process management conducted by process owners.

Chapters 10 through 16 are intended for practitioners. These chapters go into greater detail about the phases and provide lessons learned in conducting the steps of each phase.

The next three chapters deal with the associated professional areas required to manage any organizational transformation: project management, risk management, and human change management. These will round out the aspects of transformation required to succeed.

Project Management Essentials

IN THIS CHAPTER

The next three chapters cover a set of interrelated and complementary issues. Project management, risk management, and human change management must all be included in the consideration of change. If they are not addressed, they could become the cause of failure regardless of the excellence of the process management methodology you choose.

Clearly the project manager must ensure that activities for risk assessment are included in project plans. Likewise, human change can make up the lion's share of work in many initiatives, and itself become the biggest risk. Plans and control activities must allow time to deal with these changes. It's also likely that the project manager will be the one to assure that project management, risk management, and human change management happen, while conducting and keeping in sync all the activities in the process management framework.

Over the years, project management has proven to be the umbrella principle governing most professional practices and is clearly needed in all of them. Unfortunately, it seems to be recognized as valuable only when there's a huge cost of non-conformance.

NASA experienced this when the agency admitted that "Poor training and communication inside the Mars team and its failure to follow procedures allowed a tiny metric conversion mistake to destroy the $125 million Mars Climate Orbiter." Numerous IT infrastructure and application development projects have suffered from poor project management when the deadline became more important than the results, and so-called solutions were implemented only to be abandoned later.

Business process approaches are no different if they aren't managed. They fail more because of project management breakdown than because of professional methodological or technical reasons. If the wrong project structure is in place, if planning activities are short circuited, if control mechanisms aren't executed, if unskilled or uncaring people are assigned the wrong tasks, if resources aren't committed, and no time is spent on oversight—to name just a few aspects—it should be no surprise when a project fails, as it inevitably will. When it does, we must not blame the professional practices, only the organization's commitment to them.

Professional practices are unique to the type of work being performed. Writing a procedural guide is different from writing a Java program. However, all professional practices have the following attributes:

- They provide a set of guidelines for execution of defined phases and activities.
- They are conducted in a disciplined order.
- Their results are deliverables whose format and level of detail are defined. These results can be compared to objective standards.
- They define target results that will guide those responsible for the project management execution.
- They provide a common framework for communication among project players.

Project Management Essentials

CHAPTER 6

171

6
PROJECT
MANAGEMENT
ESSENTIALS

Conversely, some say that project management is an art that can't be structured. Although there is some art in it, you can't hope that a manager is a good one by nature only. Project management can be a disciplined approach and still have room for interpretation and judgment. Because every project is different, it's implicit that the project management process must be adaptable. Projects are

- **Unique**—Driven by a set of specific, one-time objectives and deliverables.
- **Temporary**—They have a definite start and finish.
- **Uncertain and therefore risky**—The product or service created varies in some distinguishing way from all other products/services, even for those initiatives that are similar.
- **Multifunctional**—They cross organizational boundaries in scope, impact, and resource consumption.
- **Dependent**—They need varying amounts of resources—such as time, money, equipment, and human resources—from organizations other than their own.
- **Of variable size**—In scope, time, participants, and business functions involved.

Consequently, the overarching project management practice can be seen as having a set of attributes different from professional practice management. Project management is the art and science of achieving project completion by doing the right things in the right way. More specifically

- It provides the process that identifies, plans, controls, and completes a change project.
- It describes the means of producing project results and gaining customer acceptance for them.
- It applies to all projects, stages, and deliverables regardless of type, size, and duration, and to all people involved in them.

This final attribute, universal application of project management, occurs in many ways:

- Through the delegation, monitoring, and sharing of responsibilities for results with a team
- Through the maintenance of personal commitments toward results and deliverables
- By providing commonly understood/accepted plans
- By establishing effective communication channels for project control and continuous improvement operating cyclically (based on a calendar)
- By establishing unambiguous hand-over/acceptance mechanisms

Regardless of the scope and size of the project or deliverable, four major stages are involved:

- Initiating (defining the work)
- Planning (planning the work)

- Controlling and improving (working the plan)
- Accepting (accepting the work)

Although project management is a wide topic, the rest of this chapter will focus on key aspects that are particularly critical for process management initiatives. I will cover some important fundamentals as well as the four major stages of making project management work. I will also cover a set of roles and structures particularly suited to this type of change.

A Few Fundamentals

If there had to be only one factor to get right in any change effort, it would be getting people to make and keep the required commitments. It sounds easy, but we often conduct process projects without it. We don't know how to figure out what to ask for. We don't know what to do when we don't get what we want and need, yet the deadlines and expectations don't change. We don't know what to do when changing conditions affect our ability to deliver or—worse— when we aren't equipped to deal with getting commitments renewed when conditions change.

Business commitments seem to be easy to make, even if done irresponsibly. Typically, expectations are set, agreements are made, dates are established, and budgets are cut before the full extent of the requirement is known and before individuals are asked to take responsibility. The corporation or business unit has formally committed to complete a job on behalf of the project's customer. This can be changed only with formal renegotiation and agreement.

The Winograd Flores Model of commitment described in Chapter 2, "Organizational Responses to Business Drivers," shows how proceeding without commitment will lead to trouble. In such a scenario, the Negotiate phase hasn't really happened yet to establish any degree of trust between the project's customer and supplier. The trust equity will start draining as soon as it's clear that the parties can't meet the expectations set.

The way to head this off is to make sure personal commitments align with the expectations implied or expressed in the business commitment. How will this occur? The answer is easy on paper, and the final criteria are easy to check. The people asked to take on a personal commitment must be empowered to achieve these business results. In doing this, successful project deliverers exhibit a number of common traits:

- They make and maintain a personal commitment to deliver expected results and are passionate about it.
- They never pretend to make commitments they know they can't keep and are sometimes brutally honest about this, like it or not.
- They communicate effectively and often with all the stakeholders of the initiative and maintain working relationships with all of them.

- They share responsibility effectively with others and don't try to do it all themselves, thereby reserving "space" for other as-yet unknown factors.
- They use sound judgment and common sense and aren't afraid to act on them.
- They empower themselves and ask for forgiveness later. rather than seek permission up front.

In summary, successful project deliverers are confident and will change anything that gets in the way of that confidence because they know that losing confidence means impending failure. As a result, they deliver consistently and can be counted on.

This sounds like you need supermen and superwomen to take on these roles. The unfortunate truth is that if you don't create a manageable situation, you will need superpowers galore. Unless you can create a project management environment that assures that all players on the project team will make and meet the required commitments, it won't be possible. The bottom line is that a successful project manager will gain and maintain commitment to the project from himself or herself and from all the other resources and stakeholders associated with it.

If commitment comes from confidence, conditions must be attached. No healthy person will be confident if he doesn't feel that he knows all appropriate factors and has them sufficiently under control. To be confident, the project deliverers must first have a commonly accepted understanding of the responsibility—that is, the project requirements. These include

- Project objectives and their fit to the business vision
- A vision of the project's results and products to be delivered
- Knowledge of the customers and other stakeholders affected and involved, along with their expectations
- Project performance indicators and targeted improvements in metrics
- The scope of the work, defining what's in and what's out
- Professional practices to be employed, such as the process management framework
- Work breakdown structure and deliverables to be produced
- Required quality levels of each deliverable and result
- The means of producing the deliverables, including knowledge and reusable enablers (human resources, technology, and facilities)
- Acceptance and decision criteria
- Team and individual incentives
- Genuine project givens and constraints

If you can't gain a reasonable understanding of these project requirements, it's unlikely that you can succeed. Otherwise, managing such a project becomes a journey without a destination on a vehicle full of passengers, each wanting to go somewhere different or not knowing where they want to end up.

In addition to knowing the destination, you must feel that you can secure appropriate control and influence over the capabilities required to conduct the project, including

- Human resources
- Financial resources
- Technology resources
- Other resources
- Sufficient time and realistic schedules
- The most effective approach
- The most appropriate tools
- The means of managing customer expectations
- The means of maintaining management awareness and involvement
- The means of motivating and managing team members

In addition to knowing the destination and having control or influence over the ways of getting there, it helps to align the business commitment with the personal commitment of someone who's motivated. Getting a "Yes" to the following questions will aid in the self-direction required from a project leader. These are also good considerations for the selection of any team member."

- Does the team member believe this change should be done?
- Does the team member believe this can be done?
- Is this something the team member wants to do?
- Does this commitment to change fit with other aspects of the team member's current personal situation?
- Does the team member believe this will be good for his/her career?
- Is there really a choice?

The predictors of success in aligning personal commitments to business commitments are a combination of some harder, more objective factors and some softer ones. Figure 6.1 shows some of the more objective considerations to take into account to determine subjective confidence. We usually make such decisions subjectively and unconsciously without even being aware of it. The result does become objective. It shows up as a sinking feeling in the pit of our stomach or a sense of euphoria. Sometimes it's a little of both.

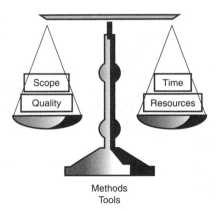

Methods
Tools

FIGURE 6.1

The project balance.

Subjectively committed project managers balance these considerations all the time. When adherence to a particular requirement dips too low, they adjust one or more factors to get back in balance and regain confidence. If it looks like they can't meet the timeframe, for example, they can reduce the expectations for results (see left side), increase the resources to meet the timeframe (see right side), or improve the means by moving the fulcrum (the balance point on the bottom). Let's briefly examine these factors:

- Time can always be moved out, although that's not a popular choice. Usually it's done as a last resort (and too late) because no one wanted to give more time earlier when some other factor went awry. Sometimes it's best to relax the time constraint when the factors on the left are non-negotiable.

- Resources can be added, either in terms of more of the same or more knowledgeable, experienced, or skilled workers. Adding resources can also mean allocating more money to a task. Not adding resources when they are needed is often the main reason for slippage and later quality problems. At some point, however, adding more resources will slow down an effort, not speed it up.

- Scope is often the factor that gets a project manager in trouble, especially if she didn't articulate it clearly and get visible acceptance up front. If a project's scope was actually bigger than anticipated or has grown beyond the current capability to manage it, the scale will tip, and the manager will lose confidence, putting the initiative in jeopardy.

- Quality is often hard to define, but you must try to do so because changes (or a lack of them) in the previous three factors often directly impact the quality of results, leading to customer expectations not being met. If scope, resources, or timeframes change but nothing else is adjusted, it will affect quality. You should encourage discussions on this aspect.

- Methods and tools can be improved to make your project more effective and efficient. This is equivalent to moving the balance point to the left and gaining leverage. The issue becomes whether it's practical to change methods and tools drastically as you progress. On the positive side, the initial approach will provide learning and hopefully feedback to enable you to improve the approach for the rest of the project. On the opposite side, changing an approach too drastically might take more time and add more risk than the potential improvements to be gained. It's always a judgment call to be shared with the sponsors of the business change.

Using the scale with its six factors can be an extremely useful way to gain initial, confident commitments from all participants and stakeholders, enabling everyone to start off on the right footing. It's also invaluable for keeping on track and staying confident throughout.

Other factors—especially personal and relationship-based ones—aren't as objective in their appearance but, nonetheless, are just as real. These factors include

- The person being asked to commit personally can only do so confidently if she has a sense of personal capability and has the appropriate time capacity given everything else that is going on in their jobs and lives. If asked to juggle a number of balls for the enterprise, the delegate must know how to juggle. However, even the world's best juggler will drop all the balls if she is already breaking the world record for the number of balls in the air and foolishly accepts four more.

- The individual must also read and affirm the project situation. If a proposed change seems like a losing proposition because of a perception of lack of support or political impossibility, the individual will go into a self-preservation mode rather than have confidence in the project. Consequently, others won't be able to take a true reading of the initiative because the individual managing will be very hard to figure out.

- Again, the individual must have sufficient authority over the six project balance factors as well as adequate influence with key resource providers and project stakeholders in order to commit to a project and succeed.

The bottom line for confident commitment can be summed up by my rules of commitment:

- Responsibility must not be accepted without access to adequate control (authority, influence, and resources).

- Responsibility must not be seen as delegated until it's accepted with a confident, visible commitment.

- The delegation and acceptance of responsibility isn't a one-time event but an ongoing relationship, which must be constantly managed to keep it alive.

- Responsibility must always be personal—it must be owned by the individual accepting the responsibility.

- Responsibility must be packaged in one size—always 100%.

- Shared responsibility must be 100% and 100%.

- Responsibility must always be associated with gaining acceptance of the "deliverable result" from an acceptor and not with the conduct of an activity (see Figure 6.2).

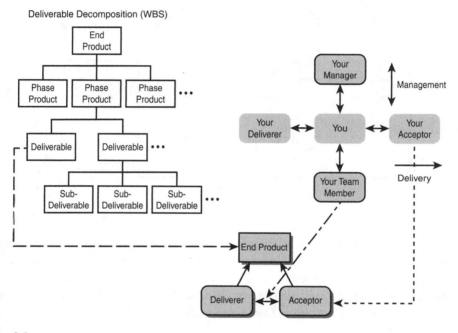

FIGURE 6.2
The project relationship triangle.

Project Management Roles and Structure

Critical to creating the right environment that ensures confidence of delivery is having a set of necessary and sufficient roles carried out in the project. Figure 6.3 depicts these roles and their interrelationships. Remember that these are project roles, not organizational line positions. Any individual can assume multiple roles except for the project manager, who can't assume the role of acceptor or champion—that would be a conflict of interest. The roles shown are the total set that could be considered. This doesn't mean that all roles have to be in place in every project, especially for a smaller initiative in a smaller organization. The core team roles, however, must be filled. The following sections will briefly cover the major responsibilities associated with these roles.

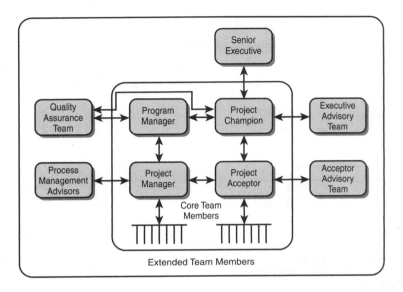

FIGURE 6.3

Project management structure.

These roles are key. Ignoring them will only result in problems later. Again, a particular individual might be involved in more that one role. An acceptance advisory team member might also sit on the quality assurance team, and the program manager might also conduct a task as a project team member. The roles aren't positions, which means that your boss could be conducting work for you as part of your team. Don't confuse project roles and job positions. Also, the communication, represented by the two-headed arrows in Figure 6.3, is two-way, not one-way. These relationships continually keep working in both directions. This takes time, which must be planned and used to ensure a common and confident set of commitments.

Core Team Roles

Project manager

- Delivers the business solution to the acceptor (that is, gains acceptance for it)
- Plans and manages the project day to day
- Motivates and manages the team
- Is the focal point for project issues

Project acceptor

- Accepts the project results on behalf of the process champion (that is, ensures delivery)
- Coordinates the multiple vested interests of the range of business stakeholders

Project Management Essentials

CHAPTER 6

179

6

PROJECT
MANAGEMENT
ESSENTIALS

- Acts as project and business conscience
- Can also be the project champion if a separate person isn't assigned to accept

Program manager

- Ensures that the project manager's delivery of the project results is consistent with an overall program of change or set of initiatives
- Clears the path and warns of roadblocks
- Assures professional and technical quality
- Resolves political and cross-organizational escalations along with the process champion
- Monitors the business and senior customer relationships
- Helps the project manager maintain the project balance factors affecting confident delivery

Project champion

- Ensures the delivery and acceptance of the project results by the acceptor
- Clears the path and warns of roadblocks
- Resolves political and cross-organizational escalations along with the program manager
- Takes responsibility for the ongoing operation of the new process subsequent to delivery
- Chairs the executive advisory team
- Might continue to be the process owner after delivery
- Assumes the role of acceptor if one isn't appointed

Project team member

- Is dedicated to conduct the day-to-day activities of the process project
- Understands the business requirements and delivers results to the acceptor on behalf of the project manager
- Brings to the project either process management professional practice knowledge and experience or subject matter expertise, knowledge, or skills
- Coordinates an ongoing relationship with an extended team of stakeholders outside the day-to-day activities of the project, gains their input, and manages their expectations

Extended Team Roles

Acceptor advisory team member

- Brings specialist knowledge and perspective to the analysis and evaluation, based on knowledge of a business function, location, or body of knowledge

- Helps create a solution as part of periodic input and review
- Acts as an agent of change going back out to the business
- Advises the acceptor on acceptability of project results, not only from his represented area, but also from the overall business

Senior executive

- Is the path for exceptions, unresolved issues, and policy changes outside the mandate of the program manager and project champion
- Is the final arbiter on direction and outside stakeholders' perspectives
- Sells the concept upward to the business owners and possibly to other outside stakeholders
- Makes the ultimate commitment
- Rallies the executive team
- Shows visible support to all internal and external stakeholders

Executive advisory team member

- Advises the champion on key acceptance issues
- Acts in the best interest of the company, not just his area
- Represents her area's perspectives on the process
- Ensures support for the new process from her area
- Provides a corporate message on the management of change in his area

Quality assurance team member

- Acts as independent advisor separate from the core team
- Helps teams plan the process change by assessing the planned approach in advance
- Brings best practices to the project through checklists and questionnaires to be used at checkpoints
- Advises team on process management and subject matter requirements before review sessions
- Assesses risk and business value at predefined checkpoints
- Recommends acceptability to pass the checkpoint to the executives based on quality and risk, not on project constraints

Process management advisor

- Has expertise in process management
- Provides process management methods, tools, templates, examples, training, and coaching to project teams

Project Management Essentials

CHAPTER 6

181

6

PROJECT
MANAGEMENT
ESSENTIALS

- Facilitates some key sessions where independence is needed
- Coordinates lessons learned and best practice feedback and knowledge-sharing across initiatives
- Provides modeling and technique support
- Helps the team plan and improve the project process on an ongoing basis

Project Management Stages

As mentioned earlier, four major stages are involved in delivering the results of a whole project, a phase of a process renewal project, or even a small deliverable. Each concept applies to everything deliverable and everyone delivering or accepting:

- Initiating (defining the work)
- Planning (planning the work)
- Controlling and Improving (working the plan)
- Accepting (accepting the work)

Initiating Stage

It's important to get a project going in the right direction. A small deflection from the right direction at this point can mean a large variance when magnified over time. Well-designed initiation documentation will give management the information necessary to authorize the planning for the upcoming project. It will provide a description of the business commitment against which personal commitments can be sought. The initiation work will provide the criteria for post-program, -project, or -phase evaluation or (in other words) guidelines for executing delivery, outlining what's required, and communicating why you are doing it. Based on this, resource allocation can take place. Initiation documentation must outline

- **Purpose**—Why are you doing this?
- **Stakeholders**—Who cares whether you do this?
- **Objectives**—What will be produced or what results are required to achieve your purpose?
- **Scope**—What are the limits to the statement of work?
- **Approach**—What methods and techniques will be used to achieve your purpose and objectives?

If these statements are specific, measurable, attainable, relevant, and time-bound, the project of delivering process management solutions will start off confidently.

The Process Management Framework addresses this aspect of project management specifically. It's the primary intent of the Vision phase (see Chapter 12, "Charting the Course of Change") to produce the deliverables and outcomes necessary in getting started on a particular process-based change.

Planning Stage

The initiating component of a project as represented by the Vision phase of the Process Management Framework describes the business commitment required. The planning stage, which is also found in the Vision phase of the Process Renewal Framework, aims to line up the personal commitments of those who will be expected to carry out desired process changes. As such, in this stage, the business will define the conditions necessary for project success based on the project manager's and team's confidence that they can meet the project requirements. They must do this by defining the combination of the six project balance variables (quality, scope, time, resources, methods, and tools) that they believe are necessary and sufficient and to which others must also commit. The result will provide identification and acceptance of the terms of empowerment for the team and establish the baseline for maintaining control and continuous improvement. Planning will provide the mechanisms to accept the personal commitment by communicating the understanding of the project. It will also show how the project work effort will be organized so that stated goals are achieved and the right results are delivered. Planning will also ensure that the right activities are conducted with the right people and responsibilities, according to the right schedule (time and cost), using the right standards and practices. The plan will help maintain personal confidence in success by establishing and communicating project direction and progress monitoring capabilities as well as project execution and continuous improvement tools. The plan will provide a context for performance measurement and decision-making about how to adjust for variances, which will surely come along.

NOTE
An initial plan must be accepted by all involved. Based on progress, this plan must be updated to reflect current realities. This planning update will be covered later in the section "Controlling and Improving."

This will provide the basis for estimating or determining the resources and effort required to complete the project. If the initiating and prior planning activities are conducted properly, an estimate will be

- Complete
- Understandable

Project Management Essentials

CHAPTER 6

183

6

PROJECT
MANAGEMENT
ESSENTIALS

- Realistic
- Supportable (because it's based on a credible approach, such as the Process Management Framework)
- Factual (based on measurable tasks that produce finite results)
- Consistent (in that it employs a standard approach)
- Reproducible (another reasonable person using the same knowledge can reproduce them)
- Reflective of possible uncertainty and risk

Although the Process Management Framework is necessary to come up with a confident estimate, relying solely on it is dangerous because each initiative will be different in all six factors (quality, scope, time, resources, methods, and tools). Because of this, estimating is difficult. Estimating is detailed, time-consuming work, and you often have to do it with incomplete data. Human factors always enter the situation. Typically, we tend to underestimate work and overestimate our ability to do work, plus we are under pressure to get going. Despite all this, estimating still needs to be done well. Sometimes those asked to make estimates are reluctant because the tasks to be estimated aren't sufficiently detailed to support accurate estimates; Those submitting estimates might do so reluctantly because the estimates can be used as weapons against them later. They are also concerned that their estimate might displease management, or the customer's management, and jeopardize approval of the project. Or, they believe that they must develop estimates based on details that don't exist.

A key reminder about estimates is that they are just that—estimates—they aren't promises or predictions. Estimates are based on a set of assumptions that can be supported by a good, repeatable framework. You can commit to doing everything possible to make estimated results become real, but if assumptions prove to be wrong or conditions change, an estimate might have to change. This doesn't mean that you can't estimate—it does mean that there should be only enough detail to provide reasonable control for the project. There should be only enough detail to adequately schedule the resources to be used in the project. There should be no more detail than the project manager can manage and maintain.

Estimating is an evolving process that can have a high degree of certainty when the details are known. Although you should have a very tight estimate on the what will happen in the next phase of a project, the results of decisions made in that phase can lead to varying amounts of time and resources needed for subsequent work. Consequently, as shown in Figure 6.4, there will always be a lower degree of accuracy in estimates for phases further out in time. As the phases are navigated, the range of variance will shrink. The overall estimates must be re-evaluated continuously as part of the re-planning that should happen at the end of each phase. The cost/benefit scenarios should then be re-examined at each checkpoint.

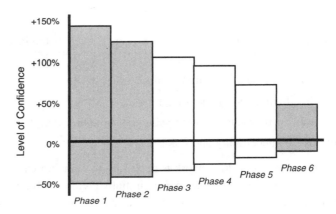

FIGURE 6.4

Levels of confidence in estimates across phases.

A Planning Process

The following planning process works particularly well and can be repeated. Some people view this as a backward approach, which it unashamedly is. It assumes that knowing your destination comes before picking your means of getting there. Each step is completely traceable to those that preceded it.

Before you start, be sure to have an acceptor. If you have to complete the project plan without an acceptor, this whole process must be reviewed again with the acceptor when he joins the team to ensure the proper commitment to the plan. The rest of this text assumes that the acceptor is "on board" and working with you in drafting the particulars of the planning cycle (shown in Figure 6.5).

12 Gain Acceptance △4	11 Set Baseline Schedule	10 Finalize & Schedule Resources △3
7 Define Communication and Control Mechanisms △2	8 Define Activities & Estimates	9 Calculate Optimum Time Schedule
6 Define Project Organization	5 Define Responsibilities for Deliverables △1	4 Define Required Skills & Sources
1 Validate Project Objectives, Scope, & Fit	2 Define End Products	3 Define Work Breakdown Structure

FIGURE 6.5

The planning cycle.

Project Management Essentials

CHAPTER 6

185

6

PROJECT
MANAGEMENT
ESSENTIALS

1. Review all the work done in the initiating stage of project management (equivalent to the Vision phase of the Process Management Framework) and make sure that it's well understood and commonly accepted. This sets the target and the criteria (objectives, scope, and fit) by which this initiative will be judged.

2. Using the Process Management Framework as the baseline, work with the acceptor to determine the end products required. Avoid interim deliverables at this point.

3. Using the Process Management Framework as the baseline, define all interim deliverables and their dependencies in a work breakdown structure for your specific initiative.

4. Determine the types of skills needed to produce the deliverables and define the potential sources of each resource.

5. With the acceptor, where possible, identify the standard to which each deliverable and sub-deliverable will be produced. This will have an effect upon the resource estimates. If a standard can't be defined, identify the individual who will determine at a later date what standard will be used. This activity will have to be added to the schedule later.

   Select those deliverables that should have a formal acceptance. Prepare a deliverable acceptance document preprinted with the name (of the deliverable acceptor, to solicit commitments regarding delivery and acceptance). Recognizing acceptance activities here can lead to adding more deliverables and tasks to the planning/estimating worksheets.

6. Identify the project organization, documenting the key individuals you will need and the specific roles that you want them to assume.

7. For each affected stakeholder type, identify and document all communication channels or avenues for sharing responsibility during the course of the project and the tools (*control mechanisms*) for keeping them open. Include the frequency of these channels' usage.

8. Identify the activities you think will be required to get the job done. Estimate resource effort by type for each activity.

9. Develop a precedence network and initial schedule for all activities with respect to elapsed time, given the assumption of availability of resources and the known constraints.

10. Negotiate to obtain required resources. Allocate actual resources to each activity and reschedule all activities with respect to resources.

11. Establish project milestones and set the baseline schedule.

12. Prepare a draft outline of the plan. Don't attempt to resolve all the questions or fill in all the blanks on this first draft. This draft should be used to facilitate a dialog between project manager, acceptor, delivery executive, and resource managers. The dialog is essential to the plan's successful completion. When the draft is complete, send a copy to everyone involved in the project. After they have had time to review it, meet with them (individually or in a group) to update the draft and approve the final plan.

There are four major checkpoints in the planning process, indicated by the numbered triangles shown in Figure 6.5. The first occurs after step 5, when acceptance of scope and quality (that is, the left side of the balance) is sought. The second occurs after step 7, when the project roles, organization, and communications are established. The third is after step 10, when time and cost are proposed. The last is after step 12, when the overall draft plan is put forward for full commitment.

Rejection at any of these checkpoints requires a revisiting of the steps prior and a renegotiation of the terms of confidence and commitment.

In planning, you need to keep a few other things in mind, including the following:

- Don't try to make the first draft too detailed. The detail will come from interaction with others (continuous improvement).

- Don't try to prepare this document in isolation. It might be hard selling the ideas, so be prepared to make changes.

- Don't go too far with the detailed work plan. Only plan in detail up to the phase where you stop feeling comfortable with your estimates due to unknowns. Allow time in each phase to do detailed planning for subsequent phases.

- Don't plan activities that last longer than two weeks.

- Don't plan activities in which the completion can't be identified by a clearly recognizable deliverable.

- Don't plan any phase without a formal acceptance at its end. Formal acceptance at the conclusion of each phase will minimize the work involved in the final acceptance. It forces re-commitment.

Controlling and Improving

With a solid plan in place, you can now execute the project and keep improving on your plan. This stage of project management is simply about that—controlling and improving the plan. Confidence is maintained through a structured approach that avoids potential chaos in the middle of project. It should be focused on understanding the current situation, replanning the rest of the project based on reality rather than wishes, rejuggling the six project balance variables (quality, scope, time, resources, methods, and tools), and sharing the responsibility with the team and stakeholders for any adjustments, according to the communications plan. In this phase, the project team attempts to come to grips with perceived and potential issues as early as possible. The team also identifies the potential for doing better as soon as possible (even if the project is under budget and ahead of schedule). Being proactive will keep everyone confident and committed and allow you to maintain your sanity.

Project Management Essentials

CHAPTER 6

187

6

PROJECT
MANAGEMENT
ESSENTIALS

At every continuous improvement cycle, such as every week, the first order is to review the actual performance and determine opportunities to do better. This requires you to understand the facts and perceptions of the project customers and to honestly determine real progress and accomplishments so far. Based on this, you can identify potential roadblocks and ways to remove or avoid them. This then finally lets you replan the rest of the initiative from where you are. Once more, you must re-examine the fragile balance among quality, scope, time, resources, methods, and tools.

To improve the plan for the rest of the project regardless of where you are, you need to look backward for the facts, review scheduled completions to see whether they happened, and look forward to those scheduled to happen to assess risk. You must review customer satisfaction and quality to date and try to spot any threats for upcoming deliverables. This enables you to examine incurred and expected costs and compare them to budgets and forecasts. At this point, you must also look at any requested and approved changes and their potential impacts and review your resource plan. If anything has changed significantly, you might also want to re-examine methods and tools for appropriateness. All of this can result in a new plan proposal or a confirmation that the current one is still valid.

More than anything else, this proactive staying on top of a project in motion requires a strong commitment to communication among project manager, acceptor, program delivery manager, and other selected stakeholders, according to the communications strategy outlined in the original plan. This communication requires a well-defined, calendar-based commitment to communicate. It demands documented status reports, project budget updates, living project plans, and in-person reviews of project management aspects, both individually and as a team. These communications should be based on feelings, perceptions, and facts. They take time and should be scheduled in advance and conducted even when there's no bad news to report.

In summary, controlling and improving is all about making sure that what you wanted to happen is happening or keeping your plan up to date. It's designed to share responsibility with the right people at the right time and avoid abdication and dropping of commitment. It keeps your client/user, your management, your team, and the other stakeholders informed. It ensures that you always have a commonly understood current schedule.

Accepting

At first blush, it might not seem as though accepting deliverables is a stage at all. It seems more like an event, a byproduct of everything else. The whole purpose of any change initiative is to deliver the results to those who expected them in the first place. All our initiating, planning, and controlling is nothing other than doing what's needed so that you can deliver the right things correctly. For this reason, I have and will continue to consider accepting deliverables a project management stage. Its purpose is to ensure that all stakeholders recognize when the deliverable is completed and the project is finished. The prime criterion that I will use for completion is the concept of acceptance. From that perspective, a result is delivered and a project is done if, and only if, the product is accepted. This acceptance must be visible and understood as completion of both the business commitment and the personal commitment. This can happen only when the acceptor has ensured that the products meet all customer requirements, and they are of appropriate quality and have clear ownership after hand-off. Only then can you consider the acceptance criteria defined in the project plan satisfied.

Acceptance won't happen if progress toward this goal isn't visible. Confidence in the product and the team is required to gain acceptance. Trust is a key component. To gain trust and confidence, the acceptor must see progress and not just promises. The best evidence of progress toward ultimate completion is through ongoing acceptance(s) of subdeliverables. To build confidence by continuously delivering, our plans must schedule planned deliverables to be accepted all along. Progress will then be eased by visibility of these sub-deliverables.

Note that the "best" professional/technical sequence isn't necessarily the best project-acceptance sequence for the business. Design your acceptances for the customer, not for the designer or technician. Plan to document and gain commitment for the acceptance criteria up front before building anything. Keep these criteria focused on deliverables, not activities. Develop a deliverable acceptance matrix that describes the product to be produced, the person producing it, the standard to be followed, and the criteria by which it will be deemed acceptable. Use clear acceptance mechanisms: the more visible and unambiguous, the better. The following are all good choices:

- A signed acceptance document starting with "I"
- A signed memo
- A personal e-mail message
- A minuted meeting acceptance with the minutes approved
- The formal session records from a workshop
- A witnessed, verbal agreement

The intent is for the acceptor to gain confidence in the product through the time of acceptance and for the project manager or deliverer to face no surprises. As with any process, the completion of any cycle also brings an opportunity to learn and share what you've learned. In the case of a project management experience, the learning should translate back to the Process Management Framework itself. What worked well and what could be improved can be turned into better methodology documentation as well as training and other guidance for the next practitioners.

Closing Project Management Guidelines

I have to thank an early mentor, Michael Howe of Oakville, Ontario, for the wealth of knowledge that I've built in project management. Many of the baseline concepts described in this chapter can be found in his teachings. They have stood the test of time. The main things that Mike taught me were to appreciate the importance of relationships, to trust my instincts, and to use common sense. I learned from him that to be successful with complex initiatives, such as process management, the practitioner can't rely on great methodologies alone. Methodologies are necessary but not sufficient. Using them doesn't mean that we will be wise. We have to have sufficient time and psychological space to show good judgment. If we don't, we will have even less time to deal with the consequences. Mike always said that a good project manager will spend his time in the following 20/20/60 mix:

- Spend 20% of your time "dreaming"—that is, looking forward, anticipating, and planning, sometimes with no productive results to show for it.
- Spend 20% of your time "worrying"—that is, monitoring, checking, and making sure that what was supposed to be happening is happening.
- Spend the remaining 60% "getting interrupted"—that is, being available to others when they need you.

The problem has become that we seem to have little time to "dream" or plan, and then all the "worrying" in the world is not sufficient. Very soon, 100 percent of the time is spent getting interrupted, and no preventative action can be taken, leading to more interruptions and zero confidence and commitment.

Summary

Project management might appear on the surface to be simple common sense that can be found in the likes of Steven Covey's habits and principles, but, if it hasn't become common practice for you or your organization, you will surely struggle. Process management isn't as simple as it looks when you get into it. It might be the toughest thing that you've ever done. By sticking to good project management approaches while you are doing it, you will reduce the risk and enjoy the journey.

By initiating, planning, controlling, improving, and accepting every project, phase, and deliverable, you can reduce project delivery risk and assist the business by delivering the capabilities it needs. By making project management everyone's job, you can work with shared confidence and commitment.

The next chapter will address a topic closely aligned with project management: how to mitigate business risk. This is an issue of great concern for many managers who are putting their businesses on the line with process projects.

Mitigating Business Risk

IN THIS CHAPTER

Professional journals and conferences abound with horror stories of business change initiatives that have gone wrong:

- One manufacturer went out of business because it couldn't implement its Enterprise Resource Planning solution, blaming it on the ineptitude of the consultants and the dishonesty of the software vendor. The owners ended up suing the participants for more than $500 million.

- In 1998, a chocolate bar manufacturer missed out on Halloween sales because the new forecasting approach and technology didn't work on time.

- A state government couldn't issue or renew drivers' licenses due to systems troubles and operational chaos.

These are just a few of the disasters that take place every year that put whole organizations at risk, sometimes for their very existence. In 1995, the Standish Group reported that companies in the United States spent $150 billion alone for cancelled or late software development.[1] Less spectacular but even more prevalent are the stories of projects that take years when they should have taken months, robbing the business of opportunity in the marketplace. In every case, it seems as though costs skyrocketed, but they weren't as costly as the lost business opportunity, often reaching hundreds of millions of dollars.

The real questions that come with these types of failures are

- What could we have done in the marketplace if we had the capability we anticipated, at the time that we were supposed to have it, and at the price we were supposed to pay for it?

- What did we miss because our scarce resources weren't available to do something additional that we had planned but couldn't do because of a lack of quality or delivery?

In these situations, it seems as though everyone feigns surprise or perhaps didn't want to face up to the horrible signs of impending failure. Looking at them in hindsight, these projects typically exhibited the warning signals of high risk and poor quality much earlier than anyone saw or wanted to see. In few cases were there any risk management strategies, checkpoints, or early off-ramps, nor were there any quality criteria put to use.

The value of good risk management was reported at Hughes Aircraft (now Raytheon) on its Peace Shield air defense project, which used a proactive risk-based approach to avoid problems. The project, seen as a potential minefield, came in 10% ahead of a 4 1/2-year schedule and significantly under budget.[2] It did this in an environment of uncertainty and doubt.

---

[1]The Standish Group. Chaos: Charting the Seas of Information Technology. *Dennis, MA: Standish Group International 1994*

[2]*"Peace Shield Risk Management." Chuck Sutherland, In Proceedings of the 5th SEI Conference on Software Risk Management, Pittsburgh: Software Engineering Institute, 1997*

Clearly, any change is inherently risky, but does this mean that we should never introduce new ideas? Of course not—the risk is usually accompanied by great opportunity. In many cases, the risk of not changing might be even greater than the risk of a major shift in direction if it means that our customers will leave us for something more exciting from a competitor. Staying the same doesn't mean being the same. Risks are part of the territory.

We have to manage the risks we have in a professional manner. Our ability to do this better than our competitors gives us a barrier to entry for our competition and great opportunity to gain advantage. One significant area of risk is that of poor quality. Today, quality isn't a differentiating factor that will gain us great advantage, but its absence will certainly cause us great loss. The management of quality and risk, like project management, must be seen as umbrella concepts that are prerequisites for process management to have a chance.

What Is at Risk?

Risk is defined as the possibility of suffering harm or loss. The higher the risk, the higher the danger or probability of harm or loss occurring. The things that can be harmed or "at risk" are first and foremost those that define the success of the business. This is the set of results that we are trying to accomplish as a result of the process change initiative itself. The work in the Business Context phase of the framework defines the future state of the "Organization-in-Focus" in terms of its vision, objectives, goals, and performance targets. It also defines the nature of the relationships that we feel we must have with our customers and other stakeholders to survive and thrive. The Vision phase defines the results of value that must be delivered to the stakeholders of the specific process within the scope of the initiative. The results of these phases tell us what to watch for to determine if a risk is truly at hand. The evaluation criteria they give us for decision making and prioritization throughout are developed based on stakeholder expectations and performance. They are the same criteria to be used in the risk evaluation process.

Although there's clearly risk to all stakeholder relationships, some will be more critical than others will. Typically, the ones to start with are those affecting the customer and owner relationships. I will examine these first.

Customer-Based Risk

We all know the importance of delivering a quality product or service. No one tries to do a bad job, and everyone says that they want to provide a quality service. Nonetheless, poor results often show up in the form of unwanted products, non-responsive processes, or unsatisfactory service performance for customers. This is the quality component of risk. If the results are unsuitable for the customer, by definition, they are of poor quality and will incur higher business risk.

The product or service might be deemed poor for several reasons. The product or service might be declared sub-standard because of its inappropriate nature, its lack of reliability or availability, or its failure to meet commitments or promises (whether perceived or real). Poor quality can also result from inadequate human capability or capacity, technological shortcomings, and myriad other possibilities.

Having acceptable *quality* is generally defined as meeting all the requirements of a product, service, or process that in some way affects its customers' satisfaction. Sometimes these requirements are explicit but often they aren't completely stated. Consequently, meeting documented standards alone usually won't suffice. Customers must be involved in the process of evaluating quality. This helps a business realize that it can't just deal with the objective factors. It must also deal with the subjective ones, such as how customers feel about what they are getting and how they are getting it. These more subjective needs should be incorporated in the stakeholder expectations so that the business can assess the risk of satisfying stakeholders.

Owner Perspective of Risk

While customers have a concern about product and service quality, owners and managers have additional concerns about other outcomes. To them, risk is associated with uncertainty. It may be uncertainty regarding the viability or customer acceptability of the products, services, or processes that will be introduced. It might be risk associated with the attention that might be paid by regulatory bodies, regarding a service that stretches the boundaries of existing practice. It might be risk due to the likelihood of labor conflict due to changed working conditions.

The starting point for all risk analysis, then, is in trying to eliminate poor quality in the outcomes to customers. Such poor quality implies that there's a lack of *fit to customer need*, which is our definition of quality in the first place. The certainties of poor quality and the uncertainties of risk will become a reality if an initiative fails to deliver the results expected. Subsequently, every other stakeholders' perspective must be taken to find all other potential areas of lack of fit. Any of these could have a direct impact on the organization's strategic intent. The possibilities are endless, but possible factors to watch out for are set out in Table 7.1, adapted from Robert Thomsett's list of risk types.

TABLE 7.1   Types of Risk[3]

Type of Risk	Effect
Commercial	The organization faces loss of market share or competitive advantage.
Strategic	The organization's strategic plan is compromised.

[3]Thomsett, Robert. "The Indiana Jones School of Risk Management." *American Programmer, Volume 5 No. 7, (September 1992) pages 10–18*

TABLE 7.1 Continued

Type of Risk	Effect
Financial	The investment in the project is lost, and the benefits aren't accrued.
Technical	Key technology platforms are compromised.
Legal	The organization is exposed to legal procedures, including prosecution.
Political	The organization violates government requirements.
Fraud	The organization is exposed to fraud and security violations.
To image	The organization faces loss of public image.
To capability	The organization can't retain or acquire the human skills and competencies to deliver or won't change its beliefs and behaviors.
To scalability	The organization won't be able to handle an increase in market share.

These risks should be evaluated in direct relationship to the project's objectives and their fit to the business vision as defined through the customers' and other stakeholders' expectations. The stakeholders' criteria provide the standards to judge whether the results of delivery have a greater or lesser chance of being met. This results-oriented aspect of risk management explains why risk management and quality management are counterparts and should be administered together in change initiatives.

Management should also be concerned about the risk in the program or project of change. They should pay attention to both the end and the means because "risky means" won't deliver a "risk-free" end. This second type of risk is affected by poor project execution. Both results-oriented and project risks must be addressed repeatedly as knowledge is gained by performing the work defined by the Process Management Framework.

Risk Factors in Business Process Management

A *risk factor* is anything or any course of action with sufficient uncertainty to potentially increase risk to the business. Risk management, then, deals with and mitigates the factors that might contribute to the risk. To manage a risk factor, we must know two major things:

- What is "at risk" and can be "harmed"?
- What factors can predict or contribute to the risk and can be managed?

While never losing sight of the risks to the initiative's outcomes, you must manage the factors within the project that can either increase or decrease the chance that the impacts will occur and reduce the likelihood of uncertainty. These are the areas to pay attention to:

7

MITIGATING BUSINESS RISK

- Project scope, to define what is to be analyzed, designed, and implemented
- Project constraints, to define what must and must not be changed or examined
- Professional practices to be employed, such as the Process Management Framework and supporting techniques
- Work breakdown structure and deliverables to be produced, including the professional standards for their acceptance
- The knowledge and capability of those assigned to do the project work to produce the deliverables
- The capacity of the human resources, in terms of both numbers and availability
- Team and individual incentives toward results with no conflicts
- Access to adequate tools and technology
- Sufficient elapsed time
- Financial resources
- Two-way communication capability and commitment with stakeholders up, down, and out
- Personal confidence and commitments to the initiative and its objectives
- Control and influence over resources of all types
- Appropriate working facilities

Gaps in any of these will raise the risk of not achieving the business results for all stakeholders.

The Process Management Framework's Contributions to Risk Mitigation

As mentioned earlier, the framework has been built to reduce uncertainty and risk. Several phases of the framework employ specific techniques intended to do this. Skipping any of the framework phases is possible if it's deemed that the risk of not undertaking the phase is low. Table 7.2 shows some of the techniques that I've found most helpful.

TABLE 7.2   Risk Reduction Through the Process Management Framework's Techniques

Practice or Technique	Contribution(s) to Risk Factor Mitigation
Business scenario analysis	Forces examination of a range of possibilities to ensure scalability and robustness of solutions.

Table 7.2   Continued

Practice or Technique	Contribution(s) to Risk Factor Mitigation
Performance and practices benchmarking	Ensures an examination of business approaches and the reasonableness of programs for change.
	Provides the agenda for urgency.
Interviewing	Helps determine true needs of stakeholders from each of their perspectives confidentially.
Workshops	Helps assure the cross-functional viability from multiple perspectives.
	Helps assure a common understanding of results and a commitment to their success.
Straw models	Ensures a focus on the process solution and provides consistent and easy-to-understand communication of the solution.
IGOE models	Makes sure that no contributing elements of a process or its components are overlooked.
	Makes sure that everyone asks the right questions.
Root cause analysis and avoidance	Makes sure that the reasons—not the symptoms—for lack of performance are found and dealt with.
	Ensures that new process designs avoid potential downstream impacts on performance.
Pareto analysis and 80/20 rule	Makes sure that the focus is on the key aspects of analysis and design, that irrelevant issues don't predominate, and that time isn't wasted.
Concerns-based change and communication	Ensures that stakeholders' issues are dealt with throughout and that those affected understand what's coming and its viability.
Process scenarios	Ensures comprehensive validation of the current situation and the proposed solution from many stakeholder points of view and under various conditions.

Obviously, there is an important relationship between quality assurance and a good methodology updated with the appropriate risk-avoiding lessons learned. One key aspect of this is the ability to trust that your well-designed approach with built-in risk prevention will mean less need to inspect later. The trustworthiness of the design approach and the standards that it offers means that some things are trusted to work because of what we did, not because every result was tested to death.

In his book *Risk-Free Business Re-engineering*,[4] Brian Dickinsen poses the business analogy of building a house, saying that, upon construction, we don't get a bunch of people with big fans to come and test to see if the house will withstand a strong wind. We don't get the fire department to come out and aim their hoses on the roof to see if it leaks. Likewise, we trust many aspects of our expected business results because we are confident that the materials used are to trustworthy standards and the methods used are professional. Trust in the methods and the people is paramount. It's cheaper and better to build a house from quality materials using proven methods than to do it by cutting corners and inspecting and correcting later. It's not easy or possible to add a bathroom after a house is built or to replace plumbing once the job is done. The same questions must be asked about business change. How much inspection, testing, and correction will we do versus good process design and early avoidance of problems? The answer to this question is at the heart of both risk and quality management.

The Risk-Management Process

In addition to a well-designed method and proven techniques, the need still remains to examine risk specifically in each initiative. My preferred approach toward assuring the quality of results for customers and other stakeholders and reducing risk for owners and managers is a preventative one.

Quality control (QC) focuses its attention on a project's "products of interest." Quality assurance (QA) focuses its effort on the "process of interest." In reality, both are needed, although a more mature organization will conduct relatively more QA." We are accustomed to a strong emphasis on quality control at the end of the production of a deliverable and the end of a project. We often see testers checking the compliance of a deliverable to a set of requirements, standards, and specifications. Corrections are then made to the deliverables if there's a gap. The main problem with this philosophy is that any shortcomings of methodology and its results are discovered late in the game when it can be expensive or even impossible to repair what has been done fast enough or cost effectively. Also, more defensiveness and blame occur the later the change is made. Refer back to the discussion of the Flores-Winograd Commitment Model in Chapter 2, "Organizational Responses to Business Drivers," to review the cost of late changes and withdrawal. The preferred approach is to avoid the problem in the first place through quality assurance and proactive risk management.

---

[4]Risk-Free Business Re-engineering. *Brian Dickinsen, LCI Press, Kings Beach, CA, 1996*

This doesn't mean that final inspections are never done, but it tries to focus on those factors that prove to be the root causes of problems in initiatives that have gone wrong in the past. Using Pareto techniques of finding the most likely causes of poor quality with the biggest impact on risk factors is commonplace. Within organizations that practice good QA, it's not unusual to find a list of the top 10 or 20 most likely reasons that things typically go wrong if not done well or dealt with. These might even be described as "Critical Success Factors," the more positive spin on risk. It's also not unusual to find a set of practices that should be conducted to assure that things don't go wrong for each reason or factor.

Taking a process perspective means that you must look at the processes or methods involved in conducting a business process initiative and be sure that they are followed intelligently. The two processes that I've defined so far are incorporated in the Framework for Business Process Management described in the majority of this book and the method of project management described in Chapter 6, "Project Management Essentials." In each case, they were designed based on the result of hundreds of projects, years of experience, and feedback so that the risk factors will be mitigated by design. By following these methods intelligently, you face far less uncertainty; much of the uncertainty has been designed out by taking a phased and complete approach. What helps is that the design of the methods doesn't just look at one aspect of the solution but also aligns them all, as defined in the Process Renewal Hexagon. The same can be said about the Project Management approach, which covers all aspects of commitment management.

What we need to have in place, then, are three things: a good framework, a good project management approach, and a good process for assessing risk on an ongoing basis. The risk assessment process should keep track of the questions to ask at defined checkpoints. A feedback mechanism from prior projects should keep these questions current, based on lessons learned from each and every initiative.

One of the best examples of the incorporation of this knowledge management approach to doing and improving work can be found in the U.S. military's use of after-action reviews. After each engagement, such as hurricane relief in Florida and refugee support in Africa, the command officers involved spend considerable time examining situations encountered. They delve into what worked well and what could have been done better. Consequently, lessons learned are consolidated into a set of expected situations and the best known approaches to deal with them. Before mobilizing the force in the next engagement, all are trained on what to do, based on what has been proven so far to optimize the results being sought. Quality is built in to doing the right things, not attached at the end to correct the risky mistakes made when it may be too late.

The following risk analysis approach is what I've found to work best in process management. The major steps are

1. Establish business requirements and stakeholder criteria that reflect the results needed for the change program or project. This is defined in the framework's Business Context phase for a program of change and the Vision phase for a specific process project.

2. For each requirement, determine the potential risks to the business that will be used to assess risk factors later. Start with the customer perspective, and then move to the owner perspective and finally look at other stakeholders' risks. Include variations in factors to assure robustness and adaptability.

3. From studying the framework, determine the necessary development steps required and the techniques and standards needed for the specific initiative at hand.

4. Determine the specific project management steps to be used and the techniques and standards needed for the specific initiative at hand.

5. Determine the specific checkpoints for risk assessment at select phase end points and start points, as well as at any other milestones that affect approvals to proceed or potential changes in direction.

6. Identify the risk management team that will assess the crucial areas of risk at each checkpoint. Understand that the team's membership might change depending on the nature of the professional work as well as the specific phase in question.

7. Determine the questions to ask to evaluate risk at each checkpoint, starting from a documented set of most likely risks and standard questions updated after the last initiative. If there is no preceding initiative, run workshops with professionals to gather their experience into explicit sets of questions.

8. Make sure that the risk mitigation strategy and plan is reflected in the action plan for the project, complete with deliverables, activities, time, and resources allocated.

9. Document these in the project plan and gain key executive and client stakeholder acceptance of the risk management plan as part of the overall strategy of delivering the project results.

10. At each checkpoint, meet with the project team to go through the questions and assess the risk of each gap along with the plan to close each gap.

11. Monitor the risk mitigation plan regularly, such as monthly or weekly, depending on the degree of risk involved and the recognized gaps.

Safety Checks

At the heart of this approach is the concept of *safety checks*. These checkpoints often coincide with updates to business case re-examinations at the end of the framework phases. They offer the opportunity to proceed or stop. At a set of key points, defined to coincide with the framework infrastructure, safety check questions are retrieved from the framework knowledge base and tuned for the risk review session with the project team and a set of independent risk reviewers. Each critical area with a potentially significant risk factor is represented on the independent risk team. These areas can include, but are not be limited to, financial, strategic, technical, legal, political, commercial, fraud, and image concerns. The team should also have representatives acting in the best interest of the customer and other key external and internal stakeholders as well as resource providers to the project itself. It's imperative that the customers, operators, and maintainers of the business process solution be there to ask the tough questions because they will inherit the implemented results.

These reviews will cover methodological steps and project management steps, both major influences over quality and risk. The reviews cover technical and managerial concerns. They will be preventative, not corrective, in nature and will look toward process improvements going forward. The sessions must be done in a spirit of co-operation, not defensiveness, accusation, or blame.

The methods and techniques will ensure that the right things are planned and completed to meet product requirements and customer expectations. They will establish quality (conformance to requirements) measurements and acceptance criteria. At checkpoints, the risk team's role is to review and provide recommendations to proceed or stop to management. Their recommendations are to be based solely on the risk factors and quality criteria and not on the project urgency or constraints. Issues of budget or timing aren't part of this forum—only risk. The project's managers will be required to assess trade-offs. They—not the risk team—should make the go/no go decisions. This is the job of the champion and business managers. This allows a graduated commitment phase by phase and for risk to be assessed periodically and in advance of its potential damage.

From a risk management point of view, safety checks will provide methods and techniques to identify, analyze, and respond to project risk. The risk team making the safety checks will develop action plans to mitigate risk, including contingency plans to deal with potential threats and uncertainties. It will focus on avoidance but will also deal with corrective actions when needed.

Safety checkpoints should be chosen based on overall complexity, cost, and potential risk impact. Clearly a three-month initiative affecting one department with little job or technology change and involving two people on a team won't have the same checkpoints as a company-wide rollout of a new way of dealing with customers around the world. The choice is one that must be made at project-planning time. Each checkpoint chosen will have its own purpose and criteria with a set of requirements and questions provided in advance for guidance. These can be used by the risk team but have even more value if used in advance by the project manager and acceptor to work together to avoid problems and surprises at the risk review sessions. This is the prime quality assurance benefit derived by a self-assurance approach.

7

MITIGATING BUSINESS RISK

If the business or process owners accept the safety check approach, they can use it as a prerequisite for formal acceptance of any framework phase conducted. If so, they must understand that safety checks don't replace proper product-acceptance procedures. They are a management tool that act visibly at predefined checkpoints when the safety checkers make go/no go recommendations to the executive based on risk and benefit criteria. These reviews occur at major milestones or when major project hand-offs are required. Also, the reviews cover professional practice methodological steps and project management steps, such as planning. The reviewers also must also understand that some safety checkpoints are required for all projects; others are conditional.

Safety Checkpoints for Business Process Change

Tables 7.3 and 7.4 describe the recommended set of checkpoints for typical process initiatives.

TABLE 7.3   Checkpoints for Business Process Strategic Alignment Initiatives

Checkpoint Number	Checkpoint	Optionality
	Business Context Phase	
1.	Business Context phase plan completed	Required, but can be combined with Architect and Align phase plan
2.	Strategic intent and stakeholder criteria completed	Conditional
	Architect and Align Phase	
3.	Architect and Align phase plan completed	Required, but can be combined with Business Context phase plan
4.	Processes identified and mapped to business and stakeholder criteria	Conditional
5.	Architecture migration strategy completed	Required

TABLE 7.4   Checkpoints for Business Process Design Initiatives

Checkpoint Number	Checkpoint	Optionality
	Vision Phase	
1.	Plan for project visioning completed	Conditional
2.	Initial business case for the project completed	Required

Number	Checkpoint	Optionality
	Understand Phase	
3.	Project plan for the "understand" analysis and "renewal" design activities completed	Required
4.	"Understand" analysis and identification of quick wins for the process completed	Conditional
	Renew Phase	
5.	Identification of the potential solutions	Conditional
6.	Renewal design, business case update, and the transition strategy completed	Required
	Develop Phase	
7.	Development and implementation plans for each professional aspect of the next release of the solution completed	Required
	Implement Phase	
8.	Activities in preparation for the pilot for each phase or iteration of implementation completed	Conditional
9.	Pilot completed and phase implementation prepared	Required
	Nurture and Continuously Improve Phase	
10.	Completion of post implementation review	Required

It also might be wise to extend the use of checkpoints wherever specific enablers are designed but not yet built and after any significant change in scope or direction is developed.

Sample Questions for a Safety Checkpoint

To clarify the concept of safety check questions, I include an example that you can use for the checkpoint at "Plan for project visioning completed." This particular set of questions can be easily adjusted and applied at any planning-oriented checkpoint. The other checkpoints will take their questions more specifically from the Process Management Framework phase relevant at the time.

Deliverables:

Plan for Project Visioning

Questions:

- Do you have a firm commitment from management for resources required for the completion of this activity to reach the next safety checkpoint?

- Is the proposed visioning team made up of knowledgeable representatives from all affected business areas? Will they work well together?

- Have all visioning team members been trained in the strategic methods and techniques of the Process Management Framework?

- Is each team member's role clearly defined, and do all members understand their responsibilities?

- Is there a project plan that describes end products, deliverables, the approach, methods and quality standards, roles and responsibilities, activities, resource allocations/estimates, schedule, control and continuous improvement tools, and schedule?

- Has the plan been accepted by all involved staff and all affected stakeholders as well as resource providers? Have all team members and management signed off on the plan and the effort required to succeed?

- Is each deliverable clearly identified as to who will be responsible for delivery, whether sign-off is required for the deliverable, and, if so, who will be responsible for accepting the deliverable?

- Does the plan include activities that will result in a "Yes" response to the questions on the QA checklist for the next safety checkpoint?

- Is a comprehensive communication plan in place to deal with management and other critical stakeholder issues?

Safety Checkpoint Assessment

At each checkpoint, the preceding types of questions should be asked. Obviously, the responses must also be evaluated and responsibilities assigned for mitigation of problems. The following form has proven useful in organizing the responses to each question.

Checkpoint Name

Safety check question

Assurance level (high, medium, low)

Potential impact of noncompliance

Person responsible for resolution

Planned action for risk reduction

Capturing this information obviously isn't sufficient. The organization must be prepared to both act on and communicate its status at each checkpoint.

Risk Management and Organizational Culture

Despite the proven value of actively managing risk, it's still not often practiced in a formalized way. Adopting and actively pursuing formal risk management brings us face to face with the same problem that comes with any new approach. The development of a process or method for doing it is easy in comparison to getting people to actually do it. For those who have attempted to raise the level of maturity of professional practices in organizations, this is no surprise. In any change, the adoption of the approach is often the limiting factor, not the availability of a process to do it. Why is this the case?

Especially in North America, organizations are typically dubious about introducing another "process" that will seem to add more overhead or non–value-added activities. Management of projects, risk, and quality—and any other formalized approach to work—is often seen as just taking time away from doing "real work," so it tends to not be supported even if it's apparently understood intellectually.

An interesting dilemma also occurs when organizations take a managed approach to projects and risk. The projects tend to be less chaotic, and heroes are not required. However, many organizations will reward the "heroes" who emerge from chaos. These same organizations do little for those who manage well in a more calm and controlled environment. Managing crisis by chasing the symptoms of preventable problems brings more visibility than by anticipating and avoiding them. The crisis managers are often rewarded highly for their apparent commitment above and beyond the call of duty. They love a challenge that recognizes action or—better yet—reaction.

In many organizations, it's even worse. *Risk* is a four-letter word that shouldn't even be mouthed. Risk is associated with uncertainty, and it can be career suicide to admit or even hint that some things aren't fully known, even though true professionals realize that not everything can be anticipated. Some initiatives might never be approved or funded if it's perceived that uncertainties and risks are involved. Hence, the issue of risk is never brought up until a problem has occurred, and the problem can't be avoided or hidden any longer. When it comes to light, everyone involved has covered his or her tracks so well that the cause can never be found. This is fertile ground for new heroes. The question is, "When would you like to deal with an issue—before it has negative consequences or after?" Experienced practitioners know that you can deal with most problems at small cost before they happen or at great cost later. It's your choice. Ignoring a risk won't make it go away. Hope and good luck won't suffice as your mitigation strategy.

In many cases, this thinking seems to be deeply rooted in the personal behavior of those running the projects. Their belief seems to be that good project managers do not need to know or apply formal risk management or project management because they are already "good project managers." Adopting organization-wide, formal methods also seems to some managers an unjust imposition on their management style that implies a lack of control or lack of competence. This might come from personal pride or even a deep-seated insecurity in their own ability to master the methods. There's also the concern that these professional methods won't be used to ensure a good process and avoid problems but that they will to be used to control people and unjustly blame or punish anyone in a position of authority later when things go wrong, even if it's not their fault. These programs must be used as, and seen as, help, not an audit of the individual. A change in methods must not be taken personally.

I can relate to this feeling that risk management is more about blame, and not risk mitigation. Once I was ordered by my CEO to take on a business improvement initiative that was already more than double the budget and tracking a year late. I was told to "get it going." One of the first things I did was to introduce a risk committee to meet at defined checkpoints to ensure some quality practices and start to gain some common commitment to what needed to be done. In the first meeting, I presented the findings that I had accumulated from my first few weeks on the job with a plan to get it on a track that I was confident could be accomplished. In that meeting, many of those involved in the fiasco leading up to that point were the ones most interested in looking backward to deflect blame onto the new person on the job. They didn't want to look forward to the factors that had to be managed. It took all my self-control, tact, and experience to let them know that I didn't particularly care about the past but was focused on what we had to do—a clean start from here.

These cultural and personal barriers have led many organizations to reactively focus on their top problems at any point in time and then call this their "risk management approach." This isn't sufficient because there will always be a long line of new problems to solve, just waiting to raise their heads as symptoms of the lack of avoidance that should have happened earlier. This behavior can be found in all aspects of life, as so eloquently recognized by Steven Covey's principle of "Putting first things first."[5] This principle advocates that we move away from doing urgent things and toward important ones. Covey strongly argues that we move to what he refers to as Quadrant II thinking and more importantly Quadrant II action. This quadrant emphasizes doing the important but, not urgent activities that will prevent us from having to do more and more of the urgent later. As Covey states, "Effective people aren't problem minded; they are opportunity minded...they think preventatively."[6] Our challenge is to get organizations to act the same way. We must overcome the attitude that "worrying about risks before acting or making commitments is wimpish..., while conveyors of bad news are...whiners."[7]

---

[5]*The Seven Habits of Highly Effective People. Steven R. Covey, New York, Simon and Schuster, 1989*
[6]*Ibid. page 154.*
[7]*"Software Risk Management: Dispatches from the Front." Robert N. Charette, Cutter IT Journal, Volume 11 No 6 (June 1998) pages 6–12*

Summary

Reducing the risk of failure is still an inexact practice that requires humans to make their best assessment of what can go wrong. However, as I have attempted to show, risk can be managed with some diligent activities that will minimize the chance of poor results and lack of performance. The challenge is, and will always be, to judge correctly how much time should be spent on this type of activity. To reduce risk to zero would mean massive overhead, and the job would never be done. This can become a risk in itself. However, just hoping and praying, that by not spending any time on a potential problem, everything will turn out fine is simply dreaming; this lack of action will come back to haunt you. Finding the balance between the extremes is the trick. It requires an approach as well as experience.

Often, the biggest reason for failure is the inability to get your stakeholders to change. Getting stuck in old beliefs and behaviors will certainly prevent success. Be sure to include an assessment of stakeholders' willingness to change in your risk evaluation. Getting people out of their past is not a trivial undertaking. Chapter 8, "Human Change," will deal specifically with how this can be accomplished.

Human Change

IN THIS CHAPTER

The challenge of getting people to change typically becomes very visible shortly after any new business models are introduced or technologies are adopted. For some strange reason, the new approach is expected to magically go in unopposed and to be greeted with open arms. When the welcome mat doesn't appear, organizations and project teams then scramble to recover and do some patch-up form of communication very late in the game—often with very poor results. A strong cultural bias exists against budgeting time and resources for activities that aren't the initiative's prime performance objective.

We seem to understand the building or conversion of the things that we are delivering. Things such as facilities are easy to see and understand in terms of their status of change. Measurements of "percentage complete" are often used to track progress. Activities such as data conversion and application migration are deemed necessary, and a budget of time and resources needed for them are expected.

But when do you convert or transform the most volatile and valuable resources: your people and your relationships with them? How can you provide new capability when the human element is the critical component, and it's not in anyone's plans or intentions? Transforming the humans can be the critical success factor in any rollout and the biggest risk factor if not done exceptionally well.

Clearly, perspectives vary on the issue of human transition, depending on whom you ask. At best, management and those charged with getting a transformation to work see human change as a necessary but bothersome task that just slows down the required "real" work. Staff and other humans affected by the change feel it as a personal impact that brings uncertainty and threatens them at the deepest levels. Managers often treat human transition—when they even acknowledge it—as a broad-based initiative involving a task sequence that must be conducted in a disciplined order and run it as a program or project. The humans expected to make the transition see it emotionally as something that will affect their jobs, careers, ability to care for their families, and their sense of competency as well as self-esteem. Management approaches the transition as a mass program. Staff members know that each one of them is different, with varying concerns that can't simply be handled with mass approaches. Management believes that staff should understand why the change is necessary and that, if they don't, better explanations will do the trick. Staff members know that, regardless of what management says, they will be uncertain as to what will really happen; there will be lots of unknowns, and changes won't go as planned.

These perspectives on human transition are totally different. Management has an intimate knowledge of external business driver realities, and staff has an unparalleled knowledge of the realities of front-line work practices. It's as if the senior management team has been equipped with only telescopes with a long future focus and can't see anything about today's details and realities up close. At the same time, the front-liners appear to have been issued microscopes to examine a tiny part of what is present and close. Neither tool helps one party see or understand the perspective of the other. It's no wonder that large divergences often exist in approaches and acceptance. This is where professionals can help bridge the gap.

There's no shortage of books and theories on getting people to change. Like the human being itself, this area is complex and often hard to understand. I won't attempt to repeat all the good academic and professional work that has gone on before me. Instead, I will focus on a few fundamental ways of thinking about the challenges and present a few approaches that I have found to work well when taken seriously. Within these there is room for innovation and refinements and a home for other techniques. Without the fundamentals, however, other techniques might look like an insincere attempt to conduct some cosmetic activity that might make the trust factor between management and staff erode, and the effort fail.

The basis of my way of viewing this issue and the approach to change is twofold:

- I believe that everyone, even in positive situations, goes through a worsening in attitude before perceptions improve, if they ever do.

- I feel that the process of navigating this type of change is a journey with ups and downs and unanticipated scenarios. Although the specific circumstances will be unknown, the types of situations can be somewhat anticipated and planned by using an approach that focuses on people's behaviors, beliefs, and concerns, whether they are rational or not. I believe this requires some active diligence to manage the journey and that it is "real work" with human behavioral change as the deliverable. It requires focussed and dedicated resources with accountabilities for transitioned people.

I will deal with these two major aspects and not delve into the other complexities. I will try to make this chapter as useful as possible by describing not only the desired conduct but also describing what to do to achieve it. Many models are descriptive but not helpful. As Sir Isaac Newton is attributed to have said, "I can describe gravity's behavior, but I don't know how it works." I will try to do a little better than Newton.

Behavioral Change

My first real awakening to the difficulties of change came a number of years ago when my wife and I attended an evening community course titled "Raising Responsible Children." We went because we felt that we could always improve our skills in raising our kids. Our children were 6 and 10 years old, and we knew that the best we could do for them was to have them grow up as responsible adults, who could cope and thrive. We felt that the way to get there was to have them learn responsible behavior as children first. To do this, we knew that they would have to change their current behaviors. We were looking forward to the 14-week course when we went to our first weeknight session with other parents just like ourselves.

In the first 10 minutes of the first session, the facilitator drew a curve on the blackboard that really got my attention. It's repeated here as Figure 8.1.

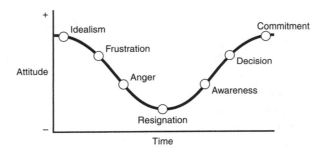

FIGURE 8.1

Attitude of participants in a change process.

The essence of what she said to us that night is that to change our children's behavior, we must change our own behavior first by doing and saying different things in different ways. It also meant that we had to do what we said we would do and stick to our commitments and promises, which seemed like a novel concept in parenting at the time. This was a real shock for some of the people in the room, and it seemed like it would be a lot of hard work that we hadn't counted on. We were hoping for some quick fixes so that we could all live happily ever after.

As it turned out, this was to be the good news. The bad news was that we could expect things to get worse before they got better, assuming that we had the fortitude and perseverance to stay with it long enough. We were warned that when we changed our actions and words, the kids would suspect that something was up and push to discover the real new limits. They would test their parents until it was clear what was acceptable, and whether the parents really meant it. We were warned that we might reach the frustration level and conclude that the transition is just not working. The facilitator said that we might even get to a point where we could just give up and abandon our program. If we stuck with it, however, we were assured that we would gradually see signs of positive results and make the intellectual decision to stick with it. With time, our children and we would then make the emotional transition and start to live the new behaviors and change our beliefs, which would lead to a change in behavior. It would be tough, require diligence, and wouldn't proceed linearly. This class made a difference and our children are growing into fine people—however, I learned as much about how to deal with people in organizations as I did about parenting.

How People React to Change: The Journey

The attitude curve that I learned in our parenting class is an example of the classic three-stage journey of human change. The journey is taken from a different perspective than the perspective we take on the transformations of most other things, such as facilities, technologies, data, and the like. Normally, the approach to change is to start with the end in mind and work backward through the activities to the current requirements. This also has some merit in changing humans because we have to know where we want them to be at the end of the journey. We must also keep in mind that they aren't starting with the new vision in mind if they suspect that it might not be their vision. Where they are today will be their dominant focus and perspective. We must end something before we can start something new, and we have to manage their transition to the new vision from that point of view.

Individuals typically have no problem starting something new, but they have great difficulty in ending something old, even if the new should be far more attractive logically. Business change drives toward a situational event. Transition is the internal process people go through to accept change and modify their behavior.

The three-stage journey, then, is composed of

- The ending state, followed by
- The transition state, followed by
- The emerging state (or the beginning)

In many ways, this journey is like a hockey game or any team sport: Figure 8.2 depicts the challenge. To be successful as a player and a team, it's essential to be able to score goals in the opponents' net. But to do that, you first have to clear your own zone and leave it behind in circumstances wherein pressure is on you all the time. When you're outside the ending zone and in the neutral transition zone, you can focus resources on the challenge of entering your opponents' zone and aim at accomplishing team objectives. Clearly, it's unlikely that games will be won, or transitions accomplished, by trying to score from the other end of the ice. Each zone requires a plan and commitment for movement to the next.

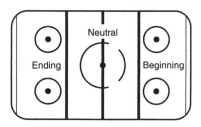

FIGURE 8.2
Leaving the past behind: The key to transition and new beginnings.

The Ending

Regardless of circumstances, people typically will think about what they have to give up more than what they will gain, even in circumstances that currently are unpleasant. Consequently, I believe that trying to sell the benefits of the change too soon is unwise. Instead, it seems to be more effective to show that you understand their situation, and to legitimize the losses and allow them to mourn those losses as they do with any passing. This is a normal human reaction and a required step in letting go, so let's not fight it.

Clearly, the ending is the hardest part for all humans to deal with. Everything that makes them valuable to the organization and the organization to them is now in question. They are concerned about having to put aside current behaviors, beliefs, friendships, relevant competencies, relationships, and many other aspects of their working situation. They are also afraid of what they don't know yet. A natural consequence of this painful time is paralysis. Humans will get caught up in their uncertainty, suspect the worst, and not move toward new action because it might be perceived as a risk personally. As a result, a valid strategy often can be to raise the visibility of the need to change from the current situation.

A Chinese proverb states, "The greatest opportunities are created out of crisis. Crisis forces people to change, and change often brings new opportunity." That might be true, but creating a crisis is just a starting point that will be a step backward if unaccompanied by a plan to transition to something new. In any event, an organization's human resources and other stakeholders must come to the realization emotionally that staying the same isn't an option. Sometimes brutal honesty and absolute proof are required to get them to move from their current beliefs.

The Change/Dissatisfaction Curve in Figure 8.3 depicts three possible states of belief for an organization's staff. Some might be in one segment, whereas others see the situation quite differently. The challenge is to get everyone to the middle, which will take different tactics and timings for different people.

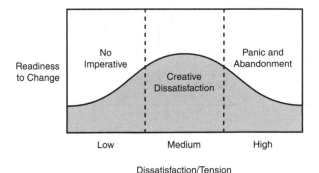

FIGURE 8.3

The relationship between dissatisfaction and readiness to change.

The high dissatisfaction segment implies that staff members truly understand that an ending has to come soon, but they have no confidence in the chance of success of the change program. These staff members might be your best workers, who will jump ship if they believe that it's sinking. In this situation, it's best to normalize the dissatisfaction level by reassuring staff and trying to build their confidence. Focus on the methods to be used in the transformation; show that the methods are professional and that they will work. It will probably mean showing how other organizations have made changes in similar circumstances. Normalizing dissatisfaction can also require communicating more information and training staff on the process of change. For these people, faster delivery efforts might be a useful approach, focusing on the long-term benefits of doing the transformation right and proving results as you go by breaking initiative into smaller scope segments. In any event, it's useful to let the staff grieve somewhat, and give them time to get it out of their system.

The low dissatisfaction segment shown in Figure 8.3 symbolizes staff members who feel that everything is OK as far as they are concerned. Why bother doing this? Clearly, the organization has to foster a deep awareness that staying the same is a threat to the organization and to the individuals in it. This can seem like a thankless job. To normalize dissatisfaction toward the middle, it might be required to increase pressure from above or to raise the bar on performance objectives based on real threats from a competitor and other external sources. This requires getting a lot of data/statistics that are irrefutable proof and dispassionately but strongly presenting them. The results of benchmarking and of customer surveys are hard to argue with. Measured stakeholder-based facts and outside perceptions of current performance cut through the suspicion of internally driven change at the whim of management. The staff might not like what they're told or thank you, but this sort of pressure is key to get the transition journey started. Tools such as industry surveys, visits to customer sites, focus groups, direct feedback through questions and complaints, market research surveys, and sales feedback information are invaluable. They allow management and project professionals to strongly make the case for change without it being quite so emotional.

The ending phase is typically short when handled well. However, it's characterized by strong feelings of pain and anger. Those affected often experience loss of identity and sometimes feel threatened. Most people value what they do and the environment that they do it in as much as what they create. For some, what they do is their whole identity. Losing it can be painful.

Transition

The transition period can be the most agonizing stage of change management and can last a long time because of frequent backsliding of morale and lack of constant attention by change agents and management. It's a time when messages can be inconsistent both over time and across messengers. This period is filled with confusion, soul searching, and doubt among those affected. It's a true test of management commitment and resolve.

This period is sometimes referred to as "between trapezes time," when individuals have let go of the old but haven't yet acquired the new. Although staff members are moving toward the future, they still tend to idealize the past and be skeptical about their destination. On the change curve in Figure 8.1, it equates to trying to climb out of the valley's depths and crawl up the right side. This slope is slippery, and it's easy to fall backward. Each retreat can lead to more reluctance to try again. The trust so important to transition can erode, and the gulf between managers and staff can widen.

The transition period is a time of self-doubt and discomfort leading to active or passive resistance and generally unproductive behavior. It's a time when people feel confused, awkward, ill at ease, and self-conscious. This is normal and to be expected. Staff and their managers must be made aware of this. This is a time to communicate what's happening so that people are better prepared and don't feel so alone. (Interestingly, these feelings of loneliness occur despite everyone else also going through the change.) At this point, we should seek to structure any activities that create involvement. We should actively encourage sharing of ideas and work together to help each other through the change.

At this point, the old and new might coincide regarding the work to be done. It's like trying to rewire your house with the lights still on. It's risky and requires extra work. It's not unusual, then, to find that people will be concerned that they don't have enough resources in terms of time, money, skills, and so on. Be sure to encourage creative problem solving in a team setting.

Be cautious about taking the pressure off to be nice; people will revert back to old behavior, and you won't be helping them in the long run, only dragging out the pain. The journey must be managed with the destination in mind. Remember to be realistic because humans can handle only so much change. Be clear about your priorities and go for the long run.

For each individual, the transition journey will vary because every person has a unique set of drivers, personality, background, and concerns. For each observation of lack of progress, it's useful to identify the holdup. Is it that the individual isn't aware of some essential information? If so, focus on communicating the what, why, how, when, who, and so on. Is it that they fear that they aren't capable? If so, focus on educating them and training them in new skills and tools. Is it that they aren't willing? If so, focus on setting clear personal and business goals and measures, provide coaching and feedback, and reward and recognize relentlessly.

The New Beginning

When the transition is well under way, we will witness the beginning of the new beliefs, commitments, and behaviors. With this comes a renewed sense of belonging and dedication. Staff demonstrate a strong ability to let go of past behavior and are filled with fresh energy and a sense of purpose. The most obvious behaviors witnessed are confidence, energy, and productivity. Staff members now anticipate the new future with a sense of excitement. The new beginning is an outcome of realizing the management of the transition phase.

Handling People's Concerns

One of the more useful models for helping plan human change as well as diagnose its current state is a concerns-based approach. Several practitioners and authors have been advocating this view in recent years. It's practical and manageable if the commitment exists to see it through.

Concerns-Based Adoption Model (CBAM)

The origin for much of today's thinking on the topic stems from pioneering work conducted at the Center for Research and Development in Teaching at the University of Texas at Austin. The foundation for this approach to managing the acceptance and adoption of change lays in the massive programs of educational renewal led by the U.S. federal government and other agencies in the 1960s. These new programs apparently failed because of the lack of attention paid to individual change. Building better curricula, researchers discovered, didn't translate to improved educational performance because the concerns and beliefs of those required to deliver the programs were neither considered nor managed. Although there has been great interest in and acceptance of the concerns-based approach within the realm of education for some time, it is just recently that many human change practitioners have come to realize that the impact of change is the same for any professionals or workers. The principles discovered in the educational world are universally relevant[1]:

- Change is a process, not an event, and it takes time to institute change.

- Individuals must be the focus if change is to be facilitated. Institutions won't change until their members change.

- The change process is an extremely personal experience. How the individual perceives it will strongly influence the outcome.

- Individuals progress through various stages regarding their emotions and capabilities relating to the innovation.

- The availability of a client-centered diagnostic/prescriptive model can enhance the individual's facilitation through staff development.

- People responsible for the change process must work in an adaptive and systematic way where progress needs to be monitored constantly.

CBAM Stages of Concern

The Concerns Based Adoption Model (CBAM) has several components. The one with the greatest relevance for planning the transition during a major initiative is usually referred to as

---

[1] *"Taking Charge of Change," Shirley M. Hord, William L. Rutherford, Leslie Huling-Austin, and Gene E. Hall, Southwest Education Development Laboratory, 1987*

the Stages of Concern (see Figure 8.4). People will navigate these transition levels as they move toward full adoption of the change. This concept is remarkably similar to Maslow's Hierarchy of Need[2] shown in Figure 8.5. Maslow's work showed that each level of personal need can be addressed only after the prior ones are satisfied. Each level has its own peculiarities and types of concerns. The Concerns Based Adoption Model works in the same way. Higher stages of concerns aren't apparent until the lower stages are dealt with.

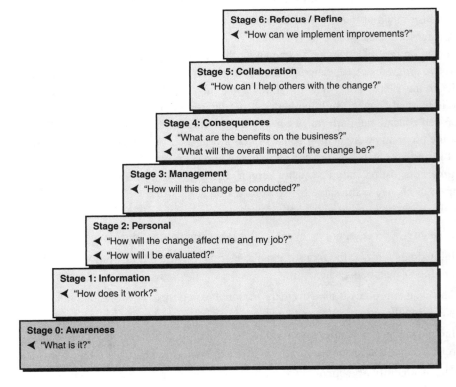

FIGURE 8.4

The CBAM Stages of Concern.

---

[2]Motivation and Personality, *2nd Edition., Abraham Maslow, Harper & Row, 1970*

FIGURE 8.5

Maslow's Hierarchy of Need.

The Stages of Concern can form the basis for the initial and ongoing change management and communications program. Communications and change tactics will vary depending on the stage in which each individual finds himself. One could easily argue that there's no point communicating to staff the benefits that will accrue to customers if the incumbent workers still don't know if they will be employed at the end of the business transformation. Their concerns are different, and they will change as the effort progresses as long as the business is diligent about moving staff members up the levels one by one. As with Maslow's hierarchy, skipping levels won't work.

Specific questionnaires can be developed to identify the stage at which an individual currently sits. If graphically represented, the concerns at the beginning of a business transformation will be skewed around the initial personal stages. During the course of the initiative, the peak set of concerns will move along to the other stages in a fashion not unlike a snake devouring its prey. The role of the change agent is to keep the meal moving by addressing the day's relevant issues.

In any event, it's appropriate to listen carefully to the things that people are saying, or to ask about and then figure out the stage at which they might be stuck. At that point, determine the needs of the individuals and answer the questions or address the concerns they might have. Actively try to get them to move to the next level. If it's premature, you will soon find out. You will have to work to get people to move from very self-oriented perspectives (What's in it for me?), through activity-oriented thinking (How will I do this work?), to result-oriented mindsets (How can I help improve on the outcomes?). Addressing these issues in the wrong order just leads to frustration, loss of credibility, and submerging of true concerns, which will only arise again when it's too late to prevent symptoms.

The position of the individuals affected by the change, as measured on Maslow's Hierarchy of Need, will also drive the nature and type of concerns that people will have. For those who are at the base level of physiological needs, concerns might center on their ability to feed, house, and clothe their families. For those at the safety need level, a focus on self-preservation issues—such as job security or being able to continue to meet physiological needs—will likely predominate. For those at the love and belonging social level, the need for meaningful relationships can be reflected in belonging to organizations, and being considered part of a group. More mature self-esteem needs show up as threats to confidence in maintaining or regaining mastery of a skill and recognition from others. At the highest level of self-actualization, the issues in focus become the challenges to being all the person can be and contributing to altruistic causes for personal satisfaction and the greater good.

It's impossible to predetermine the exact concerns that everyone might have. In addition to those common ones regarding lower level issues, which predominate early in the transition period, some other typical personal concerns are as follows:

Basic Concerns

Will I have the same job?

Will I have *any* job?

Will I have a future?

Will I like my new job?

Will I be able to do the new job?

How will my compensation be affected?

Will I have to move?

Task-Related

Will I have sufficient resources to do the new job?

Will the new work allow me to learn and increase my skills and abilities?

Will I get help with existing projects or unwanted workload during the changeover?

Will I have access to the required human and documented knowledge to do the job?

Position-Related

Will I be recognized and acknowledged for my effort, accomplishments, commitment, and capabilities?

Will I be rewarded?

Will this give me the opportunity to be seen by key influencers in the organization?

Relationship-Related

Will I be able to collaborate with others?

Will I have my concerns listened to and understood?

Will I have friends and close associates?

Will I have the support and backing of others around me?

Personal-Related

Will I have sufficient control and influence over my work?

Will this be consistent with my personal values and principles?

Will I have a sense of contribution?

Will I be able to do what I have to do without receiving too much control or aggravation?

Inspiration-Related

Will I be involved in work that will be significant for our stakeholders?

Will I be able to do these things really well?

Will I be able to do what's morally and ethically correct?

How the Process Management Framework Itself Can Help

As mentioned several times in this book, the Process Management Framework has been designed with not only business transformation and process management in mind, but also human transition. A number of the Framework's features support the human journey. Some features will make the ongoing operation of the new business approach viable for the people involved, through the design of specific deliverables required to put in place appropriate mechanisms. Other parts of the Framework address how the project is run and the roles people will play in its conduct.

Structural Changes

The intent behind a number of specific deliverables in the Framework is to design the human structures and systems required to operate according to the new business approach. These designs encompass social solutions or project approaches that change organizational culture and human behavior to align it with the desired outcomes of the envisioned business process. All of these will contribute to the knowledge of the solution and to the communication program required to satisfy concerns. The structural changes will deal with people, their relationships to one another, and their motivations. These include the following:

- Based on the envisioned new process design, appropriate supporting roles are designed, and responsibilities for them are defined. The roles and responsibilities evolve throughout the Framework as explicit deliverables.

- The organizational structure is formally articulated, in terms of who reports to whom and/or the teams to which the roles belong. Roles are cross-related to the process.

- The decision making process and the levels of decision making empowerment are articulated with clearly related accountabilities documented.

- Performance measures, rewards, and incentives for each team and role are finalized.
- Career structures and personal growth opportunities are made clear.

All these changes are defined in the Process Management Framework, and each should be designed so that humans can be successful. Structural changes must reduce the uncertainties and support the communications program. Many concerns will arise or stay if these aspects aren't actively planned and managed.

Project Management

Chapter 6, "Project Management Essentials," showed the importance of managing the progress of deliverables throughout the Process Management Framework's phases. The project management activities also are a prime vehicle to manage communications, understanding, and commitments. One of the most valuable things that we can do through project management of the framework is to seek to include and to build levels of participation. Figure 8.6 shows the philosophy that members of the core project team have a responsibility beyond their direct involvement in conducting assigned project activities of the framework. They must carry out their responsibilities representing the areas from which they were selected for the project, but they must also do more. They must be seen as facilitators of wider involvement. By coordinating an extended group of affected stakeholders at key analysis, design, and decision points, they can engage those who might otherwise be the source of concern. They have several opportunities, including the following, to ensure meaningful and appropriate involvement in the project steps:

- Stakeholder analysis and expectation setting
- Scoping
- Modeling and analysis
- Measurement
- Root cause analysis
- Problem solving
- Quick wins definition and implementation
- Decision making
- Planning and cyclical plan improvements
- Further involvement and communication

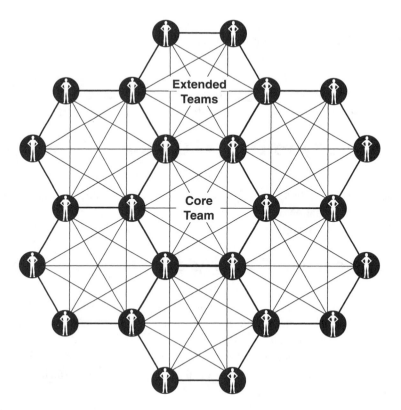

FIGURE 8.6
Extended participation through extended teamwork.

Gaining Experience

Obviously, the depth and breadth of the concerns that people will have with any change will be a factor of their degree of familiarity, understanding, and knowledge of the solution being introduced. A very good solution might still be suspect for the simple reason that those affected might not appreciate the beneficial nature of the solution or might have some degree of distrust of the developers with no reason to change their beliefs. This is especially true for situations in which people remain caught in concern stages 0, Awareness, and 1, Information, although it also applies to higher stages.

One of the most effective ways of dealing with this is to accelerate individual learning by providing lots of experience—real or simulated—as you go through the Framework. This should reduce participants' fear and feelings of being threatened. It also allows them to contribute feedback on what will or will not work and, in the process, enhance their sense of contribution to the change and their own transition.

Building such a learning environment is as much an attitude as a set of tasks. It should be controlled but non-threatening, whereby errors are perceived as "learning opportunities," not failures. Furthermore, if the feedback isn't heeded, the human transition will backslide because the effort will be seen as a sham, not as a serious attempt to include others. If the gaining of experience is done in a fun environment, a great opportunity for interaction with other stakeholders and affected departments will be achieved. It will escalate both buy-in and active cooperation.

A Methodology to Deal with Human Transition

The following approach strives to pull together the principles linking change and transition described in the previous sections. It attempts to make sense of the methods and techniques, to determine the impact of change on those affected, and to help them with the transition to a new personal beginning. In doing so, it transforms resistance to enthusiasm and commitment.

Analyze Stakeholder Concerns and Objections

Within the discussion of business context for an organization and the determination of vision for a process to be renewed, I introduced the concept and techniques for stakeholder analysis. As part of the business analysis, a set of future state attributes were defined for each relationship deemed important. It's the same set of stakeholder types that can be used to determine the set of potential concerns and responses to them at the beginning of the transition management journey. By anticipating the stakeholders' concerns, you can avoid many future obstacles. This approach recognizes that those with concerns and objections to transition won't just be your staff. Your managers, customers, suppliers, and many other stakeholders might also be concerned about the initiative, but for different reasons requiring different messages to be sent to them.

Your first step, then, is to anticipate as best you can the initial concerns and potential objections of all stakeholder types and evaluate the risks to each type should they not support the changes planned. By using the CBAM Stages of Concern, determine the beliefs that each type holds, beliefs that must change, and the kinds of responses that might get stakeholders moving on the journey from stage 0, Awareness, through to at least stage 4, Consequences, during the project. Based on this, you will be able to draft your initial transition strategy and messages as the initiative progresses and as people move through the stages of concern. This process must be repeated regularly to understand which concerns stakeholders are stuck on and whether other concerns have arisen. The changes must be reflected through the communication channels that you will establish.

Develop Statement of Principles for Renewal

From your understanding of the anticipated stakeholder concerns, you can start to develop a set of principles or commitments to your stakeholders. This doesn't mean that you will implement only changes that everyone will love because most changes will come from business necessity and might be very unattractive to some types of stakeholders. The statement of principles or change charter will lay out the rock-bottom fundamentals on which the effort will rest. This will be a set of unwavering commitments against which everyone will be expected to remain true. It's a set of mutual commitments that everyone in your organization will keep, no matter how tough, so you had better get them right and gain true support from the top. These commitments are often reusable.

Although not an exhaustive classification, some more common aspects are described in the following sections.

Core Business Principles and Values

This section revisits the beliefs, values, and principles that the organization has already committed to publicly. This is often a good starting point because it should remain stable. Reminding everyone that you will remain true to your fundamental beliefs shows constancy of leadership and cuts through potential perceptions of loss of integrity of the organization's managers. Statements such as the following aren't unusual:

- We are in business to create value for our customers. As such, it's our responsibility to provide the quality products and services they require for the lowest possible price and in the timeframes they require.
- It's also our mandate to provide an ongoing return to company owners, and to meet the requirements of other external stakeholders.
- In accomplishing these goals, it's our responsibility to provide a rewarding working environment for our staff.
- This initiative won't violate these principles.

Customer-Focused Design Principles

We all know that, in the long run, our customers pay our salaries and determine the success of our enterprise. Consequently any initiative must deliver value to them. Change principles that put the customers' perspective as the primary consideration should be made clear to everyone. You won't sway from this principle. Examples are

- End results will be measured primarily in terms of the value delivered to the customer.
- We will always make decisions on behalf of the customer as long as it doesn't violate our other corporate principles.
- We will base our solution designs on process performance and select among alternatives based on the best results.

Renewal Project Conduct Principles

A set of commitments and messages dealing with the way the project will be run is key to building confidence and serious support from the organization. Some useful statements are

- Solutions will be considered on the basis of all their implications as defined in the process renewal hexagon, not just on one aspect.

- The approach will seek to understand the current strengths and weaknesses before redesigning new processes.

- Staff at all levels will be given every opportunity to contribute insights and ideas.

- All proposals will be the subject of a properly formulated business case that takes a long-term perspective of benefits, costs, and risks.

- The business case will be revisited at major milestones, and management must authorize the subsequent phase at each.

Staff Impact Principles

At the base level of CBAM considerations and of Maslow's Hierarchy of Need is the set of personal concerns. Any set of honest principles must include a comprehensive discussion of the most common personal issues that can't be ignored no matter how difficult they are to deal with. Some examples of these principles are

- Jobs will be secure; there will be no layoffs, but people will be expected to take on new roles.

- People moving into new positions will be trained, and time will be built in to learn.

- Some people will be asked to assume positions in other units or locations.

- There might be some redundant staff as a result. If so, early retirement will be used first.

- If there have to be layoffs, those affected will be given fair treatment, including outplacement counseling and severance in accordance with the organization's collective bargaining agreements.

Management Conduct Principles

In these types of situations, many stakeholders are skeptical of management's intentions and suspect a hidden agenda. It's important, then, that management makes commitments about its own behavior that it plans to keep. The most basic of all of these is the commitment to deal continuously with all stakeholders' suspicions, fears, doubts, misunderstandings, and rumors honestly and with integrity. Managers also might want to state that they will

- Be open and share the real vision and goals.

- Communicate throughout at regular cycles and at key milestones.

- Be available for one-on-one discussions in addition to team sessions.

- Recognize and reward those who are contributing toward the project goals.

- Respond to concerns within three days.

- Give everyone a chance to input ideas and solutions.

- Always explain difficult decisions, including why and why not.
- Personally share results and findings along the way.
- Continue to challenge everyone to do better.

These categories and lists are just some of the types to be considered and are included to provoke your thinking. Each situation is different and will require unique analysis. Regardless, management must keep all stakeholders in the loop even when they think it's unnecessary. The principles listed here will cover many major and far-reaching concerns, but won't be comprehensive or specific enough for all stakeholders. A more detailed analysis will be required from the beginning through to the end of the projects, at which time the concerns at higher levels will fall into the realm of the process owner.

Develop the Communication Plan

With a solid understanding of the levels and specific types of concerns of stakeholders and a set of principles to work by, you can build a targeted communication strategy. This will determine the messages to each stakeholder group, as well as the media and timetables to be used to start and maintain the transition process.

Communication should start by addressing the set of common issues at the lowest CBAM Stage of Concern—specifically, answer questions at Stage 0, "What is the proposed change?" and Stage 1, "How does it work?" At the same time, it should develop and deliver the "Principles for Renewal." Stage 2 concerns—"How will the change affect me and my job?" and "How will I be evaluated?"—require a more targeted plan that links the stakeholder segment to the concerns addressed in the communication, as well as to the actual response, the medium, the frequency, and the messenger. An example of a communication plan for one stakeholder type, the sales staff in a district office, follows in Table 8.1.

TABLE 8.1 A Sample Communications Plan for One Stakeholder Concern

Plan Factor	Description
Stakeholder Segment	Sales staff in district offices
Concern	We will lose autonomy with the introduction of a common process and a common tracking system.
Response	It's not the solution's intent to take away any decision-making authority. The result is expected to provide better information about customers and markets so that you can be more effective. Your customers will still be your customers. You will, however, be measured and rewarded on the degree to which you share your knowledge with inside sales people and sales support organizations in the head office.

TABLE 8.1 Continued

Plan Factor	Description
Messenger	Senior VP Sales, District Sales Managers
Media	Face-to-face group presentations, sales team bulletins, personal meetings
Frequency/Timing	At project kickoff and repeatedly at quarterly sales meetings.

The communication approach listed here should start with concern management at the very beginning of the project. This is often hard for managers to swallow because they believe, "There are no problems yet. Why raise issues and open the door to problems that we would prefer not to deal with so soon?" Many also might feel that when the change management team knows all the answers, it will tell them. Management must be taught how to handle the concerns so that they are dealt with early, consistently, and credibly.

A valuable approach to dealing with this is the concept of objection management, a well-known approach in sales-oriented organizations. *Objection management* advocates anticipating objections (or concerns) and being prepared for them, instead of just responding as they occur. It goes even further, suggesting that management should bring as-yet-unstated or unrealized concerns forward. Statements such as, "Some of you might be wondering about your pension benefits under the new plan. Well, we have thought about that too, and our approach is that we will...." Even if the news might not be greeted with enthusiasm, it should be considered for a pre-emptive strike. Credibility and trust will more likely come from integrity and openness than from a perception of hiding. Consider the impact of saying that there will be no layoffs all the way through and then letting 500 staff members go at the end. Imagine the degree of cooperation and transition that wouldn't occur next time, regardless of the message.

This doesn't mean that all knowledge is present early on—it's not. But it's better to say, "We've thought about the concern and don't yet have an answer. However, consistent with our stated principles, we will let you know as soon as we do." Trust in transition comes from having proven trustworthiness, not from messages that people would love to hear—especially if the messages and messengers prove to be unreliable later.

It should be clear that you should rely on professionals with public or staff relations skills and experience to handle the actual crafting of the message and the selection of media. Producing the wrong message can have disastrous consequences.

It should likewise be clear that finding the right messenger is paramount for credibility. Those who will have ongoing business responsibility after the initiative is completed should deliver messages. This means an executive in the business area or—better yet—the process owner. In some cases, a message can come only from the CEO. I would suggest sending it down from the highest level with broad credibility that you can possibly get away with. Avoid messages of commitment about the future being sent by project team members who might not be a part of operating the solution. They might be well intentioned but have no post-initiative stake or standing.

In defining the media to be used for communications, it might be wise to use an intelligent mix of low tech and high tech. This will allow frequency and reach while engendering the trust that comes from personal delivery of messages. In any case, make sure that the mechanisms for scheduled and ad hoc communications are in place for one-on-one communication as well as for addressing a whole group. Some considerations would be formal and informal presentations, meetings and drop-in sessions, newsletters, Web sites, videos, audiotapes for the car, education sessions, e-mail, groupware, and discussion group software.

Regarding the timing and frequency of communications up, down, and out, major milestones are opportune moments—milestones as defined by key gating points and the completion of project phases. However, getting into a calendar-based routine that people can count on is also a good practice. Some communications work well monthly or bi-monthly. Each initiative will have its own pattern.

The contents of the communications must include concerns but should also cover progress. In every communication, a reminder of what you are doing and why should be present. Results of measurements, surveys, and other outside stakeholder feedback should be made known. The vision, scope, business case, plans, analysis findings, process designs, approvals, and other significant results should also be made public to build confidence. This is also a perfect opportunity to give visible credit for results, especially early wins involving front-line staff. Many concerns will disappear after stakeholders have faith that the initiative will happen successfully, is being supported, and is in good hands.

Remember that the value will come only after stakeholders see that you are really honoring the communication plan. But be careful because the plan will be discredited if it's followed blindly without genuinely listening, adjusting when necessary, and updating concerns and strategies as you progress through the project and navigate upward through the stages of concerns.

Turn Key Influencers into Change Agents

Transitioning all stakeholders at once is clearly not an option. Some will be at higher levels of readiness than others. Some will be better informed going in. Some will be more skeptical. Some will take longer. Some have fewer concerns. Within reason, a planned approach is warranted.

One factor for transitioning is trust and faith in those who are respected and trustworthy leaders. Regardless of position in the organization, certain people are looked up to for their views as a bellwether of the issues at hand. A recommended strategy is to identify the leaders whom others will follow. Treat them as the priority stakeholders to initiate the change journey.

Because they are people, too, these leaders must transition themselves through concern stages 0 through at least 4. Then, they can help do the job of getting others through their respective journeys.

To do this, you must take these priority stakeholders through the following steps and answer the appropriate questions:

- What power do the stakeholders hold, and how well are they supported?
- What will be the impact of change on them?
- What are the ranked concerns they will most likely be driven by?
- What are the responses to deal with these concerns?

You must work diligently to get these stakeholders on board by working closely with them until they are well on their way. At that point you can train them on how to navigate other stakeholders' concerns and keep the journey moving forward. At some point, a critical mass of supporters will become apparent, and the job will become easier.

Change Agent Example

In one situation with which I was involved, more than 500 front-line staff officers were affected by a project. Many specialists, then working sequentially, were to become full-service case workers. More than 50 supervisors would be the natural first line of respondents to questions from the front-line staff. Our approach was to convert the supervisors to supporting the change, and then have them play an active role in managing the transition of their team members. It was decided to take a risk and deal with all the supervisors at the same time in a one-day workshop to get the ball rolling. The concerns-based approach was adopted.

The first step that day was a presentation by the senior vice president of the unit, with questions and answers regarding stage 0 and 1 concerns. The vice president provided lots of information about the nature of the program, its reasons, and other key facts driving a particular decision. He also announced the "Principles for Renewal of the Initiative" and made a strong commitment to them. The initiative's plan also was described.

Then each group of supervisors (five to six each randomly grouped) were asked to think about themselves exclusively for a while. At round tables, they were asked to answer the question, "What are your concerns about changes that might affect you personally and as a manager?" They were given ample time to discuss and document their thoughts and feelings. Each table was asked to fill out their responses on blank transparencies with multicolored pens and to deposit them in the center of the table to be picked up during the following break. They were assured that no concern was too personal, subjective, or silly, and that full confidentiality of the author table would be maintained. The concerns sheets were then gathered and read back to the overall group of supervisors via a low-tech transparency projector. The facilitator (myself at that point) then reviewed all concerns with the whole group, and we consolidated the lists and came up with an agreed top 20 concerns of the supervisors.

At that point, the individual tables were then asked to identify a couple of appropriate responses that would deal with each concern while still meeting the objectives of the mandate and still honoring the Principles of Renewal. These, too, were reviewed as a group, and a consolidated list of actions was adopted.

Then and only then was it useful and appropriate to deal with the supervisors' staffs.

The next activity at their tables was to answer the question, "What do you anticipate will be the concerns of your staff about changes that might affect them?" These, too, were reviewed as an overall group, consolidated, and a top set defined.

The next question was, "Given what you know about the program, what are the appropriate responses to deal with your staff concerns?" After overall review, a top list of responses was developed.

The next questions dealt with the supervisors becoming change agents: "What do you think you can do to help deal with staff concerns?" and "What can you do to make the program successful?"

Subsequent to the session, the materials were consolidated, some holes filled in, and communication packages developed for the participants' use. They had become part of the solution, not the problem.

The approach worked because the participants created their own change program and, as part of the process, learned how to articulate it. A common commitment was also established among the peer supervisors to support one another with consistent messages. This would not have worked if everyone was given just a set of presentation slides through company mail.

Executing the Ongoing Communication Program

The formal communication program is effective for getting staff from concern stage 0 through to stage 4. After that point it will usually fall to the responsibility of the process owner to keep the journey alive. Stages 5, Collaboration, and 6, Refocus/Refine, are all about communicating your successes with your teammates, sharing knowledge with others, and searching for improvements in practices. These support the objectives of the Nurture and Continuously Improve phase of the Framework. This never-ending part of transition actually reflects a mindset of the incumbents that says we can always get better, no matter how good we are.

Leading up to this will be the project's development and implementation activities. During this time period, the change management team must continue to monitor concerns and continue to reinforce the responses to lower-stage concerns. The team must also craft newer and more timely responses for more recent issues and objections. This is especially important at the close of specific phases, but also on a regular calendar cycle, such as monthly. The transition of humans will progress throughout the business change and won't be done until all staff issues are dealt with.

Ten Critical Success Factors for Effective Human Transition

To summarize the key issues of this chapter, keep in mind a number of considerations in helping stakeholders navigate the often-painful journey of change. My top 10 follow:

1. **Vision.** With a well-defined destination provided by a clearly defined result or set of stakeholder criteria, the journey is never in doubt.

2. **Communications and information.** Openly providing sufficient information about who, what, when, where, why, and how reduces uncertainty, mixed messages, and confusion. The communication must be relevant and timely, and deal with the genuine concerns as they vary over time.

3. **Participation and collaboration.** Participants who create their own solutions will thereby embrace them. Collaborators create and support shared results, and will do everything necessary to make them work.

4. **Incentives.** Incentives work. Finding and committing to the right ones that are in sync with the business outcomes means that everyone is working for the business and its stakeholders.

5. **Trust.** Belief that what's being communicated is what will actually happen is a boon to navigating stages of concern. Lack of such trust can be deadly, so don't make promises you can't keep and always do what you said you would.

6. **Leadership.** Have respected leaders who make decisions and remain visible. Those who will live with the solution must make the commitments.

7. **Education and training.** Make sure that all those affected become aware and receive education on the solution and business training on the processes and enablers. Familiarity and competency break down fear and uncertainty.

8. **Resources.** Backfill the extra time required to participate and learn. Give people the tools and time to transition and become productive. They won't drop the old habits without time to pick up the new ones.

9. **Time to adapt.** No matter how positive the situation, humans need time to grieve their losses. Start the journey of transition early so that travelers can reach their destination when they need to be there.

10. **Do it yourself.** Do the projects, run the program, communicate the messages, do the work with your own staff. Outsiders producing reports and study findings can't bring transition to stakeholders. It's not their business, their commitment, or their future—it's yours. Consultants can help you with the techniques, can occasionally facilitate, and can bring outside comparisons more factually, but they should never make your decisions or try to commit to your staff.

Summary

Human change management is the hardest thing to achieve because it isn't objective. It's easy to define project steps and build plans. It's possible to get through the risk assessment with some rigor. It's virtually impossible to figure out how everyone will respond to the news that their lives will be different. Consequently, many so-called professionals ignore the issue because they are unaware of the dangers or can't deal with it. They just do the technical and procedural work instead. But you know by now that this can't be omitted. It's real work, and transitioned people are deliverables in and of themselves.

This chapter on human change management completed our look at the four aspects required for a celebration of success to take place:

- The phases and steps of the Process Management Framework
- The management of commitments and the tracking of project progress
- The careful and constant attention paid to mitigating risk
- The sensitive navigation of people through their personal journey.

These aspects must all work together.

Next is the last chapter in Part I, "A Management Guide." It provides a brief discussion of how to build a support organization to enable these four aspects to be repeated with consistency and confidence and to accelerate the learning process for all within the corporation.

8

HUMAN CHANGE

Building a Process Support Organization

IN THIS CHAPTER

Many companies have a small staff responsible for the effectiveness of process management across the organization. The nature of these groups can vary from company to company. The degree of power, control, and empowerment they have as well as the services they provide can also vary. Some of these staffs are merely advisory; others are actively involved in managing the knowledge assets produced from all process initiatives.

In setting up a process management support practice, you have to decide how far you should go and will be expected to go. This chapter examines the opportunities and possible choices that make it easier to determine what your organization should do. I will do this by treating the support group as a business in its own right and applying the Business Context and Architect and Align phases to it.

By applying the first two framework phases to your own support group, you can define your own mandate and show others that the method works. I will go through each step and examine the range of choices. You will have to choose at each point how far you should take your group.

Determining Your Business Context

At this point, your support group needs to determine its business drivers, strategic intent, stakeholder expectations, performance measurements, and critical issues.

What Are Your Business Drivers?

To work according to your accepted mission, you must understand the support group's business drivers. These are likely to include some of the group's clients' external drivers, such as market or competitive issues. They will also reflect the clients' experience with managing change, such as previous inability to adapt quickly when needed. Figure 9.1 illustrates this and other considerations in the Business Context phase.

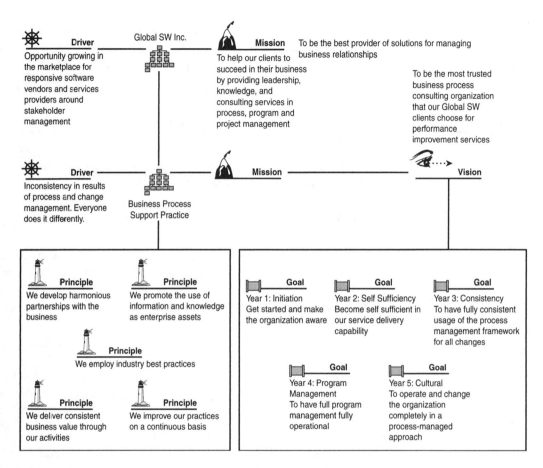

FIGURE 9.1

Process management strategic intent.

What Is Your Strategic Intent?

Strategic intent states the support group's mission, vision, goals, and principles. It also guides the choices made later concerning the group's business process and human capabilities. All design and service decisions made later must be consistent with the intent articulated in this first step.

Mission

A group's mission answers the question, "What style of operation will the support group assume?" The group might have some intense negotiations to reach a consensus on this, the most fundamental question that you must ask. The mission indicates to everyone the nature of your group's responsibility. It will show your value proposition. Figure 9.1 includes a sample mission statement for a support group.

The range of mission choices starts with a simple role to influence others' thinking about process management. Choices can extend all the way to having complete control over the design and execution of processes. Table 9.1 shows the natural progression from little involvement to complete control by a support group.

TABLE 9.1   Range of Service Styles for a Process Support Organization

Style of Service	Characteristics
Influencing	Raises awareness, runs education sessions, makes articles and references available, speaks to key managers and professionals
	Attempts to get staff to move to a process mindset and culture and to take charge of conducting process management initiatives themselves
Advising	Helps change management and project practitioners set up and conduct their own initiatives according to best process management practices
	Reviews deliverables and plans to assure quality with feedback to those responsible
	Provides standards and guidelines for use by process teams that maintain direct control
	Recommends tools
Participating	Provides people to project teams to analyze, model, interview, facilitate, document, present, and so on
	Brings own tools and recommended standards
Managing Knowledge	Manages repository of knowledge about processes, projects, and alignment to other organizational assets and structures
	Updates knowledge repository with process management outputs
	Provides reusable process knowledge to project teams
Managing	Provides project management resources and runs projects (architectural and specific processes)
	Directs process management efforts
	Manages information about programs of change on behalf of executives
Governing	Mandates standards and tools
	Runs and controls full program of aligned process and enabler change
	Vets rogue proposals against approved program
	Runs risk and quality management program

The initial value proposition is likely to be centered on innovation and provision of capability to the organization. As the support group's capability grows, it's likely to become more participatory and operational.

Vision

The vision defines where a group wants to be at the end of the planning period. This will also be affected by the choice of involvement styles in Table 9.1. Refer to Figure 9.1 for a sample vision statement.

Goals

Your support group should establish a set of specific goals to be accomplished over the planning timeframe. Some goals will be achieved earlier than others. These goals might reflect a transition in involvement style. In the early days of process renewal, it might be appropriate to plant a seed, an idea for change. Then the group can fertilize the soil with successes and key supporters to grow solid roots. The bloom of the flowers and automatic reseeding might come with a gradual culture change and the attainment of critical mass support through lessons learned. Widespread education lets the business harvest its investment benefits. Figure 9.1 illustrates how the goals support the vision and mission.

Principles

At this point, look at your corporate principles and derive a set of principles for your support group. Many will be the same as corporate's, but some will be more practice specific to your group. These are the fundamental ways of working for the process support group that will be unquestioned and that you won't violate. Naturally, management and clients must validate the group's principles.

Sample principles can be seen in Figure 9.1.

Who Cares?

Now that the support group has a reason for being, it must determine whom it will serve and with whom it must interact in order to do so. It also must be able to communicate what's required for success with its stakeholders.

A set of internal customers will receive services, and another set of internal and external providers will make this service possible. Depending on the level of style chosen while defining the mission, the service group's stakeholder groups might be widespread across the organization or narrowly focused. Figure 9.2 illustrates some stakeholders for the process support group. This set might be very similar organization to organization.

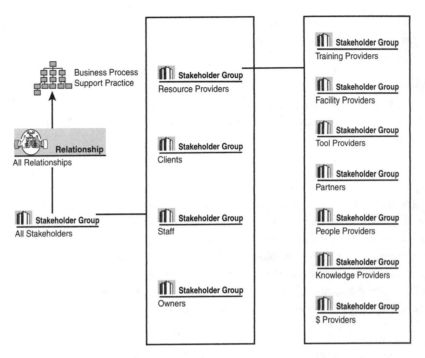

FIGURE 9.2

Process management stakeholders.

Stakeholder Expectations

To define the value of your support service, you must identify the expectations that you want to realize in your relationships with stakeholders. The same approach used in the Business Context or Vision phase should be used here. These will be affected significantly by two major decisions:

- Will use of your services be optional or mandatory? Table 9.2 shows the challenges for each option.
- Will human resources be provisioned completely from within your group? Will they come from elsewhere in the enterprise? Will they be in-sourced from outside firms? Table 9.3 shows some pros and cons for each approach.

Answers to these questions affect the relationships all around the service and your style of operation.

TABLE 9.2 Options for Use of Process Support Group Services

Group Usage Option	Challenges
Mandatory	Establishing and maintaining great relationships
	Avoiding an internal group that is not client focused
	Preventing the group from becoming non-responsive
	Mitigating a perception of non–value-added overhead
	Avoiding a no-escape perception
Optional	Maintaining a high degree of awareness and education and sense of value
	Ensuring usage and consistency of frameworks, techniques, and tools
	Getting other organizational units to document their results in common knowledge bases
	Getting teams to share
	Overcoming the perception that it will cost more to follow a disciplined approach than to just do it any way that the project team makes up

TABLE 9.3 Pros and Cons of Resourcing Options for Group Services

Pros	Cons
Business Process Support Group Resources	
Focused commitment.	Slower to build initial experience.
Consistency of method and tools and knowledge access.	Build-up of overhead cost.
Knowledge grows and remains available to service users.	Danger of internal focus and lack of currency with outside professionals.
Resources Inside the Enterprise	
Subject expertise and process capability combined.	Not main job purpose; development is sporadic.
Knowledge gained stays in company.	Distraction due to main job functions; no focus.
Low cost to initiatives.	Inconsistency of methods and tools across initiatives.

TABLE 9.3   Continued

Pros	Cons
Resources Outside the Enterprise	
Faster startup.	Lack of enterprise knowledge.
More scalable.	Loss of human knowledge from corporation.
Wider experience base and broader perspective.	Higher fees.

Critical Stakeholder Needs

To define stakeholder needs for process management services, you should define the critical success factors that must be satisfied. These factors will likely center on the accessibility of knowledgeable resources, acceptance of the whole idea from the very stakeholders you support, and management resourcing of the people and budgets.

What Are Your Products and Services?

After you somewhat solidify your group's reason for being and whom it will serve, the specific type and scope of services must be addressed. Some services can be offered initially, and others will be developed or offered later as the group learns and proves its worth.

Scope

A process management support group can enable the rest of the organization with process-oriented services. Also, as shown in Chapters 6, 7, and 8, a support group can extend its services to a much wider range of offerings that might be important to an organization undergoing change. This is especially true if transformation is expected to be difficult or risky; the organization must decide who will ensure that risky propositions are handled.

Process management, program management, project management, human change management, and risk management must have a home. The process support group must reach consensus with the rest of the organization on its role in each. Table 9.4 presents some considerations.

TABLE 9.4   Service Offering Considerations for a Process Support Group

Professional Practice	Considerations for Process Support Group
Process Management	What phases of the framework will you be involved with— just the more tactical Vision, Understand, and Renew phases, or will you participate in the more strategic Business Context and Architect and Align phases? Will your group play a role in Develop and Implement? What about ongoing Nurture and Continuously Improve phase monitoring?
	For the phases in your groups' scope, which concepts or deliverables on the maps presented in Figure 5.4 will you handle? To what degree will you advise rather than participate?
Program Management	Will you manage the project portfolio defined as a result of the architecture migration strategy and/or the process transformation strategy?
	Will you handle the process portions or all the enabler development?
	Will you be involved in defining the transformation program and defending it from unplanned initiatives?
Project Management	Will you supply support for the management of process projects?
	Will you deal with planning and control aspects?
	Will you manage the projects or just support the managers?
Human Change Management	Will you advise and help with the development of human transition plans?
	Will you develop communications strategies?
	Will you craft messages and/or deliver them?
Risk Management	Will you be involved in defining quality criteria for process project deliverables?
	Will you provide or develop questions for risk assessment checkpoints?
	Will you manage the QA team and deal with risk reduction strategies?

Specific Products and Services

Many products and services can help the process support group fulfill its service mandates.

Reference Materials

The group can make a set of reference materials available to project staff and process managers. These reference materials, such as the following, can guide efforts and ensure repeatability and sharing:

- **Methodology framework.** A comprehensive process management guide, such as described by this book, can be made available to all managers and practitioners. It could also be accessed on a company intranet.
- **Technique descriptions.** How-to guidelines for specific steps such as process modeling, process analysis, and interviewing can assist in doing detailed tasks.
- **Training materials.** Slides and other visual media describing the application and usage of methods and techniques can be made available to all qualified trainers and for reference.
- **Books, articles, and online readings.** Lists and access to other related materials can be provided to increase the knowledge of interested parties.

Tool Access

The support group can research, evaluate, select, and tailor a set of software tools to support the work in the strategic, tactical, realization, and operational modes of the framework. These tools can be low tech, or high tech and automated:

- *Low-tech tools* include templates for the various information-gathering exercises that the process analysts and designers will conduct. They also include templates of wall-chart size, forms, graphics and word processing starter kits, facilitation kits, and interview kits, all related to a specific framework phase and step.
- *High-tech tools* include software to make the framework's methods accessible to its users and guide them through the steps. Hundreds of tools on the market claim to be process-support tools, with a wide range of capabilities and prices. What you'll buy depends on what you want to do and the knowledge available as a result of the software's use. A large difference exists between various tools and technologies, as shown in Table 9.5.

TABLE 9.5   Characteristics of Various Automated Support Tools

Tool Type	Tool Characteristics
Simple drawing and flowcharting	Simple graphics tools that connect named shapes with other shapes.
	They don't manage concepts, meaning, or context in an active repository.
	Poor choice for large or complex interrelated models in which changes often have to be made.

TABLE 9.5 Continued

Tool Type	Tool Characteristics
	Good for presentations, not for knowledge management.
	Easy to learn.
	Inexpensive.
Process modeling and analysis	More sophisticated tools that manage information and graphics and keep both in sync with one another.
	Based on knowledge repository or database.
	Usually process oriented with few links to other types of asset knowledge.
	Allows graphical entry and display of results.
	Can be standalone or multiuser with check-in/check-out capability.
	Captures process knowledge, including process metrics, according to a predefined standard format or strict methodology.
	Includes various levels of model integrity checking according to modeling rules.
	Generates reports.
	Has some version control and audit trail.
	Some provide dynamic links with spreadsheets and other tools.
	Good for projects, but not as good for architecture and not very suitable for program management.
Object-oriented modeling	Models knowledge according to meta-models of your business concepts and how they relate to one another.
	Models interactions among different types of concepts, such as processes, technologies, and organization.
	Flexible and easy to change concept definitions and instances.
	Provides full integrity through conformance to built-in, defined rules.
	Model composed of business objects related to other business objects, according to defined connection types; the connectors have a specific meaning that can be queried.
	Allows many different views of the same information.
	Any change in an object is updated everywhere that the object is used—on all diagrams, reports, and in the knowledge base.

TABLE 9.5 Continued

Tool Type	Tool Characteristics
	The approach of choice for architecture and program management, where changes and impacts are significant and must be managed.
	Might provide or have links to object-oriented technology development, including C++ and Java environments.
Simulation/ animation	Models business performance variables based on extensions to the process or object models defined earlier in this table.
	Works from the assumption of variation and randomness according to statistical patterns of events and resource efficiency.
	Captures different scenarios of the process according to a set of chosen model parameters (usually time, cost, resources, and events).
	Animation graphically shows the paths being executed across the graphical process model.
	Produces statistics of performance over a sample period of time, based on assumed constraints on the variables. Tallies up an overall report for the tested timeframe.
	Allows the running of the process to examine outcomes under different "what-if?" situations.
	Good for experimenting, especially with different resource allocation alternatives.
	Only as good as the statistical assumptions applied to information.
	Deals well with only a restricted number of variables.
	Overkill for many process types but useful for those with large volume of transactions and many operational resources.

Some of these technologies are very methodology specific, encompassing specific ways of doing the work in the framework phases and steps. Business landscape, process architecture, technology architecture, organization design, stakeholder analysis, scope, process models, and scenarios are just a few of the types of models that can be captured and analyzed with the help of tools built on an integrated knowledge base. Examples of some of these models are shown in Chapter 5 and in Chapters 10 through 16. These sample models that connect many different business concepts were built with the support of an object-oriented knowledge tool from Ptech, Inc. (www.ptechinc.com).

With regard to tools, process support groups can play a number of roles depending on their choice of approach, as shown earlier in Table 9.1. The group can act as a source of knowledge about tools and recommend specific software, or it can acquire tools and make them available. It can also be the tool operator for initiatives or even the custodian of a tool, mandating its use.

Awareness, Marketing, Education, and Training

The process support group can play the key role in ensuring that an organization understands the process management environment. This can range from simple raising awareness to offering training on the business rationale and the ways of doing the work. For this aspect, your group might have to strike relationships with outside training providers if you don't do this yourself.

Business Justification Awareness

The awareness-raising aspect of the support group's responsibility will typically emphasize the business value of the process-centric approach. By using various media and messengers, it will address the questions of "What is this change?" and "Why should we do it?" The answers must deliver a consistent and compelling argument.

Methodology Education

Delivering the education required to truly understand the framework's approach and methods ensures the capability and consistency of process and project participants. You must decide whether your group will develop and run this training or have outsiders do it. If outsiders are chosen, will you hold the training in your own dedicated sessions or send staff to public training sessions offered through organizations such as DCI (www.dci.com) and IRM (www.irmuk.co.uk)? Will you mandate certain classes or just recommend them?

Techniques Training

What's true for method education is also true for the process and project participants' training in techniques. How will you deliver capability in such aspects as modeling, interviewing, facilitation, and measurement? Will it be hands-on or seminar style? Will you use automated training approaches and self-help?

Tool Training

Who will deliver training on the effective use of tools? Will your group do it, or will you ask the tool vendor to do it for you? Will it be tailored to the method steps that you have picked, or will it be off-the-shelf? Will you do it onsite or in public vendor classes? Ask these questions and make sure you are ready logistically to support technology-based training sessions.

Consulting Services

The progressions shown earlier in Table 9.1 will strongly influence the level and type of consulting service you will provide. These will range from providing management and real expertise to simply proving access to outside help:

- **Expert business consulting.** The support group can house and make available experts and leaders in the various aspects of the business. These staff members would be hired or brought into the group based on their industry-leading knowledge in one or more specific aspects of relevance to the enterprise's mandate. These subject matter experts would act as advisors and gatekeepers on the direction of the business design in their areas of expertise.

- **Process-management consulting.** The group can also be the source of world-class expertise on process management methods and techniques to be applied to any subject that the business would like to renew.

- **Facilitation.** One aspect of support often provided is access to the facilitation expertise so desperately needed on most projects. This underappreciated capability can make or break the consensus to move forward with an integral solution. A support group can provide facilitation to business-managed or support-group–managed efforts.

Business Knowledge Repository

Decisions on what business knowledge to store and make available to the business process owners and participants will be consistent with your decisions about which aspects of the Process Management Framework your group will support. If the group supports the Business Context phase, all the strategic intent and stakeholder information will be potentially available to those in the business and in projects that can leverage that information for decision making.

If the group has put its effort into the development of architectures and their alignment with one another, it will be able to support program management and resource allocation decisions.

If the results of the Vision, Understand, and Renew phases are recorded, the previous projects' knowledge and documentation can help new projects that interact with the renewed processes. Making existing process, input, guide, output, and enabler usage available can be invaluable, along with knowledge of which business rules are in place and where they are used.

Providing information about resource skills and availability will also pay off. Linking this type of information to the strategic intent and projects planned or under way will allow planners and managers to adjust and reprioritize with less risk.

Access to Process Management Framework Knowledge Sources

The process support group can also provide a great deal of know-how regarding best practices for using the framework. This knowledge, if renewed frequently, will keep the group's value intact and the organization moving forward in capability in process management. Some categories of potential knowledge that your support group can provide follow.

Framework Guidelines

Offline or online, it's potentially useful to provide step-by-step guidance through the framework of change. Help can be provided through models and documentation of the framework process and the techniques that support it. Also, other related guidelines can be added, such as help in estimating and quality assurance. Topics should cover all those areas that you've decided are in scope for your service offerings.

Practitioners find great value in visualization aids for the deliverables of the framework's steps. Templates, samples, and description of standards make it much easier to know what the results should look like. Many of the working tools and deliverables can be packaged into facilitation kits combining the training materials, workshop steps, and reusable formats for easy recording of results.

Lessons Learned Service

The framework knowledge guidance that your group provides can be valuable, but it should never be static. The process management support group can provide feedback mechanisms by which practitioners can say what worked well for them and what can be improved. These learning experiences cross-referenced to the framework steps can improve the standard references and can be used to assess risk for future projects.

Resource Contact Information

As noted earlier in this chapter, the process support group can be actively involved in the projects or can just be a conduit to resources that can help. The group can become a valuable source of knowledge regarding those who know your framework and its associated techniques. These resources and their skills and experience can show which group resources exist. It can also show others within the enterprise who could help. Qualified outside consultants and trainers can be identified as well as their rates and terms of service. The group can also establish the mechanisms for real or virtual process management communities of practice inside or outside the enterprise.

Business Process Support Group Services Directory

All the services that the support group provides should be described in a services directory. This file should provide access points for each service. Whatever choices you make as a result of considering the factors and options in this chapter should be listed. The training curriculum should be detailed and the schedule up-to-date. Descriptions of ways to engage the support team, complete with terms and conditions, should be accessible to all potential users.

How Will You Measure Your Performance?

As with all relationships and services, you will have to measure the value the support group services give to the corporation. As for any support service, this value should be measured according to the difference it makes in getting better processes working more efficiently in shorter timeframes. Because the support service delivers guidance and enablers to initiatives and projects, any glitches it experiences can hold up the delivery of the benefits defined in the business case. Depending on the choice of services your group offers, these measures could vary. Client satisfaction and management perception metrics will likely come toward the top of the list, as will the speed and quality of the overall business rollout.

Architecting Your Processes and Aligning Them

You will have defined the business requirements in the Business Context phase for the support group. Now the group must identify which processes it must put in place to run its new business. A process architecture is in order. Figure 9.3 provides a sample architecture at the highest level of details. Lower levels of detail might be called for in the areas that define services.

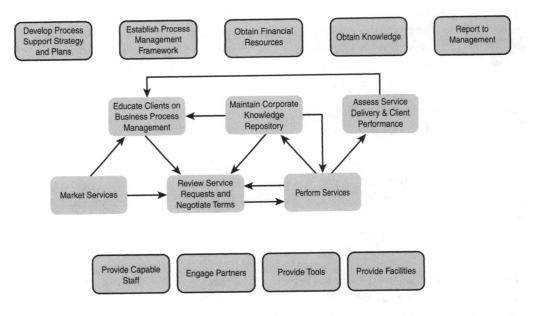

FIGURE 9.3

Sample process architecture for a process support group.

Figure out the processes in the architecture that are most important to your organization and develop them according to a definite strategy after you consider alignment with the other requirements.

For the core processes of your service, ask what information and knowledge the support group needs; find sources and distribution mechanisms for them. Consider knowledge portal technology to provide service providers and users one place to go for everything. The development of a process management portal will provide both the knowledge of the business and its process assets as well as the methods of conducting the work to produce that knowledge.

Think about where you will conduct this work and the facilities needed. Determine the roles and responsibilities that must be executed. Some of these can be found in Chapter 6 in the discussions of project management roles. Think through the reporting relationships and the organizational design for the process support group. Start to think about the skills that will be needed and where you will get workers with these skills. Your strategy might change over time as you try to find people to fill positions.

Defining Your Program to Roll Out a Support Group

Every program of change, including the startup or enhancement of a process support group, starts from the current situation. For your organization, you have to seriously consider how healthy your current relationships are. The style of implementation as described earlier in Table 9.1 might depend on earning credibility first. Consequently, you might choose to settle on your ultimate implementation gradually over time.

It might also be impossible to introduce all services initially. It might take time to become proficient, so think through what you want to accomplish over time. Table 9.6 shows a logical build sequence for a subset of services that would be delivered over two years' time.

NOTE

As with any changed process or new service, you must consider all the advice offered in Chapter 8, "Human Change." Stakeholders will have concerns that need to be dealt with. A program of communication and competency building will be of utmost importance.

9

BUILDING A PROCESS SUPPORT ORGANIZATION

TABLE 9.6   Sample Rollout of Services for a Process Support Group

6 Months	12 Months	24 Months
	Standard Reference Framework	
Requirements defined and selected	Fully operational	Framework knowledge management in place and evolving based on lessons learned
	Standard Technology Support	
Requirements defined	Technology installed and generally available	Technology used on all initiatives
Vendor shortlist finalized		

TABLE 9.6 Continued

6 Months	12 Months	24 Months
	Training Curriculum	
Curriculum defined	Training ongoing	Training ongoing
Initial training completed		

Designing Your Own Processes

Naturally, each support service process must be visioned and renewed. You must define the scope, define what work you will do, and define how you will do the work. This, too, should follow the framework as it would for any other business process that you are supporting.

Summary

You need to ask yourself many questions when setting up your internal business process support group. Tables 9.1 through 9.5 listed the essential considerations along with questions regarding what products and services a support group would offer. Your group must work through the following issues:

- What is your mission and value proposition? What style and degree of control will you strive for?
- What other related services, in addition to process management, will you take on?
- What specific process management phases will you support and what services and products will you offer?
- What tools will you select and support?
- Will use of your services be mandatory, or will your clients have an option?
- Will you build a dedicated group of staff, use other internal staff when you can get them, or use outside service providers? What mix of these do you anticipate?
- What will your own processes look like, and how will you manage them?
- Which processes and services will have priority in the near term?
- How will you develop and roll out your service offerings?

This chapter closes the first part of *Business Process Management: Profiting from Process*. The remaining chapters provide a phase-by-phase description of how to carry out the work.

A Practitioner's Guide

PART II

IN THIS PART

Discovering the Context for Business Change

IN THIS CHAPTER

The first two phases of the Process Management Framework —Business Context and Architect and Align—set the stage for understanding the who, what, when, where, why, and how of a business, so that the management team can prioritize, select, and complete projects throughout the remaining phases. The resulting knowledge, documents, and models produced during these phases should provide a "big picture" view of the organization segment being evaluated for renewal. This equates to the production of a roadmap for the business that should show how each piece fits with every other piece and what areas are affected by any given change project. This phase corresponds to delivering a complete owner's view of the business. For those familiar with the Zachman framework[1] for enterprise architecture, these two phases cover row 2 (from the top in Figure 10.1).

The first phase of the Process Management Framework, the Business Context phase, seeks to gain an understanding or confirm the criteria by which decisions will be made in the remaining phases and steps. Analysts examine the external pressures facing the organization and the values and principles, visionary expectations, measures of existing and targeted performance, and critical success factors from each stakeholder's perspective, connecting them to form an overall balanced target. The results answer the questions "Why pursue business change?" and "Who cares that you do?" Taken together, these questions provide a benchmark for all future decision making. Because a common understanding of the organization and its challenges is a key deliverable, this phase is heavily oriented toward workshop and consensus management.

The Business Context phase has eight distinct steps:

1. Validate the mission.
2. Analyze the business drivers.
3. Classify the stakeholder types.
4. Document current interactions and health.
5. Document principles and values.
6. Envision the future and set expectations.
7. Produce key performance indicators (KPIs) and targets.
8. Determine critical success factors.

These steps in Figure 10.2 are shown as a sequence of logical activities to be completed. However, much work can take place in parallel, and completing one step isn't a prerequisite for starting another. In practice, steps 1 through 3 would normally be conducted concurrently, and the organization would accept the steps 1 through 3 findings before proceeding with the remaining steps. Steps 4 through 8 can be done at the same time, and the organization can approve those results simultaneously.

---

[1] *"A Framework for Information Systems Architecture," John A. Zachman, IBM Systems Journal, vol. 26, no. 3, 1987. IBM Publication G321-5298*

Enterprise Architecture Zachman Framework View

	What?	How?	Where?	Who?	When?	Why?
Scope (Planner)	List of Things [Scope Objects]	List of Processes [Business Activities]	List of Locations [Location Objects]	List of Organizations and Enterprise Parties	List of Business Events	List of Mission, Vision, Goals, and Business Strategies
Enterprise Model (Owner)	Business Concepts and Business Entity Relations	Business Process Models, Value Chain/Business Architecture	Logistics Network	Organization Charts [Organization Structure]	Scheduled Events [Event Network]	Business Plan: Goals, Objectives, Strategies, and Requirements
System Model (Designer)	Business Objects and Data Models	Application Architecture Use Cases Analysis Models Workflow	Distributed System Architecture [Network Layout]	Model [Rule Assignment and Team Models]	Processing Structure [Sequence Diagrams]	Business Rule Model [Strategies]
Technology Model (Builder)	Logical/Physical Data Models [Object Deployment Models]	System Design [Method Diagrams]	Technology Specifications, Infrastructure Interfaces [Deployment Models]	Presentation Architecture [Team and Responsibility Models]	Control Structure [Event Models]	Rule Design Model [Requirements Models]
Components (Vendor)	Component Data Stores [Component Content Description]	3rd Party Component Class Libraries	Industry Communications Standards, HW/SW Services and Licenses	Outsourcing Services [Supplier Relationships]	Timing Definition	Industry Best Practices [Specification Models]
Functioning System (Product)	Data Stores [Object Libraries]	Integrated Component Executables [Published Processes]	File, Network, Dist Computing Services [Published Layouts]	Security: Role Access [Organization Charts]	Job and Event Schedules [Schedules]	Published Business Plans

FIGURE 10.1

The Zachman Framework for Enterprise Architecture (www.zifa.com/frmwork2.htm). Reprinted with permission from John A. Zachman.

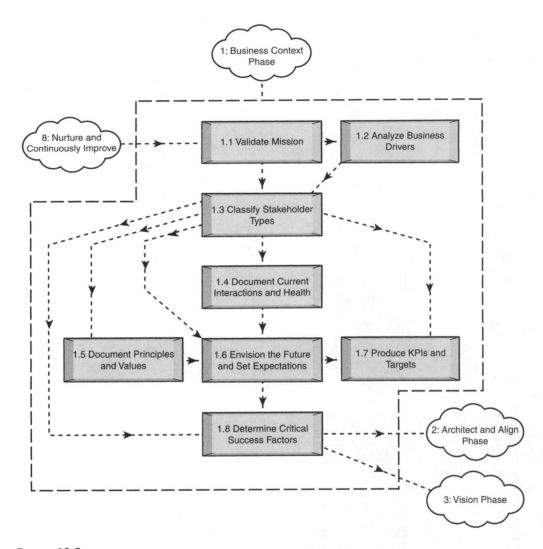

FIGURE 10.2

Process Management Framework: Steps in the Business Context phase.

The tricks and traps presented next, and lessons learned throughout this section, should be used as guides; however, they are by no means an exhaustive list. Each organization is unlike any other, having different pressures, strengths, and weaknesses, so what might be a problem for one organization might be totally nonexistent in another. As with any business decision, sound judgment should determine how important each suggestion is to your organization. However, failing to consider the knowledge presented here will increase the risk associated with the work being performed.

Each step in the framework's phases is described as to its intent and purpose with suggested techniques for accomplishing the step.

Overall Tricks and Traps for the Business Context Phase

As you complete the framework's various phases, keep in mind a number of general "rules of thumb."

Find an executive supporter or supporters for proposed transformation very early in the process. A supporter must be able to get to the top and build cross-organizational support for changing the things that senior management cares about. Management had better be fighting *with* you, not fighting *against* you!

This phase isn't intended to be an exact science. It embraces the 80/20 rule, whereby gathering 20% of the knowledge will provide 80% of the required insight. With this view, the phase will never be fully finished—only repeated over and over again every business-planning cycle. With this in mind, don't build models, study, or analyze for the sake of it; time and executive patience won't permit it. The pursuit of perfection will have a price.

The Business Context phase requires good judgment skills and self-confidence. Not every aspect has to be covered if it doesn't make sense, nor does every activity require the same degree of detailed analysis.

Conduct interviews to gather information and then validate the findings in workshops. Keep the workshops interactive all the way through and make sure there is buy-in as you go forward. Emphasize that silence is the equivalent of consent.

Maintain an outside stakeholder's perspective, not an internal political one. Never underestimate the importance of your customers and suppliers, potential staff, external regulatory organizations, and community opinion. Some perspectives might be in conflict, so balance the views by deciding what your organization wants those perspectives to be, not necessarily what the stakeholders want. You will not be able to satisfy everyone, so think through what you will have to compromise on.

Involve and collaborate with the various business units. Ivory tower efforts won't work.

Make sure the results of the Business Context phase fit into the process and are consistent with annual planning thinking and documents. Just as corporate planning today is a continuous process, this phase should also be an ongoing activity, not just a one-time project.

Always refer to the criteria developed here throughout the remaining framework activities. These will be your North Star to use for guidance and for cutting through internal power struggles.

Validating the Mission

This first step ensures that the mission, general direction, organizational purpose, and intent of the business, and other related aspects of the "Organization-in-Focus" direction are known, commonly understood, and accepted. The mission might have to be articulated formally for the first time or perhaps just reviewed and validated. During this step, examine documented statements and have the management team responsible for the initiative evaluate the statements for current appropriateness. Look for any fundamental directional change that might affect performance or the plans for process management. Without a clear answer to the fundamental question "What business are we in?", it would be impossible to chart a course of change or to manage what is put in place.

Figure 10.3 shows an example of the knowledge produced as a result of validating a business mission.

Techniques

Validation techniques are typically used in traditional strategic planning for a chosen planning horizon—typically two to five years. These involve a number of planning and analysis concepts, such as

- **Mission**—What is the organization in business to "do"?
- **Value proposition**—What is our distinguishing differentiation in the marketplace?
- **Vision**—What does the organization strive to "be" at the end of the planning period?
- **Goals**—What does the organization plan to accomplish in the planning period?
- **Objectives**—What results does the organization plan to deliver?
- **Key performance indicators**—What measures of performance will be used to set targets and evaluate progress?
- **Strategies**—What methods or approaches are used to reach the goals and performance targets?
- **Barriers**—What obstacles will have to be overcome to be successful?

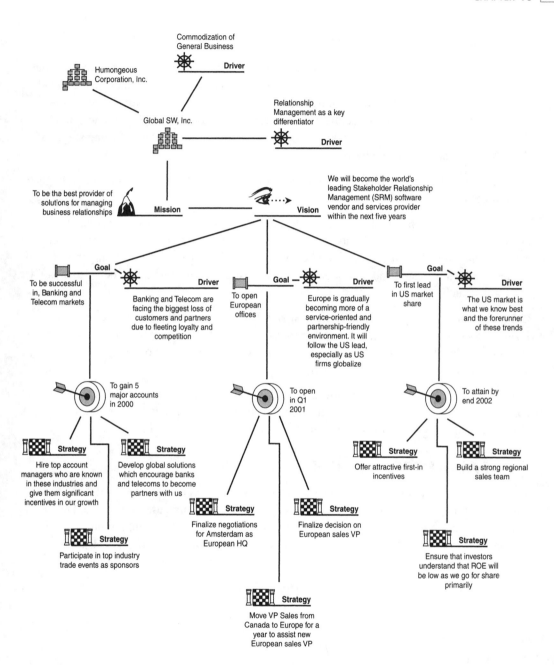

FIGURE 10.3

The mission for Global Software, Inc.

Lessons Learned

The mission validation step is inextricably linked with or dependent on the organization's business strategy. As such, those who feel that this step treads on their toes might resist. Be ready for opposition or difficulty in marshaling the required support. Remind everyone that you aren't questioning the mission statement or the business strategy, just trying to understand it, so that it can guide further decision making and direction setting within the following stages of the Process Management Framework.

The work here should cull whatever is possible from existing documents and should reference the sources.

There might have been a number of attempts at this, so don't come across as wanting to do another document review just for its own sake. Build on what already exists within the organization, validating where it's possible and creating only where it's necessary. Using mocked-up models that can be tested and reconfigured easily as starting points might be better than building from scratch.

Coordinate this activity closely with the next step in the Business Context phase, which analyzes business drivers, and the other stakeholder-based work. Use joint presentations and workshops to validate both at the same time. It will then be clearer to everyone why you are doing any of these steps.

Conduct confidential interviews followed by executive workshops for providing insight and consensus. Use techniques familiar to managers, if those techniques make them more comfortable. The technique is less important than the insight gained in the collaboration.

Analyzing the Business Drivers

This step seeks to confirm, or to gain an understanding of, the pressures facing the business today and anticipated for the future. The initiative team must gain knowledge of the factors and issues that provide either threats to be mitigated by the business or opportunities to be exploited. It must consider a range of possibilities for the planning horizon, not just a fixed guess on one possible scenario. The insights must be commonly understood and accepted.

Figure 10.4 shows an example of the knowledge produced as a result of analyzing business drivers.

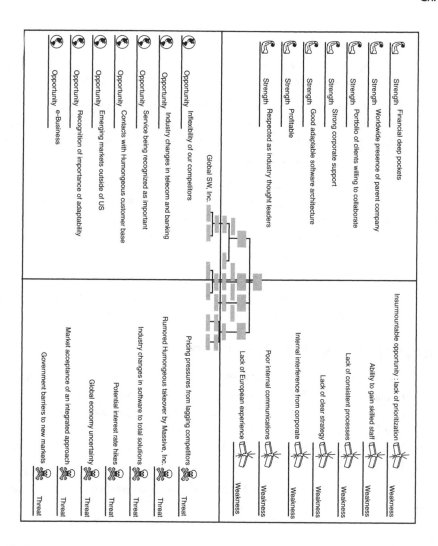

FIGURE 10.4

An analysis of Global Software, Inc.'s strengths, weaknesses, opportunities, and threats.

Techniques

The analysis techniques can be anything that the organization's management is comfortable with. The chosen technique should be able to uncover the sometimes hidden factors and perspectives that drive different managers in differing directions. Some good choices are SWOT (strengths, weaknesses, opportunities, and threats) analysis and business scenario analysis.

Lessons Learned

Gather any existing documents that relate to the pressures facing the "Organization-in-Focus," including customer surveys, market analyses, research reports, and industry journals.

Speculate on the key factors driving attainment of the organization's long-term objectives. Determine the organization's strengths, weaknesses, opportunities, and threats. Plot key leverage points in the business factors that have high impact and high uncertainty. Conclude what needs to be managed. Focus on discussion and sharing of insight, not on building pretty models.

Be careful of seeing only an internal perspective. Customers, suppliers, and other outside industry experts might know better or be able to prove perspectives as a wake-up call. Their points of view are hard to argue with. Always use external factors as the rationale for recommendations. This allows management to avoid becoming personal and makes sure that everyone doesn't get bogged down with internal issues. Make sure that your facts are correct and supportable.

Involve representatives from many organizational units that might have varying perspectives on the drivers. By involving them in the same workshops, new understanding will accrue to all.

Classifying Stakeholder Types

The third step in the Business Context phase provides the basis for the rest of this phase and for the decision-making that will follow in later phases. In this step, an organization defines the categories or types of groups and individuals with which the "Organization-in-Focus" must interact successfully now and in the future to conduct its mission and reach its vision. This step will provide the framework to discover, analyze, and organize the criteria by which options can be evaluated. It defines "who cares."

Figure 10.5 shows an example of the knowledge produced as a result of classifying stakeholder types.

Techniques

The stakeholder classification techniques can often appear to be somewhat mysterious. Sometimes stakeholder classification seems like an art. The methods used for market analysis can be helpful, such as stakeholder analysis and customer/consumer segmentation.

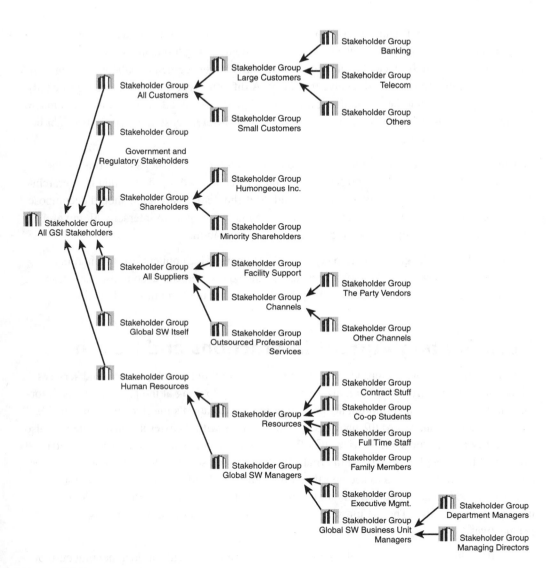

FIGURE 10.5
Stakeholder analysis for Global Software, Inc.

Lessons Learned

Gather any existing documents and information from various departments that relate to the interactions that the "Organization-in-Focus" has and should have with those parties outside its direct control. Start with Marketing and Sales, with regard to customer segmentation, and then move to the supplier side and do the same for other outside interactions.

This exercise can be difficult because you can segment customers and consumers and other interested parties many different ways. Be cautious about having too many segments or types; otherwise, further analysis can become unwieldy. Think about segmentation along the lines of how the different segments will receive treatment: A different type should require significantly different activity within the "Organization-in-Focus." It's also a good idea to move from macro segmentation to micro segmentation. For example, four different customer segments might be subtypes of All Customers.

Stakeholder classification is as much art as science. It requires workshops to be run with a wide range of internal groups represented. It should be conducted top-down (that is, hierarchically) to ensure that all stakeholders are covered. Stakeholder classification should decompose to the point of meaningful difference in the way we interact or plan to interact with the groups. Significantly different interactions require further segmentation.

Start by looking at the generic macro types All Customers, All Suppliers, All Community Stakeholders, All Owners, All Human Resources, and so on. You can decompose these into more specific types. Later analysis can then be conducted at the level of detail chosen at that point.

Documenting Current Interactions and Health

This step provides a big-picture view of the environment within which products and services are delivered to and from the "Organization-in-Focus." By looking at the physical items, information, knowledge, and commitments present at the organization's interface with the outside world, a business can record the nature of the interactions with its external stakeholders. It also can identify the products and services that flow from those interactions and assess the interactions' health. Through this step, all internal stakeholders can see that there are more views and considerations to be taken into account than just their own. Furthermore, documentation of interactions addresses the fundamental questions "What business are we in?" and "What business should we be in?" The main result is insight into the business from previously overlooked perspectives.

Figure 10.6 shows an example of the knowledge produced as a result of documenting current interactions.

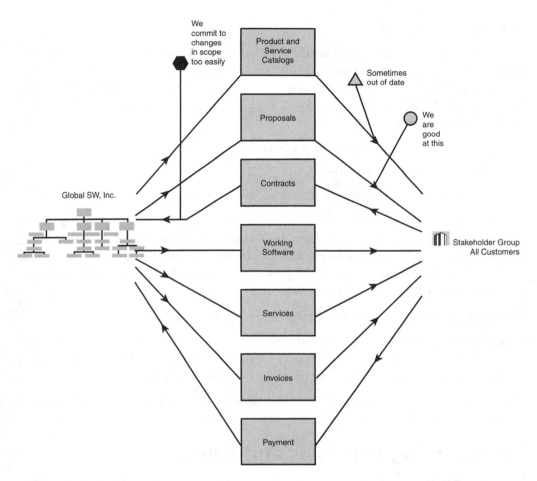

Figure 10.6

Current interactions with stakeholders for Global Software, Inc.

Techniques

The primary methods of documenting interactions aren't difficult, assuming that the key representatives of the various business areas can be brought together. The techniques are as follows:

- Inflow and outflow mapping
- Health checks
- Workshop management

Lessons Learned

Like some other steps in this phase, interacting with stakeholders is as much art as science. It requires the right, wide range of people in the facilitated session to gain different perspectives and to result in an accepted understanding of what business you are in and need to be in. Start by listing each stakeholder group at the level of detail chosen and then pose the following questions for each group:

- What goes to this group from the "Organization-in-Focus"? (outflows)
- What comes from them? (inflows)

The questions should include all current and envisioned future items.

Document the definitions of each output or input, obtaining consensus because there is rarely a common language for the terms used. Consider the health of each item listed, relative to how we would like to see its health in the planning timeframe. Mark the item appropriately as in poor, adequate, or good health today. (This relative judgement is based on the participants' experience and feedback from outside stakeholders.)

Mark each item as being a current and/or future flow, given the group's insight.

Interaction documentation isn't about model building, although the deliverable might be in the form of a chart or picture, both of which are good communication tools. It's more about the process of discussion and consensus regarding the new insights gained.

If possible, use high-touch techniques such as sticky dots to indicate health status (for example, red for poor, yellow for adequate, and green for good health).

Documenting Principles and Values

This step documents the principles and values that govern the operations and decision-making of the "Organization-in-Focus." In this step, the organization defines its core principles, beliefs, and values and then examines each stakeholder relationship at the chosen level of decomposition, linking each relationship to relevant values. This step contributes to the criteria for later selection of the most appropriate changes or decisions to be made.

An example of the knowledge produced as a result of documenting principles can be found in Figure 10.7 (see top center "Principles" section).

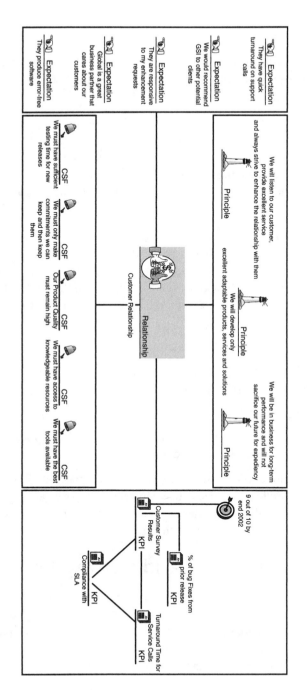

FIGURE 10.7

Stakeholder relationship criteria for customers of Global Software, Inc.

Techniques

Use whatever documentation approach you might be comfortable with to define the fundamentals of how the "Organization-in Focus" will operate. There might be a number of ways to document values and principles.

Lessons Learned

For each stakeholder group, answer the question, "What behaviors and ways of working will remain constant even beyond the planning horizon?" Consolidate all perspectives and create a "ways to work" for the business that must remain intact during and after the transformation program.

Describe the values and principles, making sure that the interests of customers, owners, and staff are considered along with other stakeholders. Principles and values represent our fundamental behavior toward each stakeholder type. They are the unwavering guidelines for human and organizational decision making and the fundamentals of designing and running the business. The principles and values should exhibit the following attributes when viewed from the stakeholders' perspectives:

- True, regardless of product and process
- True, regardless of market and conditions
- True, regardless of CEO or management team
- True over a 50+-year perspective

Look backward to see what the actual behaviors have been as well as forward to examine consistency with documented statements of core beliefs.

This step can produce a lot of directional verbiage and other materials. Try to avoid it becoming an exercise in wordsmithing sanitized statements that everyone can agree with but which don't motivate a constant pull toward a desired state of functioning. Focus more on intent and make sure that there's some emotion in it so that everyone can care about doing something.

Envisioning the Future and Setting Expectations

This step determines and documents the future state (that is, the state at the planning horizon chosen) of the "Organization-in-Focus." This occurs from the perspective of the chosen stakeholder groups, whose expectations will set the stage. Along with the principles and values, performance improvement targets, and critical success factors, this knowledge represents the target of the change initiative program and provides the criteria for later decision making.

Refer to Figure 10.7 for an example of the knowledge produced as a result of envisioning the future (see the left "Expectation" section).

Techniques

This step is best served by visioning approaches that place the observer in the future at the end of the planning horizon. Such approaches include

- Interviewing
- Workshop facilitation
- Time-machine visioning (explained in a little bit)

Lessons Learned

The stakeholder visioning technique is often referred to as *time-machine visioning* because it represents the equivalent of placing yourself in a time machine and going to the future when all is accomplished from the change program. Hypothetically, the stakeholders are asked to describe their relationship with the organization at that point, in terms of what attributes they recognize, value, and want.

For each stakeholder group at the chosen level of decomposition, answer the question "What will you say when we've delivered the new business environment at the end of the planning horizon?" Up to 10 crisp statements should be listed. Some might be the same for more than one stakeholder—for example, a customer might say something that the owners might also value. Consolidate all perspectives and create a living vision of the future of the business made possible by the successful completion of the transformation program.

NOTE

Envisioning doesn't always produce statements of desirable results from the point of view of the stakeholder because perspectives are often contradictory. What might be good for a customer might not be so good for a supplier. The exercise must balance out these conflicts and reconcile the responses as to what the "Organization-in-Focus" wants the stakeholder expectations to be, consistent with its mission, vision, and value proposition.

Producing Key Performance Indicators and Targets

This step identifies the key performance indicators (KPIs) that will be used to measure the organization's relationship with the chosen stakeholder group. Businesses should use these KPIs to determine the degree of change from where the relationship stands today to where it will need to be in the future. This step also establishes the target performance level required for these dates and delivers a path for performance improvement over a period of time.

Refer to the right section in Figure 10.7 for an example of the knowledge produced as a result setting performance indicators and targets.

Techniques

The techniques of producing KPIs and targets are some of the most elusive to master, despite their apparent simplicity. Measurements can elicit strange behavior when personal objectives clash. Conducting the following measurements should be done with care and thought:

- KPI analysis
- Balanced scorecard analysis
- Performance benchmarking
- Negotiation
- Consensus workshops

Lessons Learned

Based on the drivers and other documentation developed so far—especially the stakeholder values and expectations from the prior step—identify the KPIs for each stakeholder and determine the degree of performance improvement illustrated by each indicator. Consolidate all perspectives and create a set of future business targets that would be made possible by the transformation program's successful completion.

For each value and expectation of each stakeholder, consider indicators of efficiency, effectiveness, and adaptability.

How will these measures be obtained? If the measurement process is obtrusive, the act of measuring will affect the measurements as people change their behavior during the measurement activity.

Determining the appropriate KPIs for each relationship looks easy on the surface but, in reality, is fraught with difficulty. Numerous measures are important, but many of them don't truly reflect the required results.

Information about your current true costs might be available through your financial management group if they've conducted any activity-based cost studies. Ask the group to share early in the game.

The approach at this point closely tracks to that used in Kaplan and Norton's balanced scorecard. KPIs identify the need for measures beyond the financial ones for shareholders or owners; you'll probably also need to measure leading prognostications. These include a consideration for customer measures, process quality, and innovation and learning. In my experience, the stakeholder approach reaches beyond the balanced scorecard to link more closely to deliver performance to all those who care.

Because traditional financial measures, such as return on equity or assets, tell us only the equivalent of the score of the football game after it's over, it's key to have more leading indicators if we want to know how the game is going and what we should do about affecting the outcome before it's too late. A coach must know how the players are performing and make adjustments, if necessary. A business must know how the opposition is responding to its game plan and change strategy, if that's called for. Organizations must learn what's working and exploit the opportunity while they can. You can't win a game with actions after it's over—you need to know what signs to look for before it's too late.

One way to assess how large a change is required is to conduct a performance benchmarking exercise to see how a business compares with its peers. The invaluable aspects of this approach are that it's external and factual, and can't be disputed except at the organization's own peril. It gets management to move on the areas of stakeholder measurements with the biggest gaps and cut through the internal politics that often stand in the way of change. It's often difficult to get comparative measures but often worth the investment.

Determining Critical Success Factors

The final step identifies the factors that are critical, or the most risky, to meet the stakeholders' values, expectations, KPIs, and targets already defined. Those factors will be used later to evaluate solutions that could apply. They are also the flip side of risk assessment and can be used to get started with mitigation.

Refer to Figure 10.7 (see the bottom center "CSF" section) for an example of the knowledge produced as a result of determining critical success factors.

Techniques

The techniques of determining critical success factors are well established. and are known to management, such as

- Practices benchmarking
- Risk management

Lessons Learned

Critical success factor (CSF) analysis explores the key factors in the minds of managers when it comes to ensuring success by their organizations. It's important, however, that the exercise relate to those issues and changes agreed on as most important for the future. That is all the work that we've performed so far in the Business Context phase.

After reviewing the stakeholders' values, expectations, and performance improvement targets, a business's change initiative team should be able to complete the following statement: "To achieve the results we have defined for the chosen stakeholder group, it's vital that..." the team should obtain only three to five responses per stakeholder type from each respondent for each relationship. After that, they are no longer dealing with critical items and are delving into wants rather than needs.

After you identify the critical success factors for all relationships, consolidate all perspectives and create a set of prioritized ones for the successful completion of the transformation program. Describe the reconciled CSFs, making sure that the interests of customers, owners, and staff are considered along with other stakeholders.

Determining critical success factors is closely related to risk management. Almost by definition, the opposite of a CSF is a risk because not attaining a CSF will put the objectives of the transformation program at risk. Risk management techniques can also be used to derive CSFs.

Summary

The Business Context phase of the Process Management Framework is intended to establish a clear set of criteria that will guide the operation of a business, the establishment of priorities for change, and the management of a program of renewal. It uses the stakeholder as the basis for understanding because the stakeholder is the reason for the organization's existence.

The next phase is very closely linked to this first one. The Architect and Align phase will use the stakeholder-based criteria to establish the priorities for process, technology, organizational structure, facility, and human competency renewal. The next phase will establish a set of linked architectures and a program of change, from which specific initiatives can be resourced and launched.

Configuring Business Processes and Aligning Other Strategies

IN THIS CHAPTER

The Architect and Align phase of the Process Management Framework determines the relationships among processes, technology direction, facilities, organizational strategies, human resources, and business strategy; it also identifies likely candidates for renewal. It does this by modeling the set of processes for the "Organization-in-Focus" and cross-relating the enabling contributions of various policies, information, knowledge, technologies, skills, facilities, locations, and other aspects of change. In this phase, a business prioritizes its top processes and other change components and defines a program of design, development, and implementation.

The Architect and Align phase has eight steps:

1. Identify business processes.
2. Match processes to criteria and prioritize.
3. Identify information and knowledge needs.
4. Identify strategic technologies.
5. Identify facility requirements.
6. Determine organization strategy.
7. Determine human capabilities.
8. Determine alignment opportunities and constraints.

These steps (see Figure 11.1) appear as a sequence of logical activities to be completed. However, much work can take place in parallel, and completing one step isn't a prerequisite for starting another. In normal practice, a business would perform steps 1 and 2, and accept their outcomes before proceeding with the rest of the steps. Steps 3 through 8 can be done all at the same time, and the organization can approve those results simultaneously.

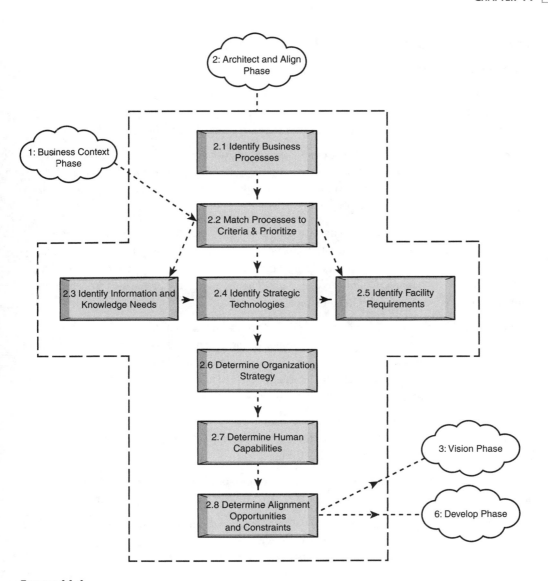

FIGURE 11.1

Process Management Framework: Steps in the Architect and Align phase.

Overall Tricks and Traps for the Architect and Align Phase

Configuring business processes is inextricably linked with or dependent on the business strategy of the "Organization-in-Focus." As such, those who feel that changes will tread on their toes might resist. Be ready for opposition or difficulty in marshaling the required support.

This phase can produce a lot of directional verbiage and other materials. Try to avoid it becoming an exercise in wordsmithing sanitized statements that everyone can agree with but which don't motivate change. Focus more on intent, and make sure that there is some emotion in it so that everyone can care about doing something.

This phase attempts to prepare everyone for the future. However, you can't predict the future with certainty, so avoid the temptation to forecast too precisely. Instead, in looking forward, try to prepare for a range of possibilities and for uncertainty. Pay particular attention to situations that, if they were to happen, would fundamentally change things for better or worse. Be prepared for change—even unanticipated change.

Be careful of seeing only an internal perspective. Always use external factors as the rationale for recommendations. Customers, suppliers, and other outside industry experts might know better or be able to provide perspectives as a wake-up call. Maintain an outside stakeholder's perspective in deciding what to do to cut through the internal politics. This tact avoids issues from becoming personal and ensures that everyone doesn't get bogged down with personal issues.

Always link processes to the reasons for their existence—that is, to the stakeholder-based criteria and the strategic drivers developed in the business context phase (as discussed in Chapter 10, "Discovering the Context for Business Change").

Throughout, use a multidisciplined team with a strong facilitator. Make sure that executives participate, make the decisions, and own the results. Build buy-in one step at a time.

The Architect and Align phase is iterative—don't strive for perfection, but go for understanding and insight. Configuring processes works better when you do it partially and quickly and then do it again. Start a mile wide and an inch deep and build downward.

Make this phase an ongoing activity synchronized with business context work. It should never end, and it will never be right.

Identifying Business Processes

This step identifies the organization's core processes and the support processes that enable or guide core processes. During this step, a process map is built, and the associated attributes of

Configuring Business Processes and Aligning Other Strategies

CHAPTER 11

279

11

CONFIGURING
BUSINESS PROCESSES
AND ALIGNING
OTHER STRATEGIES

the cross-functional processes are documented. The step should provide a common understanding and set of semantics for discussing the business of the "Organization-in-Focus." Refer to Figure 11.2 for an example of a Process Architecture diagram.

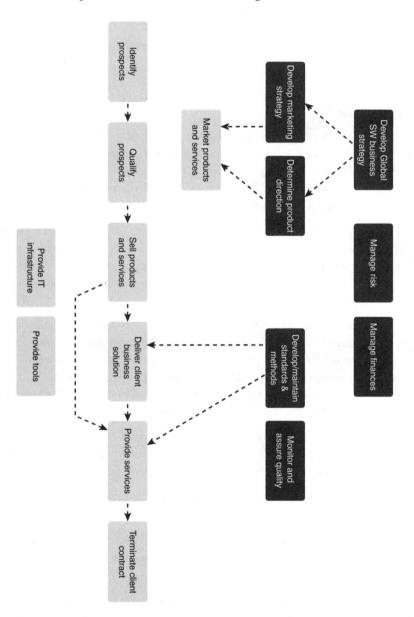

FIGURE 11.2
Process Architecture for Global Software, Inc.

Techniques

The techniques of identifying business processes include

- Architecture mapping by categorization of process types: core, guiding, and enabling
- Event/outcome analysis
- Interviews
- Workshops

Lessons Learned

Unlike with other forms of analysis, you might find defining the organization's processes very difficult to do, primarily because processes are subjective in nature and can be arbitrarily combined or disaggregated. Managers might do this according to their political whims, particularly if they see specific processes within the boundaries of their own responsibilities. Avoid such problems by keeping process analysis cross-functional and focused on customer value creation.

Always start process analysis with the customer segments and work through the lifecycle of the customer relationship, even to the time before they became customers. Keep in mind all the possible things that could happen in the relationship, whether or not they are desirable or undesirable activities—for example, include making potential customers aware of the company's services and losing customers.

By conducting interviews and information-gathering workshops for each significant customer type, you can determine the major types of events that trigger action and the possible outcomes important to the triggering stakeholder that complete the cross-functional process. Analyze these event/outcome pairings and consolidate them into a set of 4 to 10 core processes and 8 to 14 support (enabling and guiding) processes. Some high level processes will require their own architecture to be developed later (for example, the process of providing staff.)

To gather input from managers, conduct interviews and then run workshops to validate common concerns. Interviewing first helps spot sensitive issues in private and allows for more effective workshops, leading to more sensitive facilitation and consensus.

Involve the customer or a knowledgeable proxy to define what the customer values are and what performance indicators are important. Don't rely solely on insiders for knowledge and insight.

Make sure that outcome analysis examines real and final outcomes, not just intermediate results. Outcomes must be directly tied to the values of importance to customers, owners, and other outside stakeholders.

Not all process attributes can be defined at this point. These can be updated later as more knowledge is gained. Have a clear place to store the knowledge gained so that it can be accessed and updated easily.

Configuring Business Processes and Aligning Other Strategies

CHAPTER 11

281

11

CONFIGURING
BUSINESS PROCESSES
AND ALIGNING
OTHER STRATEGIES

Make sure that the architecture has a steward or custodian, whose job it is to keep the architecture maps current and help others use it effectively.

Matching Processes to Criteria and Prioritizing

This step gathers existing process performance measurements, benchmarks that performance against similar processes in other organizations, and determines which processes will contribute the most toward the achievement of stakeholders' criteria. The latter activity which processes hold the greatest opportunity for improvement. The ranking of processes for renewal begins at this point.

Techniques

The techniques for matching processes to the criteria established in the Business Context phase cross-reference process attributes to stakeholder requirements. My favorite technique is to use matrices that cross-reference the stakeholder criteria from the Business Context phase to the processes in the Identify Business Processes step in this phase.

Lessons Learned

Matching processes to criteria and prioritizing them can become very political, so it's important to get as much factual supporting information as possible. When doing this, however, remember that existing performance measures can vary greatly depending on site location and measurement technique. Use these as a guide. Don't get carried away. If you've done your homework in the previous phase and gained acceptance of proposed changes, you will find this phase much easier to execute.

Link processes to the reasons for their existence by starting with the business stakeholders' requirements and their critical success factors. Then, examining each process in the architecture for both its degree of importance or potential contribution and its opportunity for performance improvement. Remember that some stakeholders might be weighted as more important than others but also be careful to ensure a fair balance of perspectives.

Use matrices to keep the analysis and presentation simple and to keep track of what has and has not been analyzed. Map the relative importance of the processes to the relative health of the processes in a Boston grid (a 2×2 matrix) to find groupings of process improvement priorities. Show the priorities for change in the top-right corners. Create three levels of priority grouping recommendations.

Consider redoing the exercise with varying weightings to discover the sensitivity of the analysis. If small weighting changes lead to wildly different results, significant risk is involved, and a revisiting of criteria might be warranted. If not, the resulting program of change should be easier to sell.

Review the outcomes of this step with management in a cross-functional workshop using management's own previously stated, stakeholder-based criteria. Allow time for lobbying and communication because the result might exclude some people's desired initiatives and include change for others who don't want it.

Identifying Information and Knowledge Needs

This step determines the nature of the information required to support the priority processes described in the process architecture. As such, it refers to an information or data model that hopefully exists within the organization. If not, one might have to be created. The cross-reference to such models should be in the form of a "where-used" or CRUD (create, read, update, delete) type of referral.

Similarly, this step identifies the types of tacit knowledge (human, including education, experience, competencies, and skills) and explicit knowledge (documented) required to guide the organization's processes to their potential ends.

If the process areas are knowledge-intensive, a business should attempt to define or classify knowledge types by process and to prioritize each.

Techniques

Identifying information and knowledge needs can involve significant work. The following techniques are proven professional practices for such identification (which doesn't mean that they are easy):

- Information architecture
- Knowledge categorization
- Scoring and matrix analysis

Lessons Learned

Take advantage of professionals for this work, but make sure their methodology is in sync with the process strategy and cross-references to it. By evaluating the process-value chain, the information input and output should become apparent, and the knowledge required to deliver the value should be more readily definable.

Consider the help of data architects, information analysts, librarians, knowledge managers, and others with experience in categorizing and classifying concepts. Beg, borrow, and steal whatever help or previous documentation you can. There's no reward in doing it yourself if it has been done already.

Configuring Business Processes and Aligning Other Strategies

CHAPTER 11

283

11

CONFIGURING
BUSINESS PROCESSES
AND ALIGNING
OTHER STRATEGIES

Information modeling techniques are well proven and numerous. The process architects can accommodate whatever approach is accepted within the organization, so long as they can cross-reference in a where-used fashion to allow prioritization. Object/class models can also be used here.

Information-to-process matrices, showing the value of the various entities or object types, and knowledge-to-process matrices, showing the value of the various knowledge types and their accessibility, can be developed to show priorities in the areas to be dealt with first. Use a Boston grid (2×2 matrices), displaying the priorities for change in the top-right corners.

Knowledge-mapping techniques are tricky because the topic is still new. Try maps that show where knowledge is created, distributed, and used and which knowledge-management processes support other business processes.

> **NOTE**
>
> It's important not to get into analysis paralysis at this stage. High-level information models and knowledge maps will suffice to set a direction.

Identifying Strategic Technologies

This step ensuresat we understand at a high level which technologies and computer applications exist today or are promised in the future. It identifies which technologies can be instrumental in enabling the new business processes to deliver improved performance to our important stakeholders. It should also help define the priorities for a new technological infrastructure to be aligned with process/business change.

Techniques

A numberof techniques have good potential for identifying strategic technologies:

- Technology watch
- Technology principles definition
- Application architecture development
- Technology infrastructure definition
- Scoring and matrix analysis

Lessons Learned

Understand what the new processes are attempting to accomplish first, and then start with the principles of an effective technology environment (the "big rules") that must be satisfied so that technology decisions are based on business value. Complete the phrase, "If this is what must happen for the business, technologically it's vital that…." Assess the options, asking, "Can we deliver results within the existing policies, procedures, and technology plan, or do we have a compelling reason to change?" Also ask, "What are the 'big rules' that must be in place to make the change effective?" For example, you might decide that all functional applications will be designed from reusable software components.

Establish a "technology watch" team, responsible for actively searching out technologies, vendors, and examples that might stimulate ideas beyond the traditional. Ask the question, "Of all the existing and emerging technologies that we can find, which ones could help the processes reach their targets? Will they enable a different but better way of achieving performance breakthrough?" Then examine the applications (or business objects) required to support the new approach with the new technology. Finally, ask what information requirements must be managed.

Of the many ways to define or refine technology architecture, the most effective ones are business and process based. The intent of the work is to find the opportunities and enable the realignment of the technology plans and associated architectures–not to rebuild all architectures right now but to provide input for their renewal, which should be ongoing. Create or update the technology architecture by using the Critical Success Factors for technology and the total set of requirements for technology change. Identify the impact of change on applications, information, and object architectures.

Use process-to-technology grids for simplicity of tracking. Grids should have axes of "Value provided to process" and "Ease of deployment." The recommended technologies should appear in the top-right corners.

This step requires an iterative approach with refinement and feedback added each time through.

Identifying Facility Requirements

In this step, an organization gathers knowledge of the physical facilities that support existing processes, to determine the impact of possible process changes on the physical facilities, and to trigger physical working environment construction, acquisitions, or enhancements, if required.

Techniques

Performing this step requires no radically new techniques. Professionals have been identifying facility requirements for decades. The key is to link the interrelationships that facilities and process change have on one another, with techniques such as

- Facility needs analysis
- Acquisition planning and budgeting

Lessons Learned

Don't ignore this aspect of renewal—it's often overlooked. Countless books, articles, and seminar presenters talk about people, process, and technology, and miss the key role that facilities and their locations play. Even existing facilities might require renovation to accommodate new work patterns or technology infrastructure requirements.

Time-proven techniques for success exist, assuming that the appropriate business drivers are known. Allow the facility professionals to use what they know works best—get them involved.

Look for opportunities to close unneeded space, eliminate storage facilities, combine locations, or distribute work to more locations. Centralizing can cut cost, but so can decentralizing. Both can improve customer service so long as access is possible either physically or electronically. Both can occur at the same time for different aspects of renewal.

Consider remote offices, telecommuting, and mobile workforces. Facility needs might be different from what you are used to.

Consider using process-to-facility grids for simplicity of communication.

Consider the impact that facility changes can have on ways of working as well as on the staff of the organization and other stakeholders.

Determining Organization Strategy

This step helps all key internal stakeholders understand their existing roles and organizational responsibilities, as well as the potential new roles, jobs, and organizational designs. It's probably premature to design details of new organizational structures at this step, but the principles of organizational renewal should be addressed, especially those affected by new process management concepts. Determining organizational strategy helps delineate ownership or stewardship of all start-to-end processes from a process-management perspective and provides a strategy for organizational migration.

Techniques

The best techniques for determining organizational strategy are those that start with process maps and overlay organizational structure:

- Process-to-organization matrices
- Swim lane diagramming, which is placing specific subprocess activities in bands belonging to an organization, role, or person, and graphically showing an organization's process responsibilities
- Collective bargaining issue review

Lessons Learned

This sensitive and controversial step will bring out the worst politics of many people, so be careful to do this right. Start with major roles, determine logical groups of roles, and then begin to design logical organization units. Base units on complete accountability from customer-initiated events through to the customer-valued outcome.

Put in place senior process owners or stewards, even if functional groups will still exist.

Consider carefully the organization's need to adapt and maneuver quickly. If ongoing, organizational learning is critical, design for change by allocating permanent responsibility based on customers and processes, rather than on products or territories.

Consider a process-organized structure versus a hierarchical-function–organized one. Don't ignore the potential benefits of outsourcing or partnering with other firms, especially in processes that aren't the core competency of the staff.

Use human resources (HR) development professionals, along with process and business owners, to perform this step. Make sure that you consider what the organization's staff can support, given their education, experience, and attitudes.

Consider implementing the broadest cross-functional team structures, to complement different strengths and weaknesses and to build experience quickly. This is especially appropriate for internal or external customer service processes.

Involve the collective bargaining units, if excluding them from the change process means that they could become an obstacle later. Ignoring this issue could end up severely compromising the chances of a successful implementation.

You can map the organization to the process in a number of ways. Traditionally, this could have been done in a matrix, wherein the cells represented the nature of the responsibility between the work activity and the organization or role (such as "Approves" or "Is informed of"). More recently, the *swim lane* or Rummler-Brache approach has become popular, wherein organizational bands or lanes are placed on a page representing the process steps for which the particular organization has responsibility. This information can also be presented in other ways such as lists.

Determining Human Capabilities

This step determines the core competencies of the organization's staff, including the skills, strengths, weaknesses, and flexibility of workers within each business process as they currently exist. In this step, the organization identifies basic education and training required for new processes to succeed and identifies under-exploited staff capabilities. As a result, the requirements for layoff or new hiring programs will be known, and a more realistic assessment of the viability of process/technology change will be in place.

Configuring Business Processes and Aligning Other Strategies

CHAPTER 11

287

11

CONFIGURING
BUSINESS PROCESSES
AND ALIGNING
OTHER STRATEGIES

Techniques

The techniques of determining human capabilities are well-proven HR techniques that evaluate skills and competencies against a set of requirements:

- Core competency analysis
- HR skills assessment

Lessons Learned

Remember that this step involves an overall assessment of current capability, compared to the requirement for the future. It is not an individual-by-individual skills evaluation, so don't get bogged down in details. Review existing job descriptions and collective bargaining agreements and examine existing plans for staff core competency enhancement. The requirements must especially recognize the changes brought on by new work locations, especially distributed or mobile ones.

Don't delay or avoid change because the current staff isn't capable of taking on different tasks at this point. If at all possible, train rather than replace existing staff to maintain continuity, retain corporate knowledge, and alleviate fear. Build a plan to transform the staff, but don't be afraid to make the tough call of replacing individuals if they cannot learn. Go for the necessary changes even if it takes a little longer to get the staff there, and start early. At the same time, watch out for underutilized capabilities in your current staff; in some situations, doing so will enable an even greater process improvement. You'll be using the staff you already have to greater potential through the removal of constraints and the releasing of creativity and commitment. Document the approaches for education, training, layoffs, hiring, and outsourcing of staff.

Process skill requirements will affect the results, along with cultural, behavioral, and relationship management needs. Competency gaps can occur because of a lack of knowledge, especially regarding customers and the industry. Gaps can also be associated with technology change, so look at the requirements and implications of closing those gaps in terms of training time and cost.

In many cases, a key requirement to do a job isn't simply the ability to learn a new skill. The individual must be able to keep on learning forever to keep up with the new job's and the new marketplace's changing nature. Build a learning organization, not one that has to be totally renewed every two or three years.

Determining Alignment Opportunities and Constraints

The last step in the Architect and Align phase reconciles, documents, and garners commitment toward the program of change for the "Organization-in-Focus" over the planning horizon. This step shows the gaps between the existing situation and the required new business vision by identifying constraints that will hinder or prevent changes within the processes or cause supply problems with resources, tools, materials, or information. Determining alignment opportunities makes visible skills, capabilities, or capacities within the organization that might allow processes not currently being performed. It will also show the fit between required initiatives for changes to

- Processes
- Technologies
- Locations
- Facilities
- Human resources
- Policies
- Rules and regulations
- Organizational structure

This step also produces the official version of the process map. Arriving at an agreement for the candidate processes for renewal and a strategy for migration of all components completes the map. Together, these elements make up a program whose implementation can be managed by an appropriate program management office (PMO).

Techniques

The most important technique in determining alignment opportunities and constraints is a commonsense analysis of all the prior deliverables from the previous steps in this phase. Some other, more precise techniques are

- Document analysis
- Root-cause analysis
- Workshops
- Negotiation
- Communications
- Program management

Lessons Learned

Many contradictions and competing directions will likely surface. Don't become disillusioned with not being all-knowing, but use any situation when knowledge is lacking as an opportunity to openly discuss the uncertainty and facilitate a common understanding to build consensus. This is a great opportunity to become creative.

See the situation as an opportunity to learn through experience. Don't strive for perfection, but get enough direction to chart a course, and be prepared to revisit this exercise periodically. Be sure to see the results of your efforts in the short, medium, and long term, by working flexibly and iteratively to build small wins and open doors for larger wins.

Document each process's characteristic as it's currently being performed and the desired manner in which the processes are envisioned to perform. Review the total set of architectures, process by process, to ensure that each architecture, strategy, and plan is realistic and in sync with others.

Identify the sequence of the recommended top four to eight processes for renewal and the appropriate components of other architectures to support the required infrastructures.

Review the stakeholder criteria to maintain a business-outcome point-of-view. Make decisions primarily from an outside-in perspective. Look at customer values first as a criterion for selecting among competing options.

Pay particular attention to understanding the root causes of constraints and problems, but don't be limited unduly by them in moving forward. Leave room in each initiative to find creative ways around constraints.

Establish the ability to continue to manage this program of change. If there's no champion or program process owner to defend the vision, it will easily fall apart into chaos or just run out of gas. Consider establishing a program management office (PMO) to ensure that the architecture and strategies become a reality.

Summary

The amount of complexity that could come with the Architect and Align phase could be staggering if all aspects were drilled down to low levels concurrently. The secret is to focus on the process architecture and use it to determine major impacts on the other aspects of change. Then the remaining phases can take over and build the detail as part of each initiative that has been prioritized by the alignment.

The next phase, the Vision phase, deals with setting up each process project in terms of its expectations, objectives, scope, plan, and business case. It will leverage work done and will reuse the reports and results from both the Business Context and Architect and Align phases.

Charting the Course of Change

IN THIS CHAPTER

The third phase in the Process Management Framework, the Vision phase, starts to emphasize Process Design by identifying a specific process to be renewed. In the Vision phase, process owners obtain corporate commitment to the project of designing the change. They do so by defining the stakeholders for the process, their expectations for the future, ways of measuring performance, and target levels for performance improvement. They clearly identify the ins and outs of the scope and determine an approach and business case justification. They develop a change-management and communications strategy and a project plan, containing details of the next two required phases. Charting the course of change sets the scene for delivering the solution definition.

The Vision phase has eight steps, as shown in Figure 12.1:

1. Select the renewal processes and identify stakeholders.
2. Formulate a process vision.
3. Identify performance improvement targets.
4. Define project scope.
5. Develop project strategy.
6. Develop an initial business case.
7. Develop communication and human change strategy.
8. Finalize a project plan.

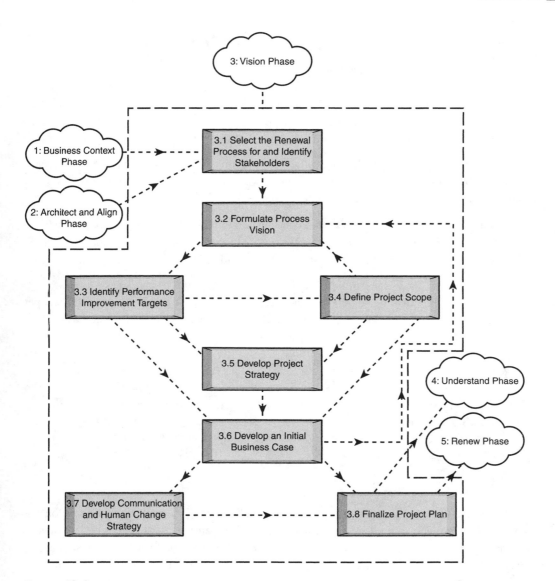

FIGURE 12.1

Process Management Framework: Steps in the Vision phase.

Overall Tricks and Traps for the Vision Phase

At this point, everyone is excited and wants to get going, but often they start by solving the wrong problem or providing the wrong solution. They don't take the time to get it right. The Vision phase is the time to get it right. If you can't spend some time on the activities in this phase, you will spend 10 times that amount of time later dealing with things that don't fit, a lack of support, resource mismatch, and other problems.

Be realistic. Don't ignore the real time available for planning change. An organization in crisis can't afford to study things to death. It must act. Also, an organization in the forefront should never stop taking time to understand how to keep ahead.

Use outsiders and outside perspectives as a constant sanity check and a remover of internal obstacles. It's hard to argue against what works best for the customer. Listen to stakeholders and conduct surveys, focus groups, and so on to better understand their needs. Use this in your communication strategy all the time.

Watch out for projects that are someone's best guess at what's wrong or someone's political pet project. Doing a project that doesn't make much of a difference, is ill conceived, or has no support can spell disaster for the organization, project participants, and process change in general.

> **NOTE**
>
> It's critical to understand the politics at play. If you don't take time for this, you will be blindsided somewhere in this phase. This doesn't mean that you must play politics, but be aware of and ready to respond to all the games and posturing that can take place.

Remember that the work in the Vision phase will benefit the project participants tremendously throughout the project, so do it well. You will benefit if you ensure management commitment. Give management choices, more than one option. Don't believe that a business case is unnecessary because the executives said to go ahead. Their commitment must be managed all the way through, and they must be very aware of what they are committing to. Sometimes, the bottleneck is clearly at the top of the bottle.

Charting the course of change can and should get everyone excited and motivated for the change. Use all this information to your advantage in the change management of the organization's human resources. If staff and managers don't change their beliefs and behaviors, nothing else matters. Build only strong cross-functional, experienced respected teams with change management skills. Don't ignore human change management issues; equip managers to be agents of change.

Pick renewal team members with different but complementary backgrounds, including downstream customers and upstream suppliers. Don't pick a monolithic set of people with a single perspective. Make sure that team members learn about other peoples' areas, not just their own.

Not everything is *top* priority, but everything is connected, so develop the scope of changes carefully. Balance the scope against the stakeholder expectations and performance targets. It's usually not possible to deliver huge performance improvements within a narrow scope.

Use the Vision phase of the renewal process to get everyone on the same page and motivated.

Communicate, communicate, communicate.

Selecting the Renewal Processes and Identifying Stakeholders

The first step in this phase identifies or confirms the key processes that are likely to hold the greatest potential for renewal, based on the findings from the architecture and alignment activities. In this step, the renewal team draws up a short list of areas for investigation, sets the pace of renewal, and provides an initial insight into the scope of the initiative to come. The team defines the "Process-in-Focus" for the project.

Figure 12.2 shows an example of the knowledge produced as a result of this step.

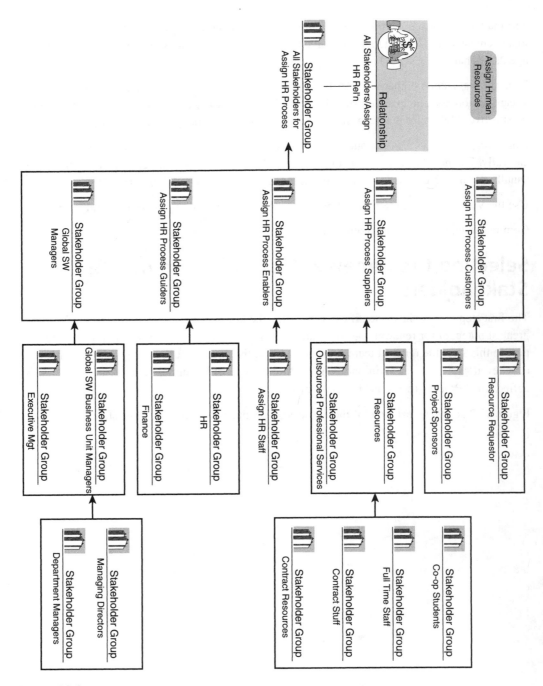

FIGURE 12.2

Stakeholders for Global Software, Inc.'s process of assigning human resources.

Techniques

As in the Business Context phase, stakeholders will be segmented and analyzed as the basis for defining project criteria, through these techniques:

- Process architecture mapping
- Stakeholder analysis

Lessons Learned

If the previous phases were done correctly, this step will simply reconfirm the findings and approach of the business context and architect and alignment activities with an update on recent events—especially if some time has passed or some key players have changed in the meantime. If no business context or process architecture phase has been conducted, conduct a fast-track version of the previous phase, emphasizing the core processes, their linkage to business performance, and the opportunities for improvement.

In the stakeholder analysis, start with the list from the business context phase and select those stakeholders who are relevant for this specific process. Then, be careful to add all internal stakeholders who are involved or affected or who can influence the process, including the workers in the process.

Gather any existing documents that relate to the interactions that the "Process-in-Focus" has (and should have) with parties outside its direct control. Gather information from various departments that interact with the process, starting with "customer-oriented" ones. Move to the supplier side and then do the same for other process interactions.

Gain support for the time, cost, and human resource requirements of the analysis and planning activities required for the startup of each possible initiative (for example, get the resources needed to complete this phase).

Formulating Process Vision

The second step of this phase defines attributes of value to the stakeholders of a specific renewal project. In this step, the organization sets the desired results of the process change that will be delivered after the project is completed. Formulating process vision provides many evaluation criteria that can be used later to appraise options for redesign.

Figure 12.3 shows an example of the knowledge produced as a result of this step.

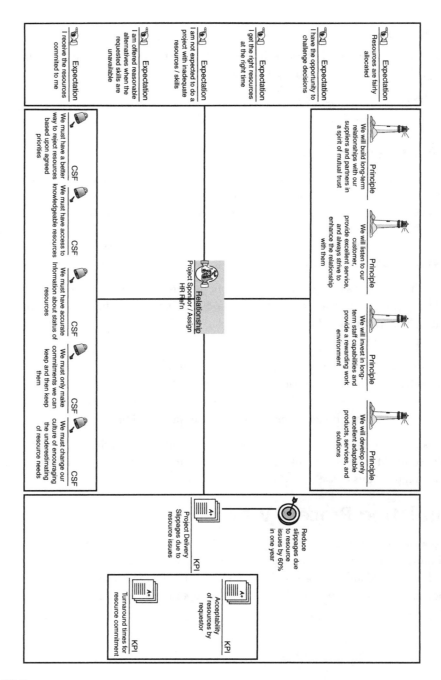

FIGURE 12.3

Stakeholder criteria for the project sponsor relationship of Global Software, Inc.'s process of assigning human resources.

Techniques

The techniques of formulating process vision are similar to those used in the business context phase, but they focus on the project's process stakeholders. Techniques include

- Interviewing

- Workshop facilitation

- Time-machine visioning, by hypothetically asking stakeholders in a future time how they regard their relationship with the company

Lessons Learned

The vision for the particular process to be renewed should refine the overall business vision developed in the business context and architect and alignment phases. However, articulating and communicating the vision is an important aspect of building a common understanding and commitment and of reducing resistance.

The vision should include descriptions of the desired future state of the organization to make sure that everyone knows almost automatically what the future will look like. Describe this state from the perspective of the process's customers (external or internal), the owners of the enterprise, the staff who will deliver process results, and the other stakeholders, if any. Use statements such as, "As a result of succeeding in this project, we will be able to say…"

Use the trends of the industry, the process type, emerging human resource concepts, and technology ideas to stimulate visionary ideas. Review and use the performance benchmark findings from earlier analysis. Ask your customers and possibly your suppliers to contribute and participate. They might have thought of things you haven't. Only they truly know their future expectations.

Express the vision in visual media, by making a video, acting out a play, or building and demonstrating a prototype. Use scenarios of standard and tricky situations to illustrate the message. Most of all, make it fun. Use this visualization to communicate, validate, and sell the future.

Identifying Performance Improvement Targets

This step defines the measurement indicators to be used to evaluate process performance today and in the future. It also targets the degrees of performance improvement based on potential and risk.

Figure 12.3 earlier in this chapter shows an example of the knowledge produced as a result of this step.

Techniques

The technique of identifying performance improvement targets resembles techniques from the business context phase but focuses on the specific expectations and needs for the project which will deliver improvements to the "Process-in-Focus." Techniques include

- Key performance indicator analysis
- Balanced scorecard analysis
- Performance benchmarking
- Negotiation
- Consensus workshops

Lessons Learned

Process performance objectives are absolutely essential to drive and guide a project forward. Targeting an 80% reduction in elapsed process time is a completely different project than trying to improve every aspect of the process by 10% (especially political and change management issues). Deciding how far a renewal project will go is the most important executive commitment made yet. It will be your source of empowerment for what you have to do, so set challenging goals but make sure that the numbers are somewhat attainable.

Start with a stakeholder relationship balanced scorecard and key performance indicators (for example, customer satisfaction) and then derive contributing process key performance indicators (KPIs —for example, on-time delivery).

For each stakeholder, identify or confirm KPIs for assessing attainment of the vision. Look for measures of effectiveness, efficiency, and adaptability. Rationalize the set of KPIs into a manageable number (maximum 5) for the overall change and compare any existing performance data against these KPIs. Determine the degree of performance improvement (*stretch goals*) in each of the KPIs that's required to meet the stakeholders' needs.

This activity looks remarkably simple on the surface, but finding KPIs that truly reflect the process under review and not a range of other processes (such as overall customer satisfaction) is very hard to do. Determining how to measure KPIs without becoming obtrusive is even harder. You can affect the performance of workers, who believe that they are being measured personally. Workers might perform better if they believe that they are being watched. If they believe that they might be held accountable for a work standard to be set by measurement, they might slow down. In both cases, they change their normal behavior, and the project moves forward based on erroneous performance results. Without reasonably accurate measures against the KPIs, decisions can be made and processes designed that won't improve the real work flow.

Defining Project Scope

This step establishes a commonly understood scope of the process to be renewed and examines its interfaces to other processes. It documents the nature of the major inputs and deliverables to ensure that critical areas receive focus and that everyone understands valid constraints.

Figure 12.4 shows an example of the knowledge produced as a result of this step.

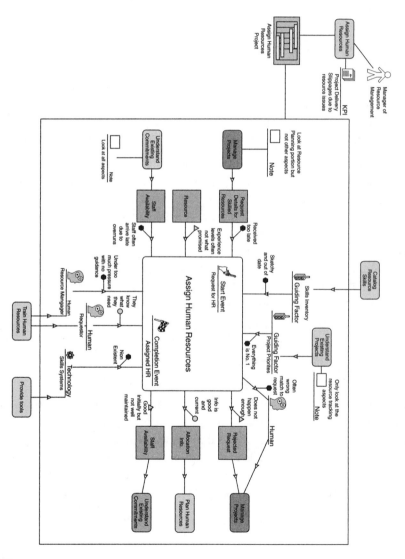

FIGURE 12.4

The scope for Global Software, Inc.'s process of assigning human resources.

Techniques

The techniques for setting project scope clearly define the edges of the project. Techniques include

- Scope modeling
- Ins and outs analysis for included and excluded aspects of the project
- Workshop facilitation
- Negotiation

Lessons Learned

Process scoping starts with the process architecture diagram and descriptions produced in the architecture and alignment phases. However, a project's scope might not coincide exactly with one process. A project might cover more than one related process or only a portion of one. It might cover the entire process but only for certain customer segments, products, or locations.

Gather an understanding of the types of triggering events, the conditions associated with them, and the desired outcomes for the renewed process. Then determine the inputs, guides, outputs, and enablers (the *IGOEs*) of the process and draw the model. An *input* is utilized, consumed, or transformed by an activity (process); it connects to the left side of a process box. A *guide* provides knowledge or direction on how or when an activity occurs; it connects to the top of a process box. An *output* is produced by or results from an activity; it flows from the right side of a process box. An *enabler* is something (a person, facility, system, tool, equipment, asset, or other resource) utilized to perform the activity; it connects to the bottom of a process box. Guides and enablers are not consumed or destroyed.

Map the IGOEs to source and destination processes, if the IGOEs are internal, or to stakeholders, if they are external. Analyze the current health of each IGOE, as relates to its role in the process. Identify the constraints each interfacing IGOE delivers to the process under renewal or places on other processes.

Commonly, the process scope will be closely aligned to interface points with other feeding or receiving processes. Examine all interfaces in and out and ask whether incoming interfaces are adequate; examine their supply as well. Ask if the receiving process gets good results and optimizes the use of what it receives. Include in the project scope those interfaces that can be accommodated without risking the project's success. Exclude from the project the analysis of interfaces that don't make too great a difference or those that can't be handled politically right now.

Think through and test the scope model by posing sample business scenarios to describe the process in a way that all stakeholders will understand.

Remember to include other aspects of scope such as locations, information types, organizational units, products, and transactions. List "What's In and What's Out" for each factor; be specific, especially with what's out. Present this and get consensus before starting analysis. You will be sorry if you don't.

Scope determination isn't an exact science—judgment is a key asset. Get some political support from the process owner or project champion at this point.

Compare the scope with the stakeholder expectations and the target levels of performance improvement. Ask yourself, "Do I feel confident that, with the currently planned scope, I can deliver the expected results for those who care?" If the answer is "No," something has to change until the scope, expectations, and target improvement levels are in balance.

Be prepared for the scope of the initiative to change as key milestones are encountered later. It might also be necessary to have a scope of analysis greater than a scope of design and of implementation. Otherwise, missing key aspects of connectivity could necessitate adding more locations or information or product types later. Be sure that the participants know the difference between what might be analyzed but not designed or implemented.

Developing Project Strategy

This step determines the initial and high-level approach and timeframe to implement the renewed process.

Techniques

Developing project strategy is as much art as science. This creative step exploits a lot of the work done before you try any of these development techniques:

- Practices benchmarking
- Technology watch
- Negotiation
- Project management

Lessons Learned

The project strategy should examine at least two and preferably three alternative solutions or approaches, considering potential technology and organizational options. These can be variations on one solution or extensions into more risk and potential reward, involving quite different strategies. The "do-nothing" solution (keep things "as-is") should always be assessed as the base case because doing nothing often isn't equivalent to staying the same in terms of business performance. Sometimes it's necessary to change dramatically to maintain your current position.

To discover new approaches, be prepared to analyze the relative market position of competitors, the availability of new technologies, or the growing scarcity of some resources.

Developing an Initial Business Case

This step documents the high-level costs and benefits of the change and shows management that business risk has been evaluated. It's intended to give managers confidence, so that the project can gain approval to proceed and obtain resource commitment.

Techniques

The techniques of developing an initial business case are the classic ones employed by organizations to justify expenditure of funds and allocation of human resources:

- Cost/benefit analysis
- Internal proposal preparation
- Negotiation

Lessons Learned

Analyze the high-level alternative approaches for potential improvement (a maximum of three), and determine the benefits associated with each alternative based on stakeholder expectations and the value added by the approach; try to quantify these benefits. Then determine the operational costs associated with each alternative. Document any nonquantifiable operational costs and benefits and examine the risks of each alternative. Add the cost of the design, development, and implementation of the solution. Work out the rate of return, cost recovery time, or whatever other decision criteria are used by the organization. Include the cost of doing nothing.

The team should carefully present the pros and cons of each approach as well as recommend one alternative as part of an internal proposal. However, the team should never defend its recommendation, only explain dispassionately. Management—not the team—should always make the final choice.

Be prepared to document and discuss the possible impact of assumptions on the return on investment. For example, would a small change in product quality lead to a huge increase in market share? What would happen if you couldn't achieve this increase?

Use the standard corporate ratios and mechanisms to prove the worthiness of the project and document the results. It's competing with other initiatives of all types for funding and management attention.

> **TIP**
>
> In this first presentation early in the project, be sure that everyone knows that this is just the first version of the business case, and that other updates will be provided later when more details are known about the solution. There will be an off-ramp, so the only risk and committed cost at this point are the resources allocated to get to the next review. In later versions, this base case will be updated with more details, specific alternatives, well-defined advantages and disadvantages, comparisons to the evaluation criteria, and overall ranking of alternatives.

Provide confidence limits (+ and – percentages) for the range of estimates of cost and benefit. Later estimates will be significantly more reliable than the initial estimates, which are made before process analysis and redesign.

In the presentations and workshops, use scenarios to help sell emotionally, and the performance evaluation criteria to avoid inappropriate non-personal biases. Use the outsider (that is, stakeholder) perspective to show why the recommended alternatives are appropriate.

Make sure that you know how decisions are really made and who really makes them before heading into working sessions and committee meetings. Do your homework and lobby in advance. This is management's real shot at making the go/no-go decision, so do lots of pre-selling one-on-one before presentations and executive workshops. Make sure that management makes the decision, or it will never fly. Their commitment is required.

Anticipate objections and be ready to deal with each. Prepare for lots of opposition and hope you don't get much.

Developing Communication and Human Change Strategy

This often-overlooked step determines the message to be sent to staff and other key stakeholders, and the media to be used to start the change management process and to create "agents of change." At this step, an organization delivers its initial message regarding change and handles initial feedback.

Techniques

Developing communication and human change strategies calls for stakeholder-based techniques such as the following, which focus on anticipated concerns:

- Stakeholder analysis
- Concerns-based change approach
- Staff and public relations

Lessons Learned

Develop and document a starting set of "principles to live by" regarding the new process and new way of running the business. Publicize this and live it. Components should include

- Core business principles and values
- Customer-focused design principles
- Project conduct principles
- Staff impact principles
- Management conduct principles

Determine commitments that will be made to the staff regarding how they will be treated as a result of changes. Identify the types of information that will be shared, how often it will be communicated, and the media and messengers for the chosen communications plan. Resolve what will be communicated to the staff and the opportunities they will have to participate in the process of making change happen. No matter what the answers are, inform the staff openly and honestly about what this change will mean to them and to the organization, so that they won't feel as though you are hiding something.

Anticipate all possible questions and objections that could come from all possible sources and build answers to them in advance. Anticipate the negatives and present them before you are asked, if possible. Make sure that all those who might be asked about the initiative and its impact know the possible questions and are prepared to answer them confidently. The responses must be credible and consistent. This won't be the case if you aren't prepared.

Commitment regarding the outcomes of the project must be made in this step. This includes what the project is attempting to do, the impact it will have on the workforce and jobs, how the project will be run, the benefits to the business, and so on. Always start messages to the staff with what a change means to them before extolling the virtues of the benefits to other stakeholders. They won't hear your message if their own concerns aren't addressed first.

Understand sales and public relations techniques such as objection management to help manage the messages and make sure that there will be time to execute the program of communication on an ongoing basis. This is real work—not something to be done in spare time. (There will be no spare time.)

Identify a person who's clearly responsible for following up and conducting the communications and change management plan.

The CEO should deliver the initial message. Commitments must be made to an ongoing communications program for the project's duration. Be prepared to repeat the message—it seldom sinks in on one go.

Be honest, no matter how painful it might be. You will pay later if you aren't.

Finalizing the Project Plan

This last (but not least) step of the Vision phase builds the project plan that will deliver performance improvement of the "Process-in-Focus." Here, the organization appoints the senior team, executive champion, project manager, and the project team members for the next two phases: the Understand phase and the Renew phase. The team undergoes training and gains commitment to the plan.

Techniques

The techniques of finalizing a project plan are based on common sense and time-proven approaches to ensuring a common understanding and assurance of support:

- Personal commitment-based project management
- Deliverable-based project planning
- Negotiation

Lessons Learned

Make sure that the commitment of all key participants is solid before starting. Build a core team of a project manager, a process owner/project champion, an acceptor, and advisors, who can support one another throughout the initiative. This group must have business experience, must have a common interest in the solution, and must be able to get along.

Assign crystal-clear responsibilities for producing deliverables before the work starts, and make sure that everyone accepts those responsibilities. Create a customer/supplier chain of deliverables inside the project. Don't manage by activity; manage by responsibilities for personal results.

Balance the results of the project (expectations, scope, and quality) against the constraints required to deliver results (time and resources), understanding which methods and tools will be employed. Always strive to balance these two competing forces. The moment the balance seems lost and the ability to deliver becomes questionable, change the balance to regain confidence. There is no other magic than to do this diligently.

Build the plan backward. Start with the envisioned project end, and select the approach to renewal by picking the appropriate steps to the end from the Process Management Framework, including management checkpoints (go/no go). Then work back through

- Deliverable end products
- Approach (work breakdown structure or project process)
- Phase deliverables
- Milestones and checkpoints for risk analysis and management review
- Project responsibility structure and reporting relationships
- Communication plan and control mechanisms
- Activity definitions
- The estimate of resource types and amounts
- The schedule

Plan to iterate this approach until all is in balance but start at what and move on to how, who, and how much. Get signed acceptance of the plan: its results, approach, and commitment to provide the resources needed.

The team composition should be cross functional with representatives from all affected business areas to assure that all aspects of the business process and its impact on other parts of the business are taken into account. The team also should include representation with project management, method, and technique experience to guide the way. Train team members together as a team to gain commitment to one approach and to build commitment to and confidence in each other.

Summary

This Vision phase sets the scene for process-based projects to be initiated properly. In many organizations, it might be seen as extra time taken away from the "real work" of the project. In reality, if this phase isn't conducted with care, significantly more work will end up being performed to correct all the confusion and lack of agreement that will surely come later. Creating the vision and scope reuses a lot of the results of the Business Context phase and Architect and Align phase. If these were not conducted and you just jumped into the Vision phase, that phase will take longer but will be worth it. Having a clear target in terms of stakeholder results, KPIs and target levels, scope, strategy, business case, plan, and communication strategy will mean that the next two phases will work well.

The Understand phase that occurs next uses the results of Vision phase to drill down into details within the provided scope. The subsequent Renew phase takes its design targets from the future state stakeholder expectations developed here. These three phases are linked and require strong integrity of models and deliverables. They cannot stand alone.

Understanding the Existing Situation

IN THIS CHAPTER

The Understand phase examines what the existing process actually does, so that you can make the right improvements and manage perceptions. In this phase, the renewal team gathers input from interviews and workshops with process participants, by measuring actual performance levels. It also analyzes what works well and not so well today. Based on this information, management and team members determine the required changes and implement some immediate improvements where feasible.

The Understand phase has six steps, as shown in Figure 13.1:

1. Confirm scope and boundaries.
2. Map existing process understanding.
3. Measure process performance.
4. Determine root causes.
5. Identify improvement priorities.
6. Implement early wins.

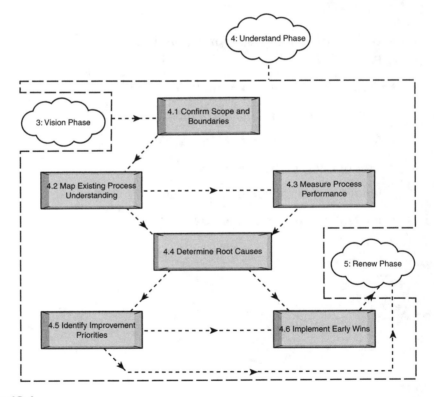

FIGURE 13.1

Process Management Framework: Steps in the Understand phase.

Overall Tricks and Traps for the Understand Phase

In the Understand phase, people often tend to work at the wrong level of detail. Some teams and individuals tend to skim along the surface, relying only on their general impressions, looking for evidence that supports their preconceived notions of the process. Others delve to the lowest level of detail in the operating procedures and don't see the overall picture at all until they've studied every aspect to death. The answer really lies in a balanced approach, in which some aspects of the process are drilled down through, but others aren't.

The objective is to *understand*, not just to build an "as-is" model. The model will be a tool and communication device—that's all.

The Understand phase must concentrate on what *actually* happens in the process, even if it's not supposed to. Don't document what the procedure guides say we should do, what the managers think is happening, or what the staff thinks you want them to be doing; instead, map the reality of how work is performed today. Gain evidence whenever you can. Some people won't like the bad news, so you have strong factual evidence of problems.

Lots of interviewing and group workshops occur during the Understand phase. It's paramount that already nervous, suspicious staff on the front lines not think that they are being evaluated personally. If they do, you will never know the truth. Evaluations must be treated as *process reviews* and not perceived as personal criticism. This means no laughing at what people do, no shaking of the head in disbelief, no suggesting other ways, and no questioning of personal motivation. Obviously, some people aren't cut out to do this type of information gathering.

This whole phase should be subject to timeboxed approaches, in which layers of the process are exposed for review and then evaluated by the team as a whole before drilling deeper. Allot a set time in each iteration for gathering facts and perceptions, work-shopping the findings, and then examining the next priority in the process. Maintain a fixed amount of time per iteration and a fixed number of iterations. Every day spent in needless detail will delay the business benefits of the solution by a day. Ask yourself if you will get more back in solution value than the effort and time you've spent in analysis.

A lot of the information gathered and analyzed in this and the next phase, Renew, can become unwieldy to coordinate and manage through conventional means. Databases, word processors, and graphic drawing packages don't help much beyond the first entry because of problems with cross-referencing and synchronization. Consider a process modeling toolkit built on an integrated repository (dictionary) to manage the information about the process and the solution. Finding the impact of a change is virtually impossible to do across many large Visio or PowerPoint diagrams.

Use common methods and tools across the team for integrity and control. Fitting the work of individuals or teams together is impossible without common means. It's confusing and annoying to reviewers when each team has to explain its own notation.

Understand and convey what you've learned. Trying to build a perfect model is dangerous and expensive! Prioritize the aspects of the process that deserve a more in-depth analysis in a timebox.

Use Pareto analysis, wherein categories of problems and issues can be examined for their frequency. Especially consider the concept of the 80/20 rule, wherein 80% of the effort and problems are found in 20% of the process steps. Focus on the right few.

Observe what you've learned but only after gathering information. You can ask tougher, more specific questions then. Ask to be shown how a particular tricky situation would be handled.

Measure at the level of granularity of change. Big change in performance usually means high-level modifications. Small change typically means minor modifications at a lower level of detail. If process steps disappear, there's no value measuring their details. The reason for measuring at the appropriate level is to be able to track performance improvements before and after the change effort.

Look for causes of flow problems and low value-added work. Especially search out situations wherein the cost of conducting existing work cannot be justified by the incremental value received by stakeholders. Ask if the extra work adds anything of value to the recipient.

Examine all guides and enablers closely, including staff competencies, motivations, and incentives. Check the official guides as well as the unofficial or undocumented ones, such as personal preferences and experience. The organizational culture is also a guide that can override a lot of great procedure manuals.

Use lots of facilitated sessions with key stakeholder involvement for validation. The objective is to get cross-functional understanding and commitment to an overall solution, not to fix problems in one person's area.

Quick wins should come early. That is, they should take no more than a few weeks or months at the outside and shouldn't wait for exhaustive redesign efforts to happen.

Confirming Scope and Boundaries

This step will challenge and confirm the scope developed in the Vision phase (see Chapter 12, "Charting the Course of Change") or create it if it hasn't yet been produced. In this step, the organization defines the boundary definitions of the process, including constraints and inter-process relationships, thereby providing controls for the analysis of the work to be conducted by the team. It is critical to confirm scope and boundaries if time has gone by since approval of the Vision phase scope approval or if new players are involved.

Techniques

The techniques used to create or validate the scope from the previous phase include

- Scope modeling
- Workshop facilitation

Lessons Learned

If a scope has been set in the Vision phase, the effort here might prove to be incidental and more of a formality. If not, the following cautions and guidelines should be taken seriously. In the best case, the scope should be examined for continued validity. This is especially true if new management and/or new project team leaders have been appointed since the original scope was conducted.

Scoping will start with the Process Architecture diagram and descriptions produced in the Architect and Align phase (see Chapter 11, "Configuring Business Processes and Aligning Other Strategies"). However, the scope of the project might not coincide exactly with earlier diagrams. The project might cover more than one related process or only a portion of one, or it might cover the entire process but only for certain customer segments, products, or locations. As mentioned earlier, this step is optional in this Understand phase if it has been adequately covered in the Vision phase and there has been little time for the business requirement to change. Validate it as a safety check.

Commonly, the process scope will be closely aligned to interface points with other feeding or receiving processes. Examine all interfaces in and out and ask whether the incoming interfaces are inadequate; also check out processes that feed the in-scope process. Ask whether the receiving process gets good results and optimizes the use of what it receives. Include those interfaces that can be accommodated without risking the project. Exclude the interfaces that don't make too great a difference or those that can't be handled right now politically.

The results of this step must be accepted by management, especially business management, because they will live with the solution, like it or not.

Scope determination isn't an exact science. Judgment is a key asset. Get some political support from the process champion at this point.

Document and draw pictures of what's in and especially list what's out. Present this and get consensus before starting analysis. You will be sorry if you don't.

Remember to include other aspects of scope such as locations, information types, organizational units, products, transactions, and so on.

Distinguish among scope of analysis, which can be greater than the scope of design and implementation. The project should be aware of its fit with other areas of the business even if it does not change them. Remind everyone that scope might change at later checkpoints as you learn more. In many cases, it might be necessary to study a wider range of characteristics than planned for initial rollout because later the solution might have to be broadened and must work when it is.

Use the scope definition for project management purposes. You will be thankful if you do. It will allow you to assure the management team's commitments and to keep your project analysts from being the cause or victim of creeping or shrinking scope change and analysis paralysis.

Make sure that all team members are intimately familiar with the scope and rationale for how decisions were made. Make it a capital offense for staff to model and analyze outside scope without an acceptor and champion's formal acceptance of the impact on the project. This means changes to time, cost, and resources must be agreed to and committed to first.

Focus on triggering events and outcomes to force an outside-in perspective that concentrates on boundaries.

Define all terms used to ensure a true understanding of what's being said. Saying that something is "in scope" can lead many people to infer completely different understandings that otherwise will only come to light much later.

Mapping Existing Process Understanding

This step obtains an *understanding* of how the existing process really is conducted and documents the understanding in a set of models and supporting notes. In this step, the project team validates and communicates the understanding to provide a baseline of understood process for gap analysis. It identifies process components to consider for measurement.

Figures 13.2 and 13.3 show examples of the knowledge produced as a result of this step.

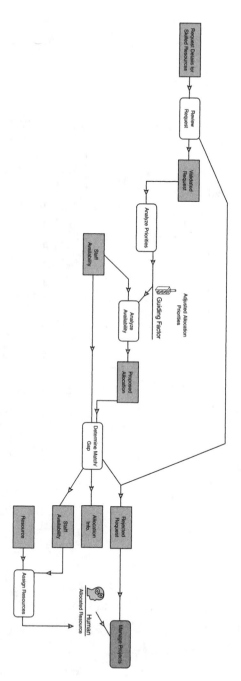

FIGURE 13.2

The current process flow for the process of assigning human resources.

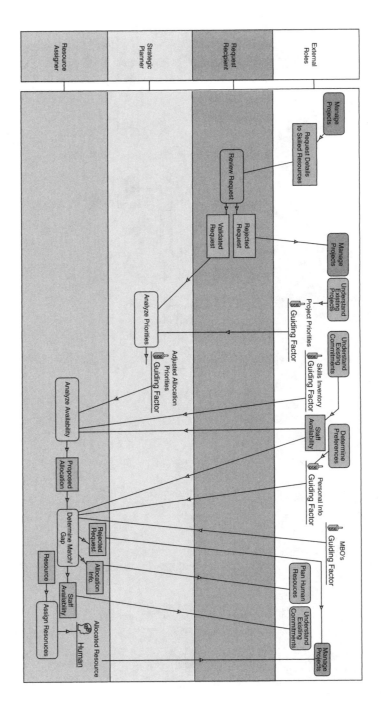

FIGURE 13.3

The current process flow with organization swim lanes.

Techniques

During this step, models of the existing process are developed by using the following techniques:

- Interviewing
- Workshop facilitation
- IGOE or swim lane process modeling

Lessons Learned

While gathering process information, focus on process flow and the objects being transformed in the process. Start from the outcomes of the process and work backward. Doing so keeps the focus on the process's purpose.

Decompose the process (step) into component subprocesses (a maximum of eight). Assign analysis responsibility to the team members to analyze components and interconnections, and to produce integrated flow and attribute models. Validate these models in a workshop.

Data models, and models or matrices of interaction between data and process, can be used. However, they won't be as beneficial at this point as they will be later when new processes are being designed. They are optional here.

Conduct process interviews with workers. Manage the time for relevance because not all details are required. For example, don't interview someone about everything she does in her job but instead discover what she does in her job that contributes to the process under study. In addition to interviewing the workers, talk to customers and suppliers. It's hard to see the impact on them from the inside looking out.

Rather than try to analyze everything before reviewing it, use layered, timeboxed analysis and prioritization that schedules all sessions in advance and reviews what has been done to date. This learning style will develop buy-in and understanding as you go and will solve the problem of getting all the key stakeholders together on short notice. You can schedule them for all sessions in advance. Make sure that all understandings and analysis are validated. Never delay a feedback or validation session. Respect the interviewee's time.

Prepare yourself to conduct interviews and run workshops. Practice before the real events, and allow sufficient time for each (two hours minimum). Document your interview results the same day you do them; otherwise, you will forget what happened. Use two staff members in information gathering interviews—one as interviewer and one as scribe. They can switch roles from session to session.

Ask these questions for each layer and process box:

- What is produced (outputs), and to which process does it go?
- What comes in (inputs), and from which process does it come?
- What determines how the work will be performed (the guides), and from which process or external stakeholder does it come?
- What is used repeatedly to do the work (enablers), and from which process or external stakeholder does it come?

Discover problems, suggestions for improvement, and opportunities for change by asking the people who do the work. They are your best source.

Don't suggest fixes as you go. Save them for the early wins and prove the savings.

Ask questions regarding the organizational aspects, such as structure, as late as possible. If this is done too early, it can result in people feeling that they have to defend the process along organizational swim lane boundaries, rather than discover opportunities to improve across the entire process.

Don't believe everything you hear. Observe the process by walking through it from beginning to end and pretending you are a customer for an order or a complaint. Walk through and challenge the troublesome situations you've heard about, not just the perfect flow.

As multiple versions and iterations of interviews are produced, an integrated process modeling software tool is invaluable for organizing the great amounts of information collected.

Measuring Process Performance

This step determines at what levels and which parts of the process to measure, and then measures the chosen aspects and steps. At this point, the renewal team determines which process steps to decompose further. The reasons for measurements and improvement priorities become clearer. This step provides a basis for tracking progress and performance incentives after process change has been implemented.

Techniques

Three techniques are used to measure the process performance:

- Interviewing
- Activity based costing (ABC)
- Various surveys and questionnaires

Lessons Learned

Measure process performance at the overall scoped level by measuring the overall key performance indicators (KPIs) performance first. Identify likely subprocesses that don't perform adequately or which show potential for improvement; then determine the subprocess performance indicators that contribute toward the overall KPIs. Finally, measure performance and document the measures in the same place as the repository of model attributes.

Find proxy measurement indicators specific to various places in the process that contribute to the overall stakeholder's relationship performance measurement if necessary. For example, customer satisfaction is a good overall KPI for the customer relationship, but the process being analyzed might be only one of several that contribute to customer satisfaction. Measuring how fast the process responds to the customer might be the best proxy.

Measure wherever the bottlenecks occur, rather than at every detailed step.

To get measurement information, consider customer surveys and other nonintrusive measures that don't affect the process being analyzed. Beware of the biasing effect that measuring can have. When staff know that you are watching and measuring, their performance changes. Depending on the staff's incentive, the results of the performance might be biased higher or lower; it won't be a true representation.

Find a quality or an effectiveness measure (such as how well are we doing what we do, and are we doing the right things for the process customer). Measure efficiency (for example, how much resource do we consume in doing what we do?). Measure adaptability (for example, how easy is it for us to change the product or service we deliver and the way we deliver it?). Common denominators are time, cost, and customer satisfaction.

If changes will occur at the macro level in the new process (that is, you've set large performance improvement objectives), measure at the macro level. Don't measure a detail that will be obliterated by the change. The counter argument also holds.

Watch for measurement variability over time. Annual, monthly, weekly, and daily transaction patterns can vary greatly. Be sure to measure the extremes, not just the averages. That's where the problems hit us hardest. Sometimes the best process solution that saves lots of frustration and reduces cost is the one that simply balances the workload.

Observed measurement problems can result in more detailed modeling having to be performed in process areas not well understood or clearly not working well. This step will iterate in time-boxes with the previous step.

Determining Root Causes

This step examines the opportunities for improvement observed during the previous mapping and measuring steps, and determines the causes or antecedents of process gaps and opportunities.

Figure 13.4 shows an example of the knowledge produced as a result of this step.

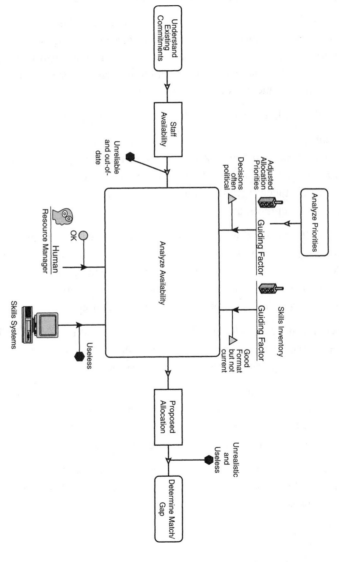

FIGURE 13.4

Root cause analysis in process flow for the Analyze Availability process.

Technique

The best technique to determine the causes of gaps is root cause analysis through approaches such as Ishikawa diagramming.[1] This diagramming traces problems backward until the problem's origin is found.

Lessons Learned

This step combines analytical and intuitive methods. Don't be afraid to use both halves of your brain—that's why the previous steps were conducted.

Identify process steps with gaps in performance and opportunities for improvement. Discovering the gaps and causes should be methodically done by examining the models and measures discovered in the preceding two steps and tracing backward to likely reasons for difficulties.

Many gaps are caused by crossing an organizational boundary where work is handed over from one unit or group to another. The earlier unit might be the cause of problems, and the latter unit might feel the effect but not know the reasons for the problems. Others are caused by passing the buck to someone else because of resource restrictions, or inappropriate measurement and reward structures.

In determining root causes, ask lots of "stupid" questions, such as

- Does the input/output flow make sense?
- Are the guides too rigid or too lax?
- What are capability and capacity of the enablers? Can they handle their assigned tasks, and are there enough enablers to get the job done?
- How do front-line workers handle typical troublesome scenarios? (To find out, role-play the scenarios with these workers and ask "What if...?")
- Are the documented procedures appropriate and, if so, does anyone use them or know how?
- Do the steps in the process contribute to the process customer values and vision? Are they necessary?
- Are the process steps performed because a customer is unhappy or another process failed to deliver? Are they a cost of having something else not done right?
- Is the sequence logical?
- Does it have to be sequential?

---

[1]*What Is Total Quality Control? The Japanese Way,* by *Kaoru Ishikawa, David J. Lu (translator), December 1988, Prentice Hall Direct*

- Do we build up unnecessary inventories? Are there queues?
- Are any resources ever idle?

Facilitated workshops that trace the cause of gaps are beneficial if a cross-functional group of front-liners is present, as well as the renewal team. Ideally, the workshop should include a facilitator, business experts, practitioners, customers, suppliers, and upstream and downstream stakeholders.

The workshops should use Ishikawa cause and effect approaches and start with the IGOEs: *inputs* and prior steps; *guides*, such as policies, methods, and procedures; *outputs* and subsequent steps; and *enablers*, such as human resources, equipment, and systems.

Build consensus on the causes before building solutions. Observe poor scenarios from beginning to end and role-play troublesome scenarios and variations.

Be sure that the removal of a constraint won't simply move the bottleneck to a later process step because the initial one was simply a governor on the flow for the overall process.

Another technique is to use red, yellow, and green stickers like traffic lights to indicate that the IGOEs in and out of a process step are healthy, of unknown quality, or in poor health. Trace backward from reds until you find the process that produces the red output.

Identifying Improvement Priorities

This step determines the potential significance and priority of improvement opportunities and defines which possible improvements could be implemented with a low degree of effort and resistance (early/quick-win candidates). In this step, the organization determines or confirms the nature of the required change program for the early win and develops an overall improvement approach.

Techniques

To determine which solutions could be implemented in the short-term and which will become part of the long-term solution, you can use three techniques:

- Application of stakeholder criteria
- Cost/benefit analysis
- Negotiation

Lessons Learned

Each solution might deliver greatly varying degrees of improvement and require greatly varying degrees of effort and implementation time. Some will entail significant overall renewal;

others will require just a simple, fast change (early win). Analyze problems, root causes, potential for improvements, and suggestions for improvements. Then determine the costs and benefits of each change against earlier stakeholder-based project evaluation criteria.

Update the evaluation criteria used for the business case to include the speed and cost of implementation. This will separate changes that need careful design and more time to achieve from those that can be implemented in the near-term.

Obtain suggestions for improvement from front-line staff as well as management. Frequently, those who perform the actual work have already thought about better ways of doing their jobs.

Some early-win changes will be maintained in the major redesign. Others won't and will be considered throwaways, providing interim benefit only and helping pay for the ultimate solution.

Early wins should impact few organizational units, be quick and inexpensive to implement, have strong support at the top and bottom of the organization, require easy enabler changes, and be low risk.

Try to implement the ideas of the front-line staff even if the benefits aren't great. This shows that you are listening and helps gain acceptance of the solution. Better yet, plan to have the front-line staff implement changes themselves; get them involved.

Implementing Early Wins

This step delivers recognized improvements early and often and markets the project team's successes. It begins delivering the returns anticipated in the business case and contributes toward staff change and executive acceptance.

Techniques

During the implementation of the early wins, four techniques will be most beneficial:

- Measurement of benefits and costs
- Project management
- Communication
- Participation

Lessons Learned

Early wins shouldn't take more than three months to implement and hopefully even less time. Plan the implementation of each early win and measure the "before" performance. After it's implemented, measure the "after" performance.

Implementing early wins can take place alternatively as part of the Understand phase or the Renew phase, if it's appropriate to delay early wins. If done now, it will be important to note the beneficial impact of early wins.

Give as much credit as possible to the staff on the front lines for their contributions and ideas. Apply these ideas toward change management objectives, letting everyone know that the ideas came from your business staff. By doing this, the staff won't let the changes fail and will be with you for what's yet to come.

Provide some project management guidance and monitoring of the business unit and other professional staff charged with implementing these wins, and make sure they do complete the changes.

Market the success as much as possible to gain support for the more long-term solutions and to begin the process of change.

Summary

Understanding the current situation with the "Process-in-Focus" is more important than many organizations realize. With their urgency to implement new systems and processes, these organizations often want to skip right past this phase. In doing so, however, they usually end up solving the wrong problem or eliminating the good things that go on today. Perhaps most importantly, they have no foundation for change, which is a journey from where you are to where you want to be. If you don't know where you are, the journey cannot begin. If you cannot show those affected why change must happen based on a sure knowledge and proof, the human change journey also won't start.

This Understand phase is important, however, in that it must not fall into analysis and modeling for its own sake. The key word is *understand*, and then move on.

Once you are ready to move, the steps in the next phase, Renew, can be initiated. The Renew phase can build on what you've learned in the Understand phase. It is the turning point from analysis to synthesis. It will build the blueprint for the future process and improved performance.

Designing the Renewed Process

IN THIS CHAPTER

In the Renew phase, an organization redesigns its business process to be able to meet the goals of the project, to accomplish the visionary expectations of the process stakeholders, and to test the design for viability. It does this by conducting research into trends and enablers of new process possibilities. It develops new concepts, models them, and then validates them in process tests. The organization re-examines the feasibility of changes and develops models to coordinate subsequent phases and a transformation strategy.

This phase has eight steps (as shown in Figure 14.1):

1. Benchmark processes and trends.
2. Gain enabler knowledge.
3. Finalize evaluation criteria.
4. Rethink the approach.
5. Model the renewed process.
6. Demonstrate/validate the renewed process.
7. Update the business case for development.
8. Develop a transformation strategy.

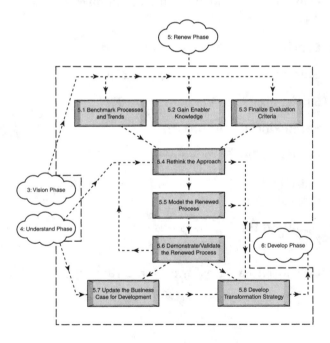

FIGURE 14.1

Process Management Framework: Steps in the Renew phase.

Overall Tricks and Traps for the Renew Phase

A lot of the information gathered and analyzed in this phase and the previous Understand phase might become unwieldy to coordinate and manage through conventional recording means. Databases, word processors, and simple graphic drawing packages don't help much beyond the first entry, due to typical changes in cross-referencing, synchronization, and impact analysis. Consider a process modeling toolkit built on an integrated repository to manage this information.

It can be tempting throughout this phase to come up with one solution and do everything possible to make sure that it sells by ignoring alternatives and pushing one view. Be careful that this doesn't occur. Give management a choice.

Use stakeholders' performance-based evaluation criteria all the way through but set the criteria at the beginning of the project. Consistently relate back all considerations and recommendations to the customer values, performance indicators, and other stakeholder criteria that have been previously defined. The magnitude of the desired performance improvements defined earlier will also ensure that the considerations for the degree of renewal can be seen as less biased. The need for improvements will be better understood if it is traced back to external business reasons rather than personal preferences.

When looking for inspiration and benchmarks, don't just look to the outside world. Often, great ideas and examples already exist internally. Learn from inside the organization as well as from others. Also, get creative—don't just copy what others do. Combine ideas in new ways that might not have been thought of in the current situation. To do this, have fun in brainstorming workshops and use the best facilitators you can afford. Don't use a team member to facilitate here. Use professionals so that team members can focus fully on what they've learned and can contribute to the innovative ideas and designs.

To test and validate the process ideas that come up, act out tricky scenarios with technology prototypes. This will allow you to conduct "what-if" walkthroughs and to communicate the essence of the solution better than you can with just charts and graphs.

Dynamic models of performance and constraints can be tried out to ensure operational feasibility. However, be sure to run these simulations carefully and use them only if it makes sense to take the extra time.

Structure the business case by fiscal year to get into the budget cycle.

Develop the master transition plan for the synchronization of all possible projects that will follow, not just the detailed schedules and work plans for each.

Benchmarking Processes and Trends

This step discovers what others have done to improve performance in the process of interest. The renewal team searches for solution ideas to remedy the gaps discovered in the Understand phase and creates new ideas based on innovative insights gleaned from others.

Techniques

The three techniques that best support the gathering of information in this step are

- Interviewing
- Focus groups
- Business practices benchmarking

Lessons Learned

To discover benchmarking trends, search the business section of newspapers, professional publications, and books on business and process change; attend conferences and professional associations; and consult with industry experts. Many organizations are members of benchmarking organizations, such as the American Productivity and Quality Center's Benchmarking Clearing House (www.apqc.com), which offer ready access to existing reports and industry analysts. Check to see if you are already paying for this service.

Lots of valuable insights can be gained by looking inside your own organization first and identifying the best way that people currently do things.

Learning from others in the same industry might prove difficult if your industry is very competitive and the source of competitive advantage is how your organization does things. If possible, learn from others through surveys and site visits. Be prepared to share your own practices and findings with those you use as a comparison. Same industry comparisons serve to make management feel more comfortable, even if the process is similar across all industries. Direct competitor knowledge will get management's attention.

Don't look in the same industry completely. Look for similar processes in other industries that still must deal with customers, suppliers, and logistics. If the desire is for breakthrough performance improvement, the best ideas can come from outside your normal business segment. Be open—quantum leaps won't come from looking in the same old places.

When reading about what others have done, don't believe it all. In many cases, those who want to make the situation sound better than it really was actually write the public relations articles. Find the project people in those organizations who were intimately involved in renewals; ask them personally about the design as well as their implementation and rollout experiences.

Your best customers and industry experts might also have ideas that you haven't yet thought of.

This activity can commence in parallel with the steps in the Understand phase (see Chapter 13, "Understanding the Existing Situation"). It doesn't have to wait until the "as-is" process model is complete.

Gaining Enabler Knowledge

This step seeks to understand the opportunities in business process change made possible by new technologies of all types. In this step, you also determine how the various combinations of computing, communications, and other technological environments can eliminate previous process constraints.

Techniques

The techniques used to obtain information on trends in technology are

- Technology watch
- Literature searches
- Technology seminars and trade shows
- Technology architecture review
- Technology vendor suggestions

Lessons Learned

Within the organization, establish an ongoing, responsible role for a staff person or team who will gather information about the enabling effects of technologies on processes of the business (technology watch). Solicit the involvement of some of these people into the project for a while.

Review industry, business, and technical literature and check out any potential technological enablers discussed or described. There's no shortage of articles these days.

Use vendors as a source of intelligence on what might be possible. Go to their presentation road shows, visit their offices, and bring them in. Ask to see what their customers have done.

Attend conferences and talk to other attendees as well as the expert speakers.

Use professional technology watch services, such as Gartner Group, Meta Group, and Giga Group. If your organization is already a subscriber, many research reports are readily available through your company contact with the group.

Look for opportunities to

- Transform unstructured processes into routine transactions with reusable and easily changed rules
- Transfer information rapidly and easily across distances, removing geographic constraints
- Reduce or eliminate human labor
- Bring complex analytical methods into the process for consistent application
- Bring significantly more information to the process as well as knowledge on how to process it better
- Change the sequence of tasks, including coordinating parallel tasks
- Capture and share knowledge to improve the process as part of the process design
- Track task status and performance, and monitor them against commitments to customers
- Connect parties directly, who would otherwise need an intermediary

Finalizing Evaluation Criteria

This step finalizes the criteria for evaluating the different options that will be submitted to the business case update later in the Renew phase. The step will produce a set of weighted requirements to be applied to all decisions on future direction and resource allocation.

Techniques

To develop evaluation criteria, use the following techniques:

- Stakeholder analysis
- Cost/benefit analysis and business case development
- Negotiation

Lessons Learned

Be sure to establish idea evaluation criteria before starting the creative design process to avoid the appearance of justifying a preconceived solution instead of evaluating several options. Base it closely on the results of the stakeholder analysis and vision, value statements/principles, KPIs, and critical success factors developed throughout the project. This step should be more of a refinement than a fresh start. Go back to the business case in the Vision phase (see Chapter 12, "Charting the Course of Change") to ensure consistency and traceability with the factors used to justify the work done to this point.

Use the external stakeholders' needs to make sense of this. It will be easier than everyone fighting for his own internal, functional biases.

Don't be afraid to consolidate and weight the components. Some will be more important than others. Some aspects will be mandatory requirements, or their lack of fit might become a showstopper. Others aren't worth fighting for. Know the difference before you start designing and gain a common understanding and acceptance up front.

Be sure to create a set of design principles based on previously defined architectural directions and on the business principles determined during the and Architect and Align phase and the Understand phase (refer to Chapters 11, "Configuring Business Processes and Aligning Other Strategies," and 13, "Understanding the Existing Situation," respectively). This will avoid esoteric forays into strange solutions that don't fit strategically, culturally, or technologically. This will also ensure that the good things we currently do that should be retained are kept and that the bad things going on are avoided. Be careful, however, since new ideas must remain alive.

Get acceptance up front from the influential players, and then communicate the criteria to everyone targeted in the communication strategy.

Rethinking the Approach

In this step, the renewal team discovers and creates ways of addressing performance gaps and opportunities, with the intent of achieving the vision, expectations, and business performance identified in the Vision phase (refer to Chapter 12). This step combines the new ideas discovered in benchmarking processes and studying technology enablers and trends and then encourages new ideas by relaxing or eliminating existing constraints discovered in the Understand phase (refer to Chapter 13). The project changes its focus at this point from analysis to synthesis.

Techniques

To rethink an approach, use

- Creativity and innovations techniques
- Workshop facilitation

Lessons Learned

The best concepts for renewal aren't new inventions but the innovative combinations of process trends, technology enablers, the relaxation of inappropriate rules, empowerment of staff, and solutions to discovered problems.

Workshops create the synergy needed to achieve these combinations. Be incredibly well prepared and plan to spend more time getting ready than actually conducting the sessions. Have all your ideas and data on wall charts and really be ready to go. Provide attendees with benchmarking data, emerging trends, and evaluation criteria before the workshop, so that they can come prepared for discussion.

Use the best facilitators you can get. The team members shouldn't facilitate; they should be part of the creative exercise. Find an outsider for pure, creative facilitation.

In the workshop, the quantity of ideas is initially more important than their merit. A discussion of quality will occur later in the session. Expand ideas before evaluating them and then narrow the list through the application of the evaluation criteria.

Initially in the workshop, focus on the following styles of discussion:

- Divergence (expanding ideas)
- "Right-brain" attitude (guesswork and intuition)
- No judgment (keeping ideas alive)
- Opportunism (turning problems into solutions)
- Acceptance (finding ways how it could work)
- Openness to options (finding multiple ways)

It's the facilitator's job to create and maintain the right order and attitude of openness.

Subsequently in the workshop, focus on the following interaction styles:

- Convergence (evaluating and reducing the list of options)
- Application of evaluation criteria
- "Left-brain" attitude (turning concepts into plans)
- Acceptance (finding ways to make it work)
- Feasibility assessment

It's the facilitator's job to switch to an approach of assessment according to the criteria established in the earlier step, "Finalizing evaluation criteria." Also the facilitator must go back and make sure that management's intentions established in the Business Context and Vision phases are well known and honored. The solution options developed at this point are there only to meet these requirements. Estimate or speculate how well the potential solutions will meet the KPI targets established earlier.

Make the workshop creative and fun, and do it away from the office. Bring toys and mind-stretching games. Laugh. Get creative.

After the workshop

- Expand the details for the short list of alternatives from the workshop
- Examine the technical feasibility of implementing the solutions
- Examine the high-level costs and benefits
- Reapply the evaluation criteria in greater detail
- Select no more than three options or variations for management consideration, further modeling, and business case evaluation
- Recommend the most appropriate option, taking into account performance objectives and risk

After the workshop, also make sure that there's sufficient time to think through each potential solution. Build a plan to evaluate each more thoroughly.

Workshop attendees should be those who've been involved in analyzing the current situation: those who will recommend acceptance of the solution, subject matter experts, and the project team. You might also choose to invite key senior managers as long as they are totally up to speed before they arrive. Observers can attend if they absolutely have to, but, if they do, they must only observe and not participate unless specifically asked to contribute something by the others in the room. The process owner, project champion, or another key player on the acceptance side of the project should kick off the session.

Modeling the Renewed Process

For small changes, this step updates the models produced in the Understand phase. In more typical situations, the renewal team creates new process models of the alternatives under consideration during this step. It also defines the implications for development of guides and enablers in the next phase, Redevelop. Modeling the renewed process provides the basis for simulation model tests, if they will be conducted.

Techniques

To create models of the alternatives under consideration, use the following techniques:

- Event analysis
- Reverse Ishikawa diagramming
- IGOE or swim lane process modeling

Lessons Learned

Assign team members to come up with models for each alternative. Then, as a group, validate or eliminate existing event triggers, and determine new event triggers where needed. Identify different and new outcomes required to satisfy the stakeholders of the initiating events, and conduct analysis of the desired events. Decompose the process (step) into component sub-processes (consider a maximum of eight per level); then analyze the components and interconnections, produce integrated flows, and document model attributes.

Models of information entities and their attributes can be used, as well as the models or matrices of interaction between data and process. However, extra time spent here will just prolong the Renew phase and might delay implementation. Create such models if you have to look for technology solutions, especially software. These models can then be used to ask vendors whether they can meet the documented process and data requirements.

Manage the time and stay focused; knowing all the details is not required.

Make sure that all designs are validated.

To have confidence in your design, ask the same questions that you asked of each layer and process box examined in the Understand phase. However, in the Renew phase, select the answer you want to see in the future, all the time designing for no disconnects. Questions should include

- What comes in (inputs) and from which process does it come?
- What is produced (outputs) and to which process does it go?
- What determines how the work will be performed (guides) and from which process does it come?
- What is used to do the work (enablers) and from which process does it come?

Deal with the organizational aspects as late as possible in this step. Stay with roles instead of positions at this point. If you try to deal with organizational structure when the process isn't designed, you will get a suboptimal result because everyone will be speculating on what changes will occur in their area, or swim lane.

The approach to modeling the new process (the "to-be") is the same as for modeling the existing process (the "as-is"). Modeling proceeds down from the top in layers, and priority for more detailed description is given to the areas of greatest uncertainty. The "to-be" model varies from the "as-is" model in that the source of information for the new model isn't a series of interviews but the concerted effort of a few staff members involved in the creative exercises and prior research activities. There's no reconciliation of gaps because the process is designed from the top down to have none.

As a check on "to-be" models, try using a reverse Ishikawa or Fishbone diagram. Rather than going backward from the problems observed, as done in the Understand phase root cause analysis, a reverse Ishikawa starts with the problems that you want to avoid or the risks that could prevent the solution from working. It then asks the question, "What do we have to have in our inputs, guides, outputs, enablers, and processes to ensure integrity and optimum performance across the entire process? This model helps you find the design principles that must be in place to avoid problems. This is a good design approach as well as a great validation technique.

An integrated process modeling software tool with a repository of process knowledge is of great assistance as versions and iterations are produced.

Demonstrating/Validating the Renewed Process

This step proves that the alternatives are viable or discovers that they aren't. It delivers buy-in to the new process design through models that demonstrate and predict behavioral and measurable performance improvements. Demonstrating the changes ensures consistent visualization of the new process and some aspects of its enablers. Through this step, the organization achieves a common understanding and acceptance of the proposed solutions.

Techniques

To validate the renewed process, use four techniques:

- Process scenarios
- Interface prototyping
- Simulation
- Workshop facilitation

Lessons Learned

Business process scenarios are a powerful way to visualize and test the new process solution. These scenarios provide paths through the process model from the perspective of the stakeholders external to the process. Each stakeholder type has a comprehensive set of events that trigger the process. When these events happen, they might bring various conditions that initiate actions in different process paths. An action ends with the accomplishment of the appropriate outcome associated with each path. These scenarios can be conveyed as a role-playing story.

To produce the scenarios, revisit the event/condition/outcome analysis conducted in the process scoping (Vision phase) or understanding (Understand phase) of the existing process. Create stories of transactions that follow different paths and test the tricky situations that the new process will have to handle. Describe the flow from the triggering event through to the final outcome from the perspective of someone or something being transformed—not from the dispassionate point of view of the boxes on a flow chart. Consider role-playing difficult scenarios to demonstrate to others what the process will really do, in terms that they can relate to. Use this to change attitudes of management and staff. Ask those reviewing the scenarios to come up with exceptions and role-play once more to either validate or discover shortcomings in the design.

The scenarios can be used as test cases in user acceptance testing and other enabler validation in the Redevelop phase.

Build prototypes of the technology interface and include these as part of the scenarios and role-plays to prove the concept of the technology-enabling role. It's unnecessary to actually construct all the underlying technical infrastructure or all the normal application links and interfaces. Focus on the interface mock-ups and stick to the script of the scenarios.

The scenarios, using the support of the prototypes, should be used to validate the human-to-machine interface. They are also a framework for the technology and procedure development activities that can then be developed more rapidly. Use them as change management tools for the affected stakeholders and staff and as training tools for change agents. They can also help validate that the simulation is testing the right things. With these, management can visualize the process solution.

Consider building simulation models that approximate the performance characteristics of the process through mathematical (statistically based) models of the process. Use these to test "what-if" situations and to find the elusive moving bottlenecks in the new process design, as well as to check on resource requirements to optimize performance.

These simulations should be used to test operational performance improvement through stochastic (that is, statistical with random variations) mathematical patterns of activity with time, cost, and resource-constrained parameters. They shouldn't just be used as equations with averages. Be cautious because simulation models can't model all performance characteristics. Typically, only a few variables are included out of a much larger set that might be in play.

To develop simulations, extend the static process models already developed by adding statistics that represent expected and possible business events, plus enabler productivity and availability, with the appropriate statistical distributions.

If using simulation to validate new process designs, be cautious. Invalid data samples, poor assumptions, and incorrect algorithms aren't unusual. Results often can give a false sense of optimism or pessimism. This tricky work requires good knowledge of statistical theory and sampling methods. Done properly, however, it can save a lot of startup time and effort. Be careful with simplistic simulation tools that can gloss over complex scenarios.

Regardless of the extent of the validation conducted or the types of testing performed, evaluate the options against evaluation criteria, and reduce and eliminate obvious nonperforming options.

When using all these validation techniques, you must keep in mind the business reasons for the process design. Validation occurs against the criteria that we worked so hard to develop. These criteria will be used extensively in the next step.

Updating the Business Case for Development

This step finalizes the decision on the alternatives for renewal and provides approval to proceed with developing and implementing guides and enablers. It is based on the re-examination of the Return on Investment or other organizational performance criteria. In this step, the organization assesses risk and undergoes a gate safety check review. Successful passage renews the executives' and staff's commitment.

Technique

To update the business case, the primary technique to use is cost/benefit analysis.

Lessons Learned

The team should carefully analyze and present the pros and cons of each approach as well as recommend one alternative. However, they should never defend their recommendation, only explain dispassionately. Management—not the team—should always make the final choice.

For each option, re-examine the benefits of the solution, review all costs of development and implementation, and determine the cost/benefit by budget cycle. Review assumptions, risks, and sensitivity of variables used in assumptions used to do financial and performance calculations. Sometimes a small variation will throw off the viability of the alternative. For example, would a small change in product quality lead to a huge increase in market share? What would happen if the organization couldn't achieve that increase?

Use the standard corporate ratios and mechanisms to prove the worthiness of the project. It's competing with other initiatives of all types for funding and management attention. It's not too late to decide not to proceed.

Make sure that you know how decisions are really made and who really makes them before heading into working sessions and committee meetings. Do your homework and lobby in advance with key influencers.

Update the prior business case with more details, specific alternatives, well-defined advantages and disadvantages, comparisons to the evaluation criteria, and an overall ranking of alternatives.

Provide new confidence limits (+ and – percentages) for the estimates of cost and benefit. Later estimates should be significantly more reliable than the internal estimates, made before process redesign.

This is management's last real shot at deciding "Go/No-go," so do lots of preselling one on one before presentations and executive workshops. In the presentations and workshops, revisit scenarios to help sell emotionally and remind managers of the performance evaluation criteria they chose at the beginning of the phase to avoid inappropriate personal biases. Use the outsider stakeholders' perspectives to show why the recommended alternatives are appropriate.

Make sure that management makes the decision, or renewal will never fly. Their commitment is required.

Anticipate objections, and be ready to deal with each. Prepare for lots of opposition, and hope you don't get much.

Use the standard cost/benefit ratios and business case mechanisms to avoid any perception of trying to "force one through."

Developing a Transformation Strategy

This step builds a framework for all the results to be accomplished in the Develop and Implement phases, which will be covered in Chapters 15, "Developing Capability for the Renewed Process," and 16, "Implementing and Rolling Out the Business Solution." In this step, the renewal champions gain management commitment to the schedule of tasks that must be accomplished and provides direction to all project teams, who must provide deliverables to overall rollout initiatives. At this point, the process owner and project manager deliver to the rest of the organization the ability to manage the remainder of the project.

Techniques

To develop a transformation strategy, the last step in the Renew phase, you need to use the following techniques:

- Commitment-based project management
- Negotiation

Lessons Learned

This step delivers an overall synchronized approach for development and rollout. It should result, not in a detailed plan, but in a directional document showing dependencies and timeframes. To accomplish this, identify the most appropriate sequence and phasing of solution implementation that delivers the optimum business benefits as soon as possible. Determine the staff's capability to accommodate changes while keeping the business operating. For each enabler area—such as human resources, technology, and facilities—determine the required solutions by business rollout stage. Then develop a professional approach and a quick-cut, high-level plan. Consolidate these approaches into an overall strategy.

Structure the deliverables and dependent projects by looking at the steps in the Develop and Implement phases. Also, use the Process Management Hexagon (refer to Chapter 3, "Principles of Process Management") to be sure that no important aspects of change are missed.

The prime driving force will be the decision regarding the major transition points toward the complete solution. These "releases" must be distinct and clear, so that each responsible manager knows exactly what has to be produced at each release point, and so that the business can accrue early beneficial results. Avoid bang solutions if at all possible.

Remember, the business must transform itself while it's still doing business. This will stress the resources unless early savings free up the time and mind-share required for change. Emphasize the importance of the early savings first.

The overall project manager shouldn't take on one of the building initiatives (facilities, systems, jobs and organization, HR, and so on) but should remain the overall driver and guider.

Don't ignore people's ability to change—it might just take more time than you think. Revolutionary ideas can be implemented in an evolutionary manner, if planned that way.

Don't ignore constraints and agreements currently in place, such as collective bargaining agreements and long-term customer or supplier arrangements. There's a lot to synchronize.

Be prepared for lots of stonewalling, negotiation, and changes. Be flexible and remember the overall objectives.

Summary

The Renew phase delivers the results that will guide the building and implementation of the business process and enabler solution. It uses all the work products delivered in earlier phases to design and evaluate options for change. It tests and then picks one approach that will best serve the goals of the business. The Renew phase is both highly technical through process model development and highly personal through creative thinking workshops and process scenarios. It is the culmination of the Process Management Framework. At the end of the Renew phase is the most important checkpoint of the framework. Before this, the cost will have been a fraction of the cost of developing and implementing the chosen solution.

The following two phases, Develop and Implement, will work out the details of the solution and build or acquire the enabling technologies and human capabilities. They will also roll out the solutions across the organization in a logical sequence. They will be the vehicle to deliver new capabilities.

Developing Capability for the Renewed Process

IN THIS CHAPTER

During the Develop phase, an organization develops and constructs all the components of the solution in detail and builds or changes all the supporting mechanisms that provide capability.

The Develop phase consists of nine steps:

1. Build physical infrastructures.
2. Provide human core capabilities.
3. Build computing infrastructure.
4. Develop processes, procedures, and rules.
5. Redefine jobs.
6. Design organizational changes.
7. Update human resources policies.
8. Develop/integrate technology and systems.
9. Develop training capability.

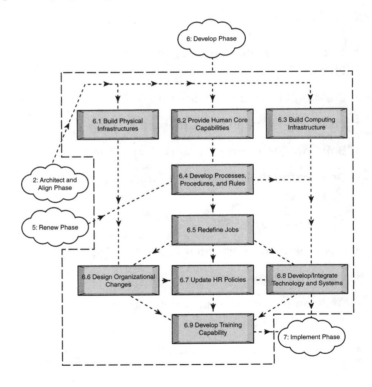

FIGURE 15.1

Process Management Framework: Steps in the Develop phase.

Overall Tricks and Traps for the Develop Phase

The Develop phase is usually the period within the Process Management Framework when the majority of time and money are spent. It can also be the point when organizations let up, thinking that they've designed the solution so there doesn't need to be a great amount of attention paid, that everything will work out. Experience has shown that nothing could be farther from the truth. Development and implementation of any one of the change factors is, by itself, a risky proposition. Making all the changes at once isn't for the faint of heart.

More than anything else, getting through the Develop phase requires exceptional project management skills and a consistent management method for planning, controlling (or continuously improving the project plan), and gaining acceptance (or hand-over) for the results produced. Part of the job of the overall project manager is to ensure that this is happening consistently.

This phase can be managed through a number of distinct programs, each of which can be the responsibility of a special team or teams:

- An Information Technology program, incorporating the steps "Build computing infrastructure" and "Develop/integrate technology and systems." It can operate under the umbrella of a technology organization or as a set of projects.

- A Human Resource Transformation program, incorporating the steps "Provide human core capabilities," "Update HR policies," and "Develop training capability." It can operate under the umbrella of a human resources organization or as a set of projects.

- A Physical Facilities Design and Construction program incorporating the step "Build physical infrastructures." It can operate under the umbrella of an engineering, construction, or maintenance organization or as a set of projects.

- A Process and Structure program, incorporating "Develop processes, procedures, and rules," "Redefine jobs," and "Design organizational changes." It can operate under the umbrella of a business or process organization or as a set of projects.

Regardless of how the work is structured, each program should have its own clearly accountable project manager/leader, under the direction of an accountable, overall change-program manager. It's critical that the overall program manager hold regular control sessions to ensure communication and commitment among these subteams.

Creating a dedicated physical project site is recommended to ensure program management coordination. Such a Process Management War Room, houses all the support tools and provides a visible focus for the program's activities.

> **NOTE**
>
> The set of measures and incentives for the Develop phase varies from those described in the earlier phases of the Process Management Framework. The Develop phase's measurements and incentives are typically oriented toward getting the deliverables produced on time, within budget, and to quality standards. They are project and program oriented. This does not mean that the business performance targets are forgotten. They are still the main driver, but every delay because of failure in the Develop phase will rob the organization of the benefits that sold the business case.
>
> It's not unusual to find that the teams working on these programs also have incentives and rewards built around the delivery process for which they are experts. Although not a process example per se, the general contractor for the rebuilding of the Los Angeles freeways after the most recent major earthquake finished many months early and received several hundreds of millions of dollars in bonuses. The value of the time saved was worth it to the city's commuters and administrators. Likewise, it's normal for contract penalties to be incorporated into agreements when outside companies build major components of solutions for large organizations.

Building Physical Infrastructures

During this step, the organization constructs and builds new physical facilities, consolidates redundant facilities, and/or eliminates unnecessary ones.

Techniques

The techniques for building physical infrastructures include

- Project management
- Professional practices for each specialty area
- Communication with other project teams

Lessons Learned

This step is part of the Physical Facilities Design and Construction program.

First, review the existing infrastructures, architectures, strategies, and project portfolios for physical modifications and the building or acquisition of new facilities and equipment. Include a review of the Architect and Align phase to see what other strategies, plans, and initiatives are planned and under way. Then, revisit the Vision phase to comprehend the enabling effect of the required infrastructure change. Use the process business case to obtain the funding/budget for infrastructure changes. When building the plan for infrastructure, include the phasing of facility introduction according to logical business sequences (define clearly the interim transition points that provide business value).

The facility component of process renewal is often overlooked, resulting in much disappointment later. Don't delay this activity. It takes time to specify, design, contract, build, acquire, and deliver the facilities. They have to be ready. One European client that I interviewed told me of the time they did everything except get the local municipality to build the road to their new processing center. Because they had given notice on the old facility, they had to get special vehicles to transport the staff during the rainy and muddy season. This was a distinct embarrassment and a productivity drain.

Building physical infrastructures can commence as soon as the Architect and Align phase is completed. If the degree of changes required is substantial—for example, buildings need to be eliminated, warehouses must be consolidated, or a new facility needs to be constructed—there will be no choice but to start as soon as possible.

Providing Human Core Capabilities

This step puts in place new ways of providing more capable and adaptable human resources. During this step, the organization educates its staff on the fundamentals required for the new process to work. It also plans the strategy for replacing staff if that will likely be required.

Techniques

As in the previous step, the techniques used to provide human core capabilities are

- Project management
- Professional practices for core HR enhancement (training, hiring, and layoffs)
- Communication with other project teams

Lessons Learned

This step is part of the Human Resource Transformation program.

Review the strategies for human resource numbers, levels, and core capabilities, as well as for hiring or laying off staff, for the duration of the process renewal project. Coordinate activities with other strategies, plans, and initiatives planned and under way. After completion of the Vision phase for required human resource change, obtain funding/budget for HR enhancements referring to the process business case.

Build the plan for HR changes, including the phasing of results, according to logical business sequences (define clearly the interim transition points that provide business value).

Developing human core capabilities can commence as soon as the Architect and Align phase is completed. If the degree of changes required is substantial—for example, completely different jobs and skills are required at higher levels—or if the responsibilities will expand to more of a customer and outcome responsibility, there will be no choice but to start as soon as possible. This would include providing staff with the basic business training required or replacing those who can't handle the new requirements with those who can. The potential ramifications of not acting include the possibility that the new process solution might not deliver the hoped-for improvements.

Implementation delays could also occur as the organization learns how to deal with raising the level of capabilities, so allow enough time for people to transition and get it wrong for a while.

Don't underestimate how long it will take to change attitudes. Give people a chance to start the journey of personal change.

Make the collective bargaining units a part of the exercise if at all possible. You will have to deal with this sooner or later. It will become more difficult if you delay or put off what will be a tricky aspect of transformation.

Put in place an overall program of internal and external opportunities for staff to learn and grow.

Building Computing Infrastructure

Building computing infrastructure includes building and testing the networks for human and data communications and the necessary interfaces among existing and new technologies. In this step, the organization evolves and tests standards consistent with the IT principles of the technology architecture. It also starts to put in place the core technologies required to support the new processes and applications.

Techniques

In building computing infrastructure, three techniques are necessary to ensure success:

- Project management
- Professional design and development practices for each specialty and profession
- Communication with other project teams

Lessons Learned

This step is part of a larger information technology program.

Building computing infrastructure can start as soon as the Architect and Align phase is completed. If the degree of changes required is substantial—for example, new wide area networks and database management systems—there will be no choice but to start as soon as possible; otherwise, the applications development might be delayed as the organization learns how to deal with the new capabilities.

Review the organization's architectures, strategies, and project portfolios for information technology, data, applications, and telecommunications. It's critical to review the Architect and Align phase to see what other strategies, plans, and initiatives are planned and under way because you will need to obtain funding for the initiative by showing how cross-functional solutions can be delivered. Don't try to justify the infrastructure based on one process alone.

Developing Processes, Procedures, and Rules

During this step, the "To-Be" process models developed in the Renew phase are expanded into greater levels of operational detail to assist staff to perform new jobs. The organization writes policies required for new processes to be effective. It terminates old policies, procedures, and practices, and writes new business rules and procedures.

Techniques

A high-level of communication with the other subproject teams is necessary when using the following techniques for this step:

- Process modeling to the workflow level
- Policy writing
- Business rules design
- Procedure guide preparation
- Multimedia (text, graphics, images, voice, or video) reference material design
- Negotiation
- Project management

Lessons Learned

This step is a natural extension of the Renew phase and is part of the larger Process and Structure program.

The basic approach to develop processes, procedures, and rules is to continue the process design work conducted in the Renew phase. Drill down each process step of the "To-Be" model to its elementary level of detail, so that all boxes are at the bottom level and assigned to a role in the organization. This finalizes the flow of work from role to role.

As you drill down to the detailed process levels, many policy issues have to be reviewed. These will likely surface as challenges to the existing definition of business rules that might no longer be appropriate for the new process. Have a policy/rules committee in place during this activity to resolve these challenges quickly. This group of empowered decision-makers must meet regularly (weekly at the very least) and make decisions without delay. The new business rules might also have to be encapsulated in formal organizational policy to become official. Don't ignore this formality if it's required.

Procedure guides should flow easily from the process descriptions; however, an understanding of how the roles and jobs will be structured (although they won't be final yet) is also necessary to ensure that they link and flow. Be careful to write job and role descriptions in as modular a style as possible for ease of change later. Use event triggers as the initiator of the process step, response definition as the description of what gets done, and outcome as the result that must be achieved. Together these will form the basis for job descriptions and accountability.

If the procedures will be automated and put online for multimedia real-time access, you will have to develop and test the mechanism for population, ongoing update, and distribution of these instructions. The procedures must be written with additional linkage information built in. Coordination with the systems team throughout this step is critical.

Redefining Jobs

This step defines the roles to be played in the new process. In this step, the organization groups the roles into whole jobs, makes clear the initial relationships between roles and between players, and writes new role descriptions. It also ensures or finalizes agreements with collective bargaining units.

Techniques

The techniques of redefining jobs include

- Event/outcome analysis
- Customer/supplier chain analysis
- Job description preparation
- Collective bargaining
- Negotiation
- Project management

Lessons Learned

This step is a natural extension of the Renew phase and is part of the larger Process and Structure project.

Starting with the process descriptions, define logical roles before looking at job descriptions. Roles can then be assembled into jobs, and changes can easily be accommodated. Look at logical roles by examining triggers and outcomes first and then looking at staff capability to conduct all the process steps linking the two. Look for logical breaks in professional practice or expertise if hand-offs must be incorporated.

Determine the style of organizational structure anticipated, such as team or hierarchical. Based on the style, determine the degree of empowerment and accountability each role and job should have. Would the employee

- Completely follow the steps, rigorously going by the book(employee doesn't exercise judgment)?

- Be completely empowered to make decisions on the job, with little in the way of rigorous procedures to follow?

- Operate under some combination of following the rules and exercising judgment? If so, how?

At each logical node or hand-off in the process from job to job or person to person, be sure to define the method by which the hand-off or transfer of responsibility is to be handled. Don't assume that it will just happen or that people will know what to do. Consistent with the Flores–Winograd Commitment Model described in Chapter 2, "Organizational Responses to Business Drivers," make sure that the following steps in the customer supplier protocol are in place:

1. Prepare for the initiation of the hand-off (determine what to propose or to request of the other party and how to do it).

2. Negotiate and understand the conditions of mutual satisfaction (including counter-proposals and requests) until a common commitment is negotiated.

3. Perform the work, monitor progress, and deliver the results.

4. Assess the results of delivery (including measuring performance).

Evaluate the relationship between the supplier of the work and the customer for breakdown in delivery or satisfaction and improvement potential.

Make sure that the collective bargaining representatives are aware and involved early on, as appropriate. It's paramount to prevent collective bargaining conflicts from becoming an unresolvable issue.

Here are some guiding principles for situations in which roles and jobs must support a more flexible and empowered environment:

- Jobs become resources to serve other jobs. People must see themselves as nodes on a horizontal value chain or flow chart, not hierarchical boxes on an organization chart.

15

DEVELOPING CAPABILITY FOR THE RENEWED PROCESS

- As you make the processes simpler, jobs will cover more responsibilities and might be more complex.
- Job enrichment should occur as a result of this broadening of responsibilities. Make sure that everyone can become worker and middle manager combined.
- Support people in teams—don't leave them as isolated individuals.
- Flatten decision-making by reducing organizational levels and empowering staff but establish measurement of and clear accountability for the results.
- Encourage natural leaders to emerge and play key roles.
- Transform managers into coaches, consultants, and facilitators who help teams and develop staff potential. Hold managers accountable for the same results as the teams.
- Give executives incentives to become closer to the customer and the process, as well as to lead and influence more.
- Through process ownership, expand senior managers' scope of influence, to cover those who don't work for them.

Designing Organizational Changes

In this step, the most appropriate organizational structure is designed, given the requirements of business performance and process design. The step provides a framework to accommodate the desired new job definitions to ensure that the organization becomes more flexible and responsive. Arriving at a good organizational structure adds to the building of consensus on change.

Techniques

The techniques to consider for designing organizational changes are

- Team-based organization design
- Collective bargaining
- Negotiation
- Project management
- Thick skin

Lessons Learned

This step is a natural extension of the Renew phase and is part of a larger Process and Structure program.

Determine the appropriate organizational style, based on the nature of expected products and services and on the emerging logical roles and job definitions. Will the style involve

- Mass production and punctuated innovation, long business cycles with a low skilled work force—that is, the traditional hierarchical structure around specialized functions?

- Continuous improvement in processes and mass customization (variation) in products and services for each customer—that is, a process organized from customer event trigger through customer outcome and satisfaction?

- Mass production transitioning to continuous improvement and mass customization—that is, a mixed function and process orientation?

The second option, a process organized from event trigger through to outcome, features

- Well-designed, natural organizational units that should send finished products, or complete logical services, to one another.

- Process teams that manage completely from business event through business outcome.

- Strong "customer" orientation and accountability for results. This means managing from the outside stakeholder back into the organization, even if the customer or stakeholder is "internal."

- Administrative functions incorporated as part of the workflow.

- Information shared broadly across the process organization, especially results and measurements.

The third option can be an intermediate step to full process organization, which can evolve later. It is a mixed function/process approach, bearing these hallmarks

- Product or function management is stovepipe-oriented in a traditional vertical product expertise fashion. Process management is laid horizontally across all product and service organizations.

- Traditional professional excellence (in product and function management) and process orientation (in cross-functional ownership) are both required but must work together for the good of the corporation.

- Any difficulty in finding the right process owner—one without conflicting goals—must be overcome and reconciled.

- Consideration should given to turning over the process ownership to the customer of the process—that is, the one with the greatest vested interest in the result, not the supplier.

A mixed function/process approach might be the only realistic option in situations where process change and organization change aren't simultaneously possible because multiple processes flow across multiple organizational units.

Consider contracting out those tasks that aren't your core competencies for the future, such as

- Backroom operations that can be performed better, faster, and cheaper by a third party than you can do them. This includes operations from which you can reallocate your staff to more core business functions.

- Non-strategic processes of little direct value to customers.

- Commodity functions that aren't part of your value proposition.

- Activities that will draw key resources away from the opportunities or threats in the marketplace.

- Processes that, to do well, require significant growth in organizational resources or investment in new capabilities that might not be possible for your organization.

- Operations subject to disruptive industry changes, to which your internal organization won't be able respond quickly enough.

- Operations that, because of uncertainty in the market, pose too great a risk in overhead structures and long-term commitments.

- Functions that haven't succeeded in changing or delivering expected outcomes in the past.

Consider partnerships with other organizations of trust if fast-changing relationships exist between customers and suppliers, or if business cycles change faster than your ability to respond internally. Investigate new partnerships if the risk of overhead structures and long-term commitments becomes too great.

If you are outsourcing parts of your business, be sure not to let your key resources go to the partner organization. Those staff members who know what's required to make the new relationship work and who can keep the supplier honest must remain on your team. This is an all too frequent experience with outsourcing arrangements. If you can't maintain your ability to remain a smart customer or buyer, you will be constrained in being a good supplier to your customers. Make sure that your suppliers have an incentive to make their customers' customers—that is, *your* customers—successful.

Updating Human Resources Policies

Updating human resources (HR) policies eliminates the existing constraints on process management imposed by employee guidelines crafted to fit the old work model. An update also enables the new style of organization to function effectively. This step provides incentives to staff to move toward the required behavior and team performance. It allows a more flexible allocation of staff and broader definitions of jobs. It also deals with displacement of existing staff and hiring of new employees.

Techniques

To update HR policies, use the five following techniques:

- Collective bargaining re-negotiation
- Team incentives and performance measurement
- HR policy writing
- Negotiation
- Project management

Lessons Learned

This step is part of a larger Human Resource Transformation project program.

Get the HR staff working with the renewal team as soon as reasonably possible—long before you reach the Develop phase. An HR staff's own processes of change are often very slow and cautious. They need time to think of the ramifications of this specific process and the policy changes it will require in other areas not yet progressing through renewal. HR must consider the implications of some staff changing, but all. HR must become part of the process renewal solution, and not an obstacle.

Negotiations with collective bargaining units or staff representatives could slow down changes in HR policy, so start early and build trust and support, no matter how unpleasant the negotiations might be.

Incentive systems work; however, for process-oriented approaches, they will be different than they are going into the project. Incentives must be aligned with the improved performance targets that the process change is attempting to deliver. They must be directly tied to actual customer satisfaction and the other Key Performance Indicators as defined earlier in the Business Context and Vision phases.

New incentive systems might orient payment and recognition more toward team-based, process-value creation and performance. Sharing rewards and recognition within the team would be based only on the degree of overall team performance. The bigger the pie, the more there will be for everyone, although some might be entitled to a bigger portion than others based on other factors. However, recognition should also be more than just financial rewards. Providing positive feedback to successful teams, time away for personal needs, visible published recognition of superior performance, opportunities for advancement, and other acknowledgments can go a long way toward keeping the process working well.

Individual evaluations might take into account advancement and contribution to teamwork objectives and become more peer-based, instead of just supervisory appraisals.

Under HR policies updated to fit the new organization, positions should be filled according to the expertise, capability, and character of the individual, and not be based on seniority.

With flattening of the levels of the organization, employees might be promoted into more responsibility within the process and not to positions away from the customer or outside the day-to-day process operation. A new team member might serve simple everyday customers and then be trained and promoted to take on mid-sized clients. With continued progression, he might become a major customer representative and, ultimately, perhaps a global account manager. All the time, however, the role is one of serving customers.

Developing/Integrating Technology and Systems

This step levers the process vision and process design into a set of systems solutions that will enable improved performance and support the new job definitions. In this step, the organization develops these solutions based on the models and prototypes developed in the prior phases; this accelerates the systems development process and reduces systems development time and business risk. Managers will incrementally release versions of the systems solution, keeping in mind the need to provide maneuverable solutions.

Techniques

Use the following techniques to develop and integrate the new technologies and systems:

- Systems requirements modeling
- Prototyping/rapid application development
- Workshop management
- Project management
- Quality assurance

Lessons Learned

This step is part of a larger Information Technology program.

The process models developed in the Renew phase and further expanded in the "Develop processes, procedures, and rules" step should be used as the basis for applications to be developed. Each model will outline the rules of off-the-shelf software solutions to be acquired. The needed transformation from inputs to outputs and the content of the guides will define the enablers' roles. Also, the role and job descriptions will help define staff technology requirements.

The scenarios developed earlier to validate the process designs should also be used to check dialog flows, script development, and user testing of technology support. They should also be used to evaluate software vendors' packages applications for suitability toward the whole process under all situations.

Use evolutionary prototyping and rapid application development to build applications. There will be pressure to deliver something fast and to see it evolving. Maintain high user involvement as was the case for the iterative process design.

The prototypes used to validate the process/people/technology interface should be the basis for the development of application prototypes. Iterate through the prototypes to final validation of user requirements and evolve them rapidly into robust applications suitable for production purposes.

Iterate using time-box techniques; schedule reviews and feedback sessions well in advance. Never delay a session to validate what has been developed so far. Instead, prioritize the work, and show what has been done to date.

Develop data models in detail with full attribution if this was not done in the Renew phase. Data models can be evolved iteratively along with the prototypes.

All models developed earlier will undergo a transformation from conceptual business-oriented models to physical application system or object models, specifying precisely what the system must do in the prototype and final solution.

Don't ignore the documentation or later support requirements.

The applications must be designed to change easily as the business changes. Design for flexibility. Use techniques that allow for changes without changing a lot of code or data designs, such as business rule separation from program logic.

Developing Training Capability

In this step, the organization develops the materials required to train staff members in their new jobs. It produces the facility to transfer knowledge regarding the use of new processes, rules, and systems. It creates the mechanisms to increase awareness of customers and new business realities. It also provides a vehicle for ongoing training.

Techniques

To develop training capability, or modules, the following techniques should be used:

- Training needs analysis
- Training media analysis
- Training material development
- Population of just-in-time training vehicles

15

DEVELOPING
CAPABILITY FOR
THE RENEWED
PROCESS

- Workshop management
- Project management

Lessons Learned

This step is part of a larger Human Resource Transformation program.

Before developing the actual training modules, confirm all course objectives and audience needs, produce an outline for each module incorporating the teaching points, and determine training evaluation methods. Formulate the instructional media and strategies to be used and identify text, graphic, and multimedia design methodologies. As you develop the modules, construct and validate a set of mechanisms used to evaluate the training's effectiveness and the capability of those trained. These mechanisms can take the form of work projects, role-playing, quizzes, or question-and-answer sessions.

Training must cover all aspects of change and build on the core competency education delivered already in the "Providing human core capabilities" step earlier in the Develop phase.

Incorporate new processes, new roles and jobs, new communication methods, and the use of the new systems and technology, as well as all the new soft skills required to work and cope in a process-oriented, team-based environment. Teach people to use their professional judgement.

Run pilot training to ensure that it's effective. Be prepared to change whatever can be improved.

Incorporate why change is taking place, not just what and how.

Train people on how to learn and keep learning and changing. Instruct them in how to work in teams providing human core capabilities.

Use training professionals to develop the courses and to keep them going.

Summary

The Develop phase is a lot of work and can cost a lot of money. It's success depends heavily on the results of prior phases, to be sure that the organization is solving the right problem in the right way. A number of programs must work together. An Information Technology program, a Human Resource Transformation program, a Physical Facilities Design and Construction program, and a Process and Structure program all might be happening concurrently. If any of these fail, the whole initiative is at risk, and the business and its stakeholders won't gain the benefits so eagerly anticipated. Failure in the Develop phase is usually because of poor project and program management. Diligence and sticking to commonsense practices is warranted.

The next phase, Implement, is also a time of hard work. Everything must roll out according to plan. There will be many human change issues if the change management strategy hasn't been honored. The Implement phase can be exciting, but, if you do everything that has been covered to this point, that excitement will be for the right reasons.

Implementing and Rolling Out the Business Solution

IN THIS CHAPTER

The Implement phase puts in place all the changes necessary to achieve initial performance improvements and to continue to improve on them over time. The organization delivers the early and ongoing results in this phase by running trials and pilot tests, educating key stakeholders, and rolling out the solution in a series of releases.

The Implement phase has eight steps (see Figure 16.1):

1. Prepare for business testing.
2. Complete business tests and pilots.
3. Update deliverables.
4. Educate management.
5. Develop rollout plans.
6. Train staff.
7. Develop and run marketing programs.
8. Roll out changes.

FIGURE 16.1

Process Management Framework: Steps in the Implement phase.

Overall Tricks and Traps for the Implement Phase

For best effect, the whole Implement phase must be treated as a series of solution releases wherein the transition points of the transformation strategy are viewed as distinct steps toward overall implementation. Each transition point will deliver more and more of the solution of each required aspect of change. At some points, changes to some aspects, such as systems or organization, will be complete or more advanced in comparison to other aspects. Each aspect should be managed as its own complete project within the overall program of change.

Project management will be a critical requirement because things will go wrong if not diligently planned and scrupulously monitored and controlled. Pressures from other priority work and unanticipated stresses on the human resources will arise because business must go on while the changes occur. Managing this ruthlessly must be the prerogative of the overall process owner, process renewal project manager, acceptor, and champion.

Communication must be kept up as well as at any point. Staff and customers will need to know what's happening now as reality starts to sink in that this is no longer some project with a future impact. It's happening now.

Human change management is no longer avoidable. The change is here, and will affect everyone. Denial is no longer an option. Provide support mechanisms to help staff through the difficulties.

Business unit managers might try to delay the implementation because they feel they are too busy or don't have sufficient resources. They have to be assisted to make the change. A lot of this concern is genuine, and negotiation will be required. However, watch for stonewalling and be prepared to be direct and tough with these tactics.

Make sure that the managers send the message that the implementation will be realistic and compassionate. Provide feedback mechanisms for the improvement of the solution when needed. Act and be flexible. Treat feedback and changes as part of continuous process improvement and not an admission of failure.

Each operating unit must support the schedule dependencies or risk the whole program. Make individual expectations clear. Make sure that someone is always on top of this issue.

Be sure to phase in the solutions by business strategy, not by technical convenience, meaning that business results are delivered early and often, even if it's not as convenient to the solution developers. Remember why and for whom this is being done.

Use appropriate and different communication tactics for different audiences internally and externally. Meet locally and cross-functionally often. Treat the process participants as team members.

Be fair and honest but decisive with the people affected. This is no time to back down. Let them know through your actions that the change will happen but that you will support them in achieving personal as well as business success. The human transformation should be focused on training, hiring, and lastly layoffs. Implement interim rewards and celebrations to make success visible and to maintain commitment.

Despite the need to be strong, be willing to change based on experience as you go. Real issues and constraints will come along. Be ready to negotiate but watch for unreasonable objections.

Do everything within your power to do what you said you would do. This is the essence of trust. Everyone is watching.

Preparing for Business Testing

This step puts in place all the guidance and enablers for the real business test, which will provide confidence that the new solution is viable. In preparing business testing, the organization builds the plans to ensure that everything has been considered in the last validation exercise before implementation. It plans all related activities, roles, and responsibilities, and ensures commitment from all participants to avoid any last-minute surprises. The organization finalizes evaluation criteria to be used subsequently to evaluate success.

Techniques

To prepare for business testing, use the following techniques:

- Project management
- Building test plans
- Communication with other project teams
- Training development methods

Lessons Learned

Identify the criteria for an ideal pilot location, examine the potential sites, and then gain agreement in principle to one or more sites with the managers affected. Pick a site that will be assured of success—one that isn't too risky in terms of jeopardizing the whole process and business renewal. It must work, but be sure to also test the essential elements of the solution, which must have credibility with the rest of the organization.

Build a plan for the pilot test that includes resource implications and funding scenarios, and gain approval for pilot operation from managers to ensure commitment. Make sure that all participants in the pilots understand their expected involvement and commit to completing their assigned activities.

Implementing and Rolling Out the Business Solution

CHAPTER 16

363

16

IMPLEMENTING AND
ROLLING OUT THE
BUSINESS
SOLUTION

Because additional work will be required from the pilot participants, make sure that the affected staff is well trained before beginning the pilot. Test-run the training program and invite the participants to contribute to its redesign before rolling it out to the entire staff.

The planning for the testing uses the results of many of the prior phases' deliverables. From the Business Context phase and the Vision phase, the future state stakeholder principles, expectations, KPIs, target performance levels, and CSFs provide the criteria to drive the assessment of the results produced in the pilot. From the Architect and Align phase, the process, knowledge sharing, technology, organization, skills, and facility and location strategies provide guidance and constraints that must be honored. The Vision phase also provides scoping constraints and the business case parameters (updated in the Renew phase) to assess fit and outcome compliance. The Understand phase provides a definition of the problems to be solved and current performance levels to be improved on. The Renew phase provides the agreed upon evaluation criteria for testing the business solution and the process models of the solution that has been built and is ready for testing. Perhaps most important for business testing, the Renew phase provides the set of scenarios that now act as test cases to be tried out using the real solutions that have been assembled into an integrated business solution. These scenarios would have been used to test the different components created in the Develop phase, but this is the first real test of how they all work together. The process scenarios developed earlier in the project and used throughout to validate the process designs should continue to be used for test plan and script development and user testing of systems' technology support.

The test plan for the business test, and especially for the pilot operation, must search for real situations that mimic the scenarios but are more specific. It must also add others as they come up in testing with real customers, suppliers, and staff.

Completing Business Tests and Pilots

Completing the business tests and pilots evaluates and proves the viability of the designed solution. This step eliminates specific objections and changes middle manager and staff attitudes.

Techniques

The techniques to use during the testing step include

- Local management commitment building
- Customer and supplier involvement
- Project management
- Honest listening and communication
- Establishment of feedback mechanisms

Lessons Learned

Measure, measure, measure. You will need to know how well the trial is working, and will need irrefutable proof for the nay-sayers and skeptics as well as management in general.

Be prepared to make changes on-the-fly and re-evaluate the impacts. Testing should be a learning lab as well as a proof of concept, after all. There is no point kidding yourself that it's working if it isn't.

Publicize the results as part of the ongoing communications strategy for the stakeholders. Get testimonials from the staff as well as the customers and suppliers and use them because they are as real as anything you will find.

Keep the feedback loops open and running efficiently so that the parallel development projects delivering the capability to the other upcoming releases know about appropriate modifications quickly enough to respond.

Celebrate success as you go and reward the staff for improved business performance.

Updating Deliverables

In this step, the organization strives to understand what has worked based on the feedback from the pilots and trials, and what can be improved. It updates all appropriate deliverables developed in the Develop phase, improving improves all deliverables, approaches, and plans going forward.

Techniques

To update deliverables, use the following techniques:

- Project management
- Cross-functional workshops

Lessons Learned

Gather and analyze the feedback from the pilot operation, taking into account all stakeholders' perspectives. Determine which deliverables need to be revamped to reflect the outcomes of the "Completing business tests and pilots" step.

Build a plan for updating the deliverables, including any new resource implications and funding requirements; gain approval for changes from project funders and approvers to ensure commitment.

After modifying each deliverable, test the results to ensure that they meet the expected outcomes.

Implementing and Rolling Out the Business Solution

CHAPTER 16

365

16

IMPLEMENTING AND
ROLLING OUT THE
BUSINESS
SOLUTION

Prepare updates in the communication strategy aimed at affected staff, customers, suppliers, and other stakeholders, and then deliver the message, handle objections, and manage perceptions.

Educating Management

This step deals with any concerns that managers might have regarding their own futures. These managers will be the first people questioned by the staff about the changes in the new process. Consequently, it's imperative that they be on board first. They must have the knowledge to ensure consistency of response across the organization. Educating management creates agents of change.

Techniques

The techniques to educate management include

- Human change management practices
- Professional training development
- Offsite retreats
- Professional workshop management
- Public relations approaches

Lessons Learned

Before attempting to educate management on the changes, gain a holistic (from all perspectives) understanding of the changes that will be made based on all previous project results. From the human resource changes, understand the specific impacts on the management structure and players and their staff.

In this step, it's important to make sure that key managers and those in influence are truly committed to the solution. Having done so will help create a domino effect of positively changed attitudes toward this change and toward change in general.

Prepare materials for a workshop session with managers regarding the process changes and the impact that the changes and their new roles will have on them. Conduct the workshops off-site without distractions.

It's crucial to get the managers through their own personal change first. Only then can they help others deal with change. If they are overly concerned about themselves, they will be of little help to their staff and can even be a negative influence. Anticipate the concerns and expose the bad and the good before being asked. Set up a communications channel for ongoing support of managers.

Take the time to do it right and do it again if necessary.

Developing Rollout Plans

This step recognizes the specific deficiencies in capabilities and resources and identifies constraints to implementation and change by creating detailed, individual departmental plans for integrated change. In developing rollout plans, the organization defines how and when support departments will conduct the necessary support activities. It finalizes the organizational structure and responsibilities with specific names and roles. It consolidates the individual plans into a coordinated set.

Techniques

In developing the rollout plans, use the following techniques:

- Project planning
- Win-win negotiation
- Presentations
- Communications
- Broad participation

Lessons Learned

Review the Transformation Strategy developed in the Renew phase in detail to determine the overall coordination and schedule required, taking special note of any transition points when the business will implement a major release of an integrated solution. Examine the current state of enabler development is under way in the Develop phase, and then review the plan with staff and managers to discover areas of risk and constraints.

Negotiate the delicate balance between what must be done and what quality level is required within the allowed time, resources, and cost. Consider the effectiveness of tools and approaches for change itself.

Each plan should cover an organizational unit and deal with all aspects of change implementation. Working with the overall project manager, plan the specific transformation required in the solution for every piece of the new organization and everyone in it. The plan must answer this question for all staff: "What does this mean for me and what renewal program will I go through?"

For best results, plans should be developed collaboratively with the staff, based on appropriate guidance from the project team according to a planning template. In that way, all plans can be consolidated.

Avoid planning for one-shot perfection. Instead, accommodate mistakes, learning, and improvement over time.

Implementing and Rolling Out the Business Solution

CHAPTER 16

367

16

IMPLEMENTING AND
ROLLING OUT THE
BUSINESS
SOLUTION

Determine roles and backup resources for the existing work that the resources would normally be conducting for the period of transition to keep the business going as change occurs. Make individual expectations crystal-clear.

Training Staff

This step ensures a correct and consistent understanding by transferring information and knowledge to staff and continuing to change attitudes. Staff training makes the implementation run more smoothly by delivering an ongoing training strategy.

Techniques

To ensure the success of the training program, use these techniques:

- Strong coaching of workshop leaders
- Consistent materials and messages
- Formal presentations
- Workshops

Lessons Learned

Based on changes recommended during the pilot testing, update training materials so that they will be ready for the training classes.

Training sessions should be scheduled for those who will use the new knowledge just before the time that they will need to apply it. Follow the practice of small doses of just-in-time training sessions when needed, instead of massive training programs that will be forgotten quickly if not applied.

Use multiple media and training approaches, so that trainees can "Read it, hear it, see pictures, experience examples, try it, and try it again."

Arrange individual schedules for training. Make sure that everyone knows their own personal training schedule and has a mentor outside the classroom and following any automated training programs.

Test competencies as part of the training rollout. After training, monitor job performance right away, and after a set time.

Set aside enough time to conduct training properly. This human enabler of change and process performance is the only one practice that can carry accountability and make all the others work. Trainers can make up for shortcomings in all other enablers if they know what they are doing and care to do it right.

Developing and Running Marketing Programs

This step makes the marketplace aware of the renewal programs, by revealing new strengths and competitiveness. This allows the organization to start to take advantage of new capabilities.

Techniques

To prepare for and announce changes to your customers, use the following techniques:

- Formal marketing campaigns
- Meetings with key customers and suppliers
- A project in the marketing or public relations department

Lessons Learned

Review the results achieved so far in design and testing of the new process; determine the reality of the Transformation Strategy from the Renew phase and the organization's true readiness for rollout. Whatever date is announced to the marketplace, it must be realistic; otherwise, credibility is lost. Don't commit to dates and schedules until you are absolutely confident that you will make them, or unless you have a really good contingency plan for the project (or your career).

Share the renewal plans in confidence (under nondisclosure terms, possibly) with your best customers and suppliers as early as possible. It will boost their confidence in you and might buy time. Customers' and suppliers' positive responses can act as testimonials later during the larger rollout.

Use multiple approaches to educating the marketplace. Top customers can be informed in person by top executives. At the opposite extreme, most customers will learn about proposed business changes through a press release, newspaper story, or marketing brochure.

Train the message conveyers really well and consistently. Prepare them for the difficult questions and how to handle them. Provide role-playing opportunities to test their readiness.

Be prepared to change tactics, if necessary.

Rolling Out Changes

This step finally puts in place new processes, new jobs, new organizations, new systems and technologies, new incentive programs, ongoing training programs, and new measurement systems.

Techniques

During the final rollout of the entire set of changes, use the following techniques:

- Empowered work teams
- Measurement-based recognition
- Coaching and hand-holding
- Removal of old mechanisms
- Phasing in of changes
- Continuous improvement of teams and mechanisms
- Groupware environments

Lessons Learned

Plan your work and work your plan. Repeat as necessary. Manage to the transition points. Each point commences its own rollout.

As you implement new technologies and make new facilities available, be sure to remove old technologies and facilities. Likewise, retire old policies and rules. You will be sorry if you don't.

Change reporting relationships and organizational structure. Initiate new jobs and incentive schemes based on performance results.

Implement the measurements and incentives early to gauge progress. Reward and celebrate successes and progress.

Provide ongoing training, hand-holding, coaching, and support until people get it.

Never stop communicating.

Institute staff teams to assist each other as part of an ongoing cross-functional, continuous improvement team.

Summary

The work in the Implement phase finally delivers the benefits to the business. This phase is difficult even if it is eagerly anticipated, because the transition takes time and it is easy to get frustrated while moving out of your comfort zone. The Implement phase typically places an even greater demand on everyone's time than in earlier phases. At this point, backsliding in terms of human transition can occur. The steps in the Implement phase require a lot of attention to the stakeholders, both internal and external because they will be experiencing the reality of the new process. A lot of the activity in this phase gets them ready and capable to move forward.

The next phase, Nurture and Continuously Improve, is not really a phase at all. It is the ongoing execution of the process with a process owner in place and the environment of continuously searching for opportunities to improve even more.

INDEX

SYMBOLS

NUMBERS

A

M

**Macintosh, Apple
Computers, 45**
management. *See also*
processes, managing;
project management
   business process holistic,
      88-90
   business process, 73-74
   business rule, 80
   colleagues (The
      Morningstar Packing
      Company), 104
   conduct principles,
      226-227
   customer relations,
      model, 49
   data, integrity, 31
   educating, 365
   human changes, support
      groups, 243
   information, business
      process view, 31
   KM (knowledge manage-
      ment), 77-79
   objection, 228
   programs, support
      groups, 243
   quality, 70-71
   Return on Management®
      (ROM), 25, 71
   risks, support groups, 243
managers
   program, core team role,
      179
   project, responsibilities,
      170
**Managing (support
   group service style),
   238**
**Managing Knowledge
   (support group service
   style), 238**

**mapping existing
   process understanding,
   314-318**
**maps, knowledge-
   mapping techniques,
   283**
**marketing programs,
   developing and run-
   ning, 368**
markets
   forces, effects on organi-
      zations, 69
   investment, 25-26
   place changes, handling,
      8-11
Maslow, Abraham, 218
**Maslow's Hierarchy of
   Need, 218-219**
materials, training, 244
matrices
   information-to-process,
      283
   process performance
      measurements, 281
measuring
   performance, products or
      services, 249-250
   process performance,
      281-282, 318-319
   renewed processes, 344
**"Measuring and
   Managing Knowledge
   Capital"** (*Knowledge
   Executive Report*)**, 26,
   71**
members. *See* **team
   members**
mergers, 20-21
**messages to staff, word-
   ing of, 306**
methodologies
   human transitions to
      change
      *change agents,
         229-231*

   *communications,
      227-232*
   *renewal principles,
      224-227*
   *stakeholders, analyz-
      ing, 224*
   *ten factors for team
      transition, 232-233*
   education, products or
      services, 247
   framework, 244
**methods, project man-
   agement, 176**
Microsoft, 46
Microsoft Office, 15
**military, after-action
   reviews, 199**
missions, 237-239
   Global Software, Inc.,
      260
   Morningstar Packing
      Company (The), 101
   Rexall.com, 115-116
   Stanford University FAO
      (Financial Aid Office),
      106
   statements
      *Process Renewal
         Group, 38*
      questioning, 38-40
   validation technique,
      260-262
**mistakes, learning from,
   60**
**mitigation of risks,
   196-198**
Mobil, 20
modeling
   object-oriented, 245
   processes, 245
   renewed processes,
      333-335

relationships
business customers, 280
criteria for customers
(Global Software, Inc.
stakeholders), 268
dissatisfaction and readiness to change, 214-215
equity (customers and
suppliers), 49
process management
methods and informa-
tion systems develop-
ment, 167
**reliability of products
and services, 14-17**
**Renew (Process
Management
Framework), 127, 139,
326-327**
business case, updating,
337-338
enabler knowledge, find-
ing, 329-330
evaluation criteria, finalizing, 330-331
performance, rethinking,
331-333
process designs, renew-
ing, 153-156
processes, benchmarking,
328-329
renewed processes,
333-337
transformation strategy,
developing, 338-339
trends, benchmarking,
328-329
**renewal principles for
human transitions to
change, 224-227**
renewal team, 295, 310
**renewed processes. See
also processes**
computing infrastruc-
tures, building, 346-347

demonstrating, 335-337
designs, 153-156
evolutionary prototyping,
355
HR (human resources)
policies, updating,
352-354
human core capabilities,
providing, 345-346
Human Resource
Transformation pro-
gram, 343
incentives, 344
Information Technology
program, 343
jobs, redefining, 348-350
measures, 344
modeling, 333-335
organizational
changes, designing,
350-352
partnerships, 352
Physical Facilities
Design and
Construction program,
343
physical infrastructures,
building, 344-345
procedures, developing,
347-348
Process and Structure
program, 343
processes, developing,
347-348
rapid application devel-
opment, 355
rules, developing,
347-348
scaling, 166-167
selecting, 295-297
systems, updating,
354-355
tasks, contracting out,
351-352
technology, updating,
354-355

training capability, developing, 355-356
validating, 335-337
**repositories, business
knowledge, 248**
requirements
customers, fitting, 194
facilities, 284-285
information needs,
282-283
stakeholders, 242
resources
contact information,
products or services,
249
project management, 175
support groups, 241-242
team transition factor,
232
responsibilities
people on projects,
173-177
project managers, 170
results
Architect and Align
(Process Management
Framework), 144
Business Context
(Process Management
Framework), defining
for change, 140
business strategies, aligning, 144
change, implementing,
160
Develop (Process
Management
Framework), developing
enablers or support
mechanisms, 157
Implement (Process
Management
Framework), imple-
menting change, 160